AMERICAN
TOUGH

RUPERT WILKINSON

AMERICAN TOUGH

THE TOUGH-GUY TRADITION AND AMERICAN CHARACTER

CONTRIBUTIONS IN
AMERICAN STUDIES,
NUMBER 69

GREENWOOD PRESS
WESTPORT, CONNECTICUT · LONDON, ENGLAND

Library of Congress Cataloging in Publication Data

Wilkinson, Rupert.
  American tough.

  (Contributions in American studies, ISSN 0084-9227; no. 69)
  Bibliography: p.
  Includes index.
  1. National characteristics, American. 2. United
States—Popular culture. 3. Toughness (Personality
trait) 4. Personality and culture—United States—
History. I. Title. II. Title: Tough-guy tradition and
American character. III. Series.
E169.1.W487 1984   302.5′4′0973   83-10794
ISBN 0-313-23797-2

Library of Congress Catalog Card Number: 83-10794
ISBN: 0-313-23797-2
ISSN: 0084-9227

First published in 1984

Greenwood Press
A division of Congressional Information Service, Inc.
88 Post Road West
Westport, Connecticut 06881

Printed in the United States of America

10 9 8 7 6 5 4 3 2 1

For Lorna Wilkinson

If you don't move with the times, the times will mow you down. . . . Everything good always starts with self-interest, haven't you learned that yet? Altruists crack under pressure.
> —Businessman and community leader, "Little Italy,"
> Manhattan, 1979

This is not a matter of sitting down at the dinner table and talking about it. . . . I belong to the school that does not talk about things—you *do* them.
> —Harry Hopkins, on the prospect of war, 1940

BACKBONE HINTS for the Prevention of Jelly-Spine Curvature and Mental Squint. A Straight-up Antidote for the Blues and a Straight-ahead Sure Cure for Grouch.
> —Title of a 1908 inspirational anthology

Parties are not built up by deportment, or by ladies' magazines, or by gush.
> —Sen. Roscoe Conkling, New York State Republican
> Convention, 1877

[The men of the States come], just matured, certain, numerous and capable enough, with egotistical tongues, with sinewed wrists, seizing openly what belongs to them. . . . Their shadows are projected in employments, in books, in the cities, in trade; their feet are on the flights of the steps of the Capital; they dilate, a larger, brawnier, more democratic, lawless, . . . sweet-bodied, completer, dauntless, flowing, masterful, beard-faced, new race of men.
> —Walt Whitman to Ralph Waldo Emerson, August 1856

CONTENTS

PREFACE

This book started life in the notes of an earlier book on drinking in American culture (Wilkinson, *The Prevention of Drinking Problems* [1970], pp. 241–42). I remarked there on some conflicting traditions that seemed to exacerbate male concerns about ruggedness versus consumer indulgence. It was my first attempt to articulate something I had sensed for a long time: that the meanings and pressures of toughness were different in America and Britain; that this was true especially for males but due to wider causes than any theories of masculinity could supply. The problem was one for cultural history in the broadest sense.

One difficulty with the subject is that every American above the age of two is, knowingly or not, an expert on it. The trick is to avoid saying the obvious without confining oneself to a mere collection of insights. I decided to center this book on three essays (chapters 1–3), each dealing with a set of paradoxes that has complicated and shaped American ideas of toughness. Chapter 1, "Contrary Strains," explores traditional dualities within those ideas. "Producers and Consumers," chapter 2, looks more chronologically at an old but continuing source of conflict: the tension between strenuous producer values and indulgent consumer ones. "Organized Individuals," chapter 3, uses the theme of toughness to connect some familiar but disparate writings on individuality and conformity in America and then examines the trade-offs between ideals of self-reliance and self-assertion and the pressures and attractions of modern organization. The last chapter pulls together other aspects of toughness in America—including the sociological and historical—and compares American toughness to toughness elsewhere. The book as a whole takes its story up through the 1970s with occasional forays into the eighties, and it deals mainly with middle– and upper–class groups.

A number of people have sustained me in this work over many years. Without Marcus Cunliffe I am not sure what would have become of it: he gave me ideas and encouragement at every stage of my journey, in the valleys as well as on the plains. My wife Mary provided a support that meant all the more because it was founded on critical judgment and a journalist's impatience with turgidity. Other people who have given exceptional help include Craig Comstock, Ricky Elliott, David Riesman, and Daniel Snowman; Robert Walker, the series editor for Greenwood Press; and my colleague and dean, John Whitley. My more specialized creditors reflect the range I have tried to cover: Christopher Chaffin on the Roman moralists; Malcolm Kitch and William Lamont on medieval and Stuart England; Colin Brooks on seventeenth– and eighteenth–century England and America; Michael C. Adams, Christopher Gerry, Robert Gross, and Karen Putnam on nineteenth–century America; Cynthia Hamilton on Westerns; Sherry Marker and Maryan Talbot Roberts on adolescence and masculinity; Douglas Tallack on technology and Mexican machismo; and David English on Australian culture. Heather Dubrow informed me on a wide variety of things, from Friday night poker games in an English department to comparisons of British and American child-rearing. Howard Nenner supplied the book's first two words. I am indebted to Jane South and Bessie White for discussion as well as highly competent typing; to Ayako Firsing of the Princeton University Store for her splendid book service and lively correspondence over the years; to the arts deans of Sussex University for research support and leaves; to the staffs of Sussex University Library and the U.S. Library, London; to Marie Smith of Greenwood Press for her careful and sensitive editing, and to James Sabin and Susan Baker at Greenwood for guiding the book through its various stages.

Part of chapter 2 was given as a lecture to the American Studies faculty and students of Nottingham and East Anglia Universities and King Alfred's College, Winchester. I am grateful for their response. I am also grateful to the editors of *Encounter* and the *Journal of American Studies* for encouraging the work by publishing preview articles by me, and to the political scientist (I must omit his name) who read my *Encounter* piece and wrote: "I very much enjoyed your article and cannot contribute useful criticism since I have just discovered that *I* am an American tough guy."

AMERICAN TOUGH

INTRODUCTION

Everybody knows the modern tough guy—the bottom–line realist, a man to joke with but not mess with, nobody's fool. Assertive, crisp, and definite, he projects a cool confidence, seems capable of handling any practical situation. Writ large on the screen, he is most obviously a Bogart, a Wayne, an Eastwood. Dramatized by political columnists, he is, diversely, a Jack or Robert Kennedy, a Richard Daley, or the man Richard Nixon wanted to be. It takes no book to argue that the toughness he stands for, in real life as well as myth, is something that Americans have traditionally, if uneasily, admired.

But *do* we know him? The images and role models that make up the American tough-guy tradition are highly complex. They connect with many things in American culture, yet their place in that culture is ambiguous and contested. While Americans know that they have a tough-guy tradition, there is some vagueness about the precise nature of that tradition and a great deal of disagreement and confusion about its modern relevance. At the heart of the confusion lie questions that have seldom been asked.

What values shape American notions of toughness? Images and models of toughness are so diffusely woven into American culture that nobody has tried to define them as concepts, to show how they connect and where they conflict. This is partly because personal concerns with toughness often come through to us as a matter of style and aura— a wisecrack, a grimace, or a tone of voice—rather than in systematic statements that invite analysis. Yet styles and mannerisms reflect cultural values no less than do explicit declarations.

When did it all begin? The term itself, "tough guy," capturing in extreme form several American notions of toughness, did not reach general currency until about 1925. It still has a modern ring derived from its initial association with gangsters and detectives. Yet the quotations at the start of this book suggest that some of the American concern with toughness is much older. How much of it in fact is old; how much is new? What developments and changes have the basic conceptions of toughness undergone?

What exactly has created the tough-guy tradition and made it distinctively American? In working on this book I have found that most people who ask me about it—European as well as American—connect its subject with one or both of two things: masculinity and the frontier. Both are crucial but neither provides an easy explanation of American concerns with toughness. The traditional association of masculinity with assertiveness, hardness, and mastery is not peculiar to Americans. Conversely, American tough-guy styles and attitudes have never been the total monopoly of men: from Florence Kelley to Bella Abzug, from Rosalynn Carter to Jodie Foster, the various forms the American tough guy takes are not bound by gender. A full understanding of tough-guy attitudes in America must go beyond the feminist critique of macho values that flourished in the 1970s.

The frontier explanation of American concerns with toughness sometimes includes immigration and its selective rigors. Yet even in this expanded form there are problems. Other countries have had testing experiences of frontier settlement and immigrant journeying into unknown lands. And if American models of toughness are just a product of pioneer self-reliance and immigrant courage and hardship, then what on earth are they doing in today's society of organized ease and "31 Flavors" affluence? Do they simply survive on nostalgia? Where, for that matter, does any tough-guy model belong in a culture that, according to several commentators, has become more sensate, expressive, and narcissistic?

This brings us to questions about acceptance. Personal toughness continues to be respected, even while ambivalence and disagreement exist about its proper place in the culture. The most obvious idealizations of toughness have been embodied in countless movie and television heroes, each with his own package of combat prowess, savvy, and crisp-talking confidence. If these components are now stylized and exaggerated to the point of spoofery, no one could say that they have been foisted onto an unattracted public. Yet the term "tough-guy" has always carried bad as well as good connotations—of unpleasant intimidation as well as enviable thrust. "Tough," used as a noun, was an American invention of the 1870s. Its connotation was wholly unfavorable: it meant a thug or rowdy. Among heroes, too, some of America's toughest—from Andrew Jackson to George Patton—have had controversial reputations. The very attraction of people to tough and assertive behavior has exacerbated fears about aggression. One remedy has been to build notions of self-control into the popular idea of toughness, but this has not allayed all anxieties.

In day-to-day life Americans have responded to their tough-guy models in a number of ways. Some honor them wholeheartedly and for the most part consistently. Others do so more sporadically, often in conjunction with styles that are not at all tough. Still others develop wholly different modes of behavior, sometimes in reaction *against* the tough guy. Even so, notions of dynamic toughness represent a cultural force with which virtually all Americans have to deal in some way.

This mixture of salience and ambiguity has nowhere appeared more vividly than in journalistic debates about the merits of presidents and presidential candidates. In April 1972, when Senator George Mc-Govern had become the leading contender for the Democratic party nomination, Washington columnist David Broder declared that "toughness" was the essential quality of McGovern which reporters had overlooked. Leaving aside his World War II record as a bomber pilot, the fact remained that this "soft-voiced sometime minister and college teacher" had risked his family's economic security to build a successful Democratic organization in the Republican stronghold of South Dakota and was now making a serious, well-prepared bid for the presidency. "Tough. Very tough," was Broder's conclusion. Nine months later, after McGovern's landslide defeat by Nixon, another Washington columnist, Joseph Kraft, blamed the disaster on the candidate's tactical errors and personality. He simply lacked "the toughness of mind, the breadth of experience, the judgment of men and the personal presence that are required for the White House." And so "he never had the enthusiastic support of the strong men who have been the mainstays of the Democratic Party."[1]

The distance between these two comments does not represent just a difference of opinion about McGovern himself, nor the change in McGovern's fortunes and image during the election. The articles themselves reflect the importance to the media of contests of strength and toughness, yet they show some disagreement about what toughness demanded. It happened again in 1980 when Jimmy Carter's re-election campaign became so embroiled in the issue of "leadership." Was Carter naive, incompetent, passive, a pushover for the Russians and Iranians, or was he "calm in crisis," "steely-eyed" with subordinates, physically vigorous (all that jogging) and "whip-his-ass" competitive? The very phrases used in and around the beleaguered Carter White House were revealing; and the question of toughness soon became crucial for other candidates too—in their own eyes at least. Yet, as John Connally discovered to his cost, a candidate could disturb his audiences by seeming *too* tough and masterful, too hard-line, even too charismatic. If the voters wanted a promise of dynamism and direction, they also wanted a relaxed, kindly reassurance, and in the end it was Ronald Reagan who offered both.[2]

There was, obviously, a close relationship betweeen this bundle of concerns and the circumstances in which Americans found themselves at the end of the seventies. The 1980 election came at a postimperial moment, when Americans were not at all sure what role they wanted or could obtain either for their presidents or for their country in world affairs. In crises affecting sensitive national honor, many Americans wanted their president to get tough yet realized the past costs and current limits of such toughness. Economically, too, the idea was growing that America had entered a period of fundamental decline, reversing its history. This prompted new worries about the people's vigor and ambition, industriousness and will.

The scope of this book goes beyond and behind these developments. American ideas about toughness, for all the confusion surrounding them, represent a definable and long-evolving tradition. Their historical sources, however, are diverse, and their styles and values are pulled like elastic in opposite directions—toward expansiveness and laconic plainness, self-reliance and covert submission, moral strenuosity and mean-guy cynicism, and so on. These opposite tugs have been meshed and concealed in rich and wondrous ways, ranging from institutional arrangements to tricks of language and organized fantasy. It follows from all this that America's tough-guy tradition is too full of paradoxes to be a guide for the future, yet too entrenched in the culture to be simply rejected. In the 1980s, especially if the energy crisis returns, some of the tradition will be relevant and useful. And some will be destructive.

Let us start with definitions. American culture has expanded formal dictionary meanings of toughness—resilience, intractability—to include mastery, competence, informal assertiveness, and self-defense. Within the scope of these values, different individuals and groups place different emphases, but they commonly assume a dangerous but exploitable environment. Posed against this environment is *the guy who can take care of himself* ("handle himself"), physically, economically, and socially. This formula incorporates and connects every feature of toughness most admired by Americans in the twentieth century. To wit:

The tough guy is masterful. He can manage situations; he can manage himself. Calculation and self-control increase his effectiveness. He is the "can-do guy," the guy who delivers, who gets things done. In tight situations he demonstrates technical competence.[3]

The tough guy is dynamic. His style celebrates action, impact, and the power of speed. He is the mobile operator geared to survival and success in a fluid society.

The tough guy can take it. He can cope with many kinds of stress. In physically demanding conditions his equipment includes willpower as well as muscle tone. Indeed, in some romantic versions, the will takes over from physique, driving a sick or exhausted body to the limits of endurance. He seeks self-knowledge by testing himself—*proving* himself in both senses of the word. In curricula vitae no less than political rhetoric, he talks of meeting challenges.

The tough guy is, above all, the stand-up guy, a living reproach to the approval-seeking and plastic soothings of modern social life. (Here more than anywhere he embodies a counternorm against other values that are equally strong in the society.) Not afraid to face down rivals and aggressors, he sees almost everyone as a potential adversary. Competence and self-defense unite in the hard-headed realist, unfooled by sentiment or trickery. The sap as much as the sissy has become an antithesis of the tough guy. Being no sucker, the tough guy must show some irreverence for authority, while, beneath his hard shell, he is usually supposed to retain a benign, democratic core. Individually, through aura and performance, the tough guy must have class; sociologically, he must project a classlessness. His styles draw from ethnic and lower-class idiom, but they are not manifestly proletarian.

These, then, are the values that surround the American concern with toughness. They operate on a range of levels, from that of myth and collective fantasy to styles and preferences adopted in everyday behavior. I propose to use the acronym "ACT" for the basic concern and the phrase "ACT values" for the surrounding values and beliefs.

In depicting ACT values through tough-guy stereotypes, I have consciously used the pronoun, "he," not "she." This accurately reflects the historical connections between ACT and masculinity, but it does not do justice to the double relationship that has long existed between American notions of toughness and women. By using femininity as a defining opposite, the tough-guy tradition put pressure on women to be wholesome, sweet, and ultimately submissive, whether as Victorian wives and mothers or as cute majorettes. Yet Calamity Jane did exist, and her ilk were not to be put down by labeling them "tomboys." From the early nineteenth century, it was a characteristic of American child-rearing that it encouraged girls as well as boys to talk up and assert themselves.[4] I speak here not only of a real, underlying toughness— many a "baby doll" has had plenty of that—but of widespread conventions that encouraged women to be openly aggressive, dynamic, and independent. Of course the balances and nuances betweeen sweet submissiveness and "the guy who can take care of herself" have varied. Alexis de Tocqueville claimed of American business-class women in the 1830s that before marriage they were bold and free, enjoying democratic relationships with their parents; once married, however, they bent themselves to their husbands' ventures and led more constrained lives than their European counterparts.[5] Again, the frontier conditions that associated ruggedness with masculinity also required women to be visibly strong and independent, managing stores and farms as well as their homes.[6]

In a broader, historical sense, the problem lies with the dual function performed by ACT values. As in other countries, *men* used their culture's notions of toughness and strength to define their masculinity vis-à-vis women. Yet, from an early point in their history (as we shall see), *Americans* as a whole used the same notions to define their national identity. Although the definition was often put in masculine terms (as republican and democratic "manliness"), various factors, ranging from the speed of westward expansion to ideas of freedom and equality, made it impossible for American men to shut women out of that definition. The result was ambiguity. Women who adopted tough styles were sometimes resented and sometimes admired, by men as well as by other women.[7]

Modern theories about American culture and social character divide sharply into those claiming that American character has fundamentally changed and those which argue (or imply) that it has not. Some have hedged their choice, acknowledging old elements in the new or secondary changes in the old. But even those have gone mainly for one or the other; unlike some theories of American political history, there has been little attempt to interweave the forces of change and tradition.[8]

Since the early 1970s the "change" school has predominated. Though differing about the causes and social stances of a new American individualism, the leaders of this school agree that it is largely focused on psychological fulfillment and emotional and expressive freedom. One of them, Daniel Yankelovich, claims that these attitudes will survive Reagan conservatism and will adjust, in more outward-reaching forms, to new economic constraints.[9]

My conception of the theme of toughness in America goes against the grain of these theories. It does not contradict them, but it is concerned with aspects of American character that more obviously have a long lineage. At the heart of the matter lies a traditional concern with dynamic strength. Around this concern a weight of attitudes and images has accumulated. It is like a snowball rolling through time. As the snowball rolls along, it grows unevenly; bits fall off but more sticks on, sometimes suddenly, sometimes slowly, till its shape and size bear little resemblance to the original lump. Yet it is still snow!

Historically, the American concern with toughness has three main sources: a plain man, anticourtier tradition that goes back to Tudor and Stuart England; a complex of frontier myths and images; and the tension in a business society between striving and self-indulgence. (This last factor is explored at length in chapter 2, and a general history of the tough-guy tradition is presented in the last chapter.) From these diverse but interconnected sources, American ideas of toughness came together in the early 1900s; they were further shaped in the twentieth century by notions of professionalism and technical mastery.

In all these historical developments, child-rearing patterns played a part, but only a minor one. They did not create the conflicting messages of the culture; they merely transmitted and modified them. The main sources of ACT (its American dimensions as opposed to universal concerns with strength and aggressiveness) lie in broad social and economic developments and a heritage of ideas and symbols rather than sexual training or family background. I would argue, indeed, that ACT cannot be defined on the level of deep intrapsychic or psychodynamic feelings and processes, nor are tough guys invariably neurotic. With their many permutations, ACT values can fit a number of personality structures. Tough styles and attitudes, even anxieties about physical and social softness, are largely learned and imitated; they must involve some deep processes, but concern with toughness is not necessarily a compensation for feelings of inadequacy or unsureness about basic identity. I do not deny that runt experiences—early years of frailty and handicap, plus the goad of vigorous parents and older siblings—have influenced some renowned exponents of toughness. More generally, too, conflicts over dependency and sex roles, reaching well back into childhood, explain some of the American attraction to toughness. I still do not see these aspects as *defining* features.

1
CONTRARY STRAINS

Ideas of toughness cut across American culture in contradictory pairs. Each idea engages with a counterpoint that equally claims the authority of toughness. Most are traditional, with historic roots of varying length, but the culture is constantly reworking them. It decks them out in new forms; it finds new ways of bridging and masking their contradictions.

Whether these pairs of opposites can be boiled down to one essential conflict in American culture is a problem best left to the end of the chapter. A recurrent theme, however, is that of ambivalence toward aggressiveness and a wish to look for controls on aggression inside as well as outside the value system of toughness.

MIND AND MUSCLE

Although many societies have had their strong-man hereos, only America has developed in such loving, muscular detail the superhero tradition of Tarzan and Superman. American action novels throughout the twentieth century have lavished more attention on bodily grace and power than have their European equivalents. It is the same in public life and political journalism. The jogging and dieting boom of the 1970s has perpetuated the image of the trim public figure, reputed to weigh little more than he did on his college team.

In everyday life there is a related phenomenon that is difficult to describe in words. It has a narcissistic overtone, and I would like to call it ''body-consciousness,'' except that it often seems to be unconscious. More pronounced in the 1940s and 1950s than today, it appeared in styles of walking—a hefting of shoulders, a slight swivelling of the waist, a relaxed strut—which often distinguished Americans, especially men, in a crowd of Europeans.[1] Some of it has been institutionalized in uniforms and equipment that emphasize or exaggerate parts of the male body—for instance, the football uniform, especially when displayed for the photographer in the de rigueur crouch; or the uniforms of soldiers, police, and some security guards, which are tailored around the hips and stomach.

Yet for all the fuss about physique, jocks and he-men have long been ridiculed as well as admired, not simply because people fear violence or want relief from heartiness but because they recognize that physical assets are seldom enough for survival and success. From the 1820s on, an increasingly dominant figure in American sports was the rule-bending gamesman who went all out to win through calculation and psychology (disconcerting the opponent) as much as physical ability.[2] The term "gorilla," used from the 1860s, was derogatory because it meant physical threat at the expense of brainpower. In our own time even Robert Ringer, the best-selling exponent of *Winning through Intimidation* and *Looking Out for Number One*, employs the term "tough guy" unfavorably, to mean a fight-happy neurotic who wastes his time on "physical prowess."[3]

The tension between body-power and other kinds of toughness has been coped with in various ways. The commonest is to suppose that a record of physical vigor, even the slightest claim to past athleticism, indicates a more general dynamism. This is not unique to Americans; *mens sana in corpore sano* means the same thing in other corners of the globe. Americans, however, have enshrined it in diverse institutions, from the downtown athletic club to the presidential campaign, whose length and pace is supposed to be a gruelling test of character and fitness for office. The historic American concern with energy has cemented the assumption that physical vigor supports mental vigor.[4]

Brainpower, conversely, has been even more systematically applied to athletic training. The professionalizing and commercializing of sport in the early 1900s promoted the idea of the scientifically trained athlete. Its epitome in the twenties was Gene Tunney's "academic" approach to boxing (though Tunney the writer sported an irreverence that did not charm the ring's moguls and pundits). In the 1960s and 1970s computers and videotapes took it all a stage further; plays were replayed, quantified, analyzed. Body and brain were united in sports technology and "sportsmedicine."[5]

Symbol and metaphor, too, blurred the distinction between physical and mental toughness. The massive, firm jaws developed by comic-strip heroes in the 1930s and 1940s implicitly connected character with physique. In language the traditional, American preference for vivid, down-to-earth images has propelled violent metaphor ("eyeballing," "toe to toe," "blood on the floor") into the most flannel-suited occasions, and it is not always clear that the image *is* purely metaphor; there are hints, sometimes, of a real fist in the eye.[6] There are also strains to narcissism. These surface in distinctively American expressions about job performance ("you're looking good," "we're in good shape," "if I handle myself well") and power ("defense posture," "a low profile," and that hoary term, "muscle").[7] Such expressions sublimate but also keep alive the idea of physical prowess in a world whose tests of toughness are mainly nonphysical.

EXPANSIVE/LACONIC

Inflation of expression and economy of expression are equally characteristic of American culture. Out of both have come styles of toughness nurtured by frontier life and business incentives.

Expansiveness in American speech goes back to nationalist bragging about the continent's richness and grandeur. The tall tales of southwestern humor dealt with a frightening environment by transforming its gargantuan and devouring properties into mighty individuals—men–alligators, ring–tailed roarers, and mythical superheroes like Pecos Bill.[8] The genre also created a small vocabulary of long, knobbly words—"rambunctious," for "obstreperous"; "hornswoggle," "to cheat." The expansive tradition survived most obviously in ten-gallon Texanism and the sexual boasting of male groups, from athletic club locker rooms to college fraternities. The salesman and booster gave personal expansiveness a bottom–line value: to sell a product you must sell yourself; mastery means confident communication.

Nevertheless, when expansiveness spawns toughness, there are likely to be paradoxes. What, for instance, are we to make of the tough-guy rooster in American history? His showiness brought him close to the tough-guy's antithesis, the dandy. The rooster is commonly associated with the West and frontier South, but the East too had its versions, and did so long before the ghetto hipster made his mark. The epitome in the 1870s was Roscoe Conkling, the strutting, pigeon-chested boss of the New York Republicans. A keen boxer and physical fitness enthusiast, Conkling disparaged his opponents in the reform clubs as effeminate and genteel, yet he himself was a vain and gaudy dresser.[9] Tough (or would-be tough) expansiveness, pushed to the point of contradiction, crops up again in the media appetite for heroes, drama, and exaggerated adversity. From World War II propaganda films romanticizing the least military task to the public feting of the returned Iran hostages, the media has indulged a fussy hysteria, a projected self-pity, the very opposite of stoic values. Likewise, profane and detailed self-pity marks many American war novels and stories, from World War II through Vietnam. Underlying the tough-talking, hard-swearing cynicism and fear is a tone of civilian surprise and victimization. A more tepid version of pseudoheroic self-pity occurs among those psychobabblers who speak of "traumas" and "survival skills" in ordinary living.

The laconic mode of toughness drew from frontier and rural conditions too: from the self-restraint required when small, isolated numbers of people had to live austerely and work with each other, year in, year out; and from the life of the dirt farmer who had to spend great tracts of time by himself.[10] The taciturnity of the countryman, whose speech does not hurry the seasons, is not of course confined to America; but it gathered virtue from the American myth of rural strength, simplicity, and integrity versus the affectations of smooth-talking city folk. Laconic speech symbolized honest, functionally stripped leanness against the corrupting flab of urban living. In business, it represented efficiency and authority. The dignity of the colonial New England merchant—an air of command based on calm assurance, self–control, and the suggestion of hidden reserves—survived through the nineteenth century in some of the very people who employed effusive salesmen. George Lorimer, meat canner turned editor, advised young businessmen in 1902 to use few words and make them count, lest they gave too much away. It was easier to look wise than to be wise.[11] In subsequent decades the very expansion of organized salesmanship and noisy public relations campaigns prompted the kind of sales resistance that ridiculed "ballyhoo." Efficiency values—"time is money"—were invoked against bureaucratic verbiage, and this reached through into the world of selling. By the 1970s some marketing departments had developed a cult of curt aggressiveness backed by slogans such as "NET"

(No Extra Talk) and "Don't Give Me Paragraphs! Give Me Bullets."[12]

The laconic mode fits a competitive view of the world. Whether for winning or mere self-defense, toughness here requires a low profile, close-to-the-ground wariness. The less you tell others about yourself and where you are going, the less you enable others to contradict, upstage, outwit and emotionally manipulate you. The theme of vulnerability reduced by self-control, the idea of the strong person who can keep his feelings and designs to himself, runs through popular phrases from that very American game, poker—the "poker-faced" man who "plays his cards close to his vest." The laconic mode stands for self-sufficient confidence, but in fact it can also cover up the traditional western male's *lack* of confidence about expressing sensibility, having been taught that fine feelings are for women. Perhaps it takes a Hemingway to use functional brevity and silence itself—like a good architect's use of space—to convey sensitive feelings.

Today the laconic mode remains attractive because it contrasts with the approval-seeking and fashion-following promoted by other forces of the culture, old and new: democracy, puritan prying, fear of violence and social conflict, systematic organization, public relations. The laconic tough guy is free of the need to placate others or justify his actions with elaborate words. "A man's gotta do what he's gotta do." In films and fiction, the laconic hero often represents an antibureaucratic ideal—Clint Eastwood's Dirty Harry, the unorthodox but ultimately humane detective cutting through the phoney rules and excuses of officialdom with brief, hard, flat statements.

But who of us can be Dirty Harry? Isn't it conceivable that most Americans enjoy toughly laconic individualism in their fantasies only? They may admire Mr. Eastwood, but in their day-to-day lives they scurry around placating the boss, their colleagues, and their relatives. There is some truth in this. Even the type of assertiveness training that tells people how to stick up for themselves against unfair demands by repeating plain statements sometimes assumes that the would-be assertive will be unable to get away from placatory language: "I understand how you feel but. . . ." "I may have made a mistake, but. . . ."[13] It does not follow, however, that *all* leanings to laconic toughness are displaced onto fantasy figures. The tendencies to terseness and curtness in ordinary language and in business behavior refute this. American corporate life, indeed, produces verbal extremes from placatory beatings around the bush to the bruising put-down or joke. A certain democratic informality between ranks may actually encourage a kind of bullying to show who is boss.[14] Other styles mix the appeasing with the tough and terse. In the high reaches of Washington's national security agencies, largely manned by exbusiness executives and lawyers, Richard Barnet has described "the style of talking to a subordinate: the driving command masked by superficial informality; or to a superior: fact-loaded, quantitative, gutsy."[15]

As Barnet's example indicates, the American language of toughness has produced various styles that put together the expansive and laconic. An exponent of one such formula is the quiet, pragmatic movie hero who bursts into eloquence at a climactic moment, quelling his audience with forceful home truths. A very different style, found in politics and bureaucracy, is that of the slow talker who deploys heavy phrases: "We shall make a determination on that." The exact reverse is the habitual fast talker who uses terse language. This comes in several overlapping variants—New Yorker, Jewish, detective hero, and so on—and it has still another converse, a less wordy style that uses terse language but inflates its images. So, Mickey Spillane tells us that Mike Hammer "fired a cig," "killed a quart," "punched Lola's number out [after] working the phone book," "threw a buck on the counter," and "grabbed a cab."[16] The first page of Robert Penn Warren's *All the King's Men* (1946) provides another classic mixture: terse-sounding language exaggerating danger and excitement in the commonplace. American popular writing, indeed, has evolved several kinds of expansive/laconic combinations. In the Gold Rush era, far western humor often used laconic exaggeration.[17] Another tradition, ranging from Twain to Chandler, uses a wordy narration to highlight terse dialogue; and some authors effusively celebrate their tough heroes' very lack of effusiveness.

Within words themselves, American language has gone in for a Meccano approach, coupling a verb with a preposition ("kickback," "smashup," "rollback"), or connecting a noun with another noun connoting action or impact ("bookmobile," "trustbuster"). Often crisp and dynamic in sound, these terms paradoxically condense meaning by expanding the initial word. Mixtures such as these conceal a tension within ACT between the imperial and the armored: the impulse to move out, to reach, to incorporate, and the impulse to "hunker down," conserve, and defend.

"HIT THE LINE"/"TOUGH IT OUT"

The tough guy's need for action cuts across a more universal definition of toughness that Americans also honor. The American belief in dynamism and grand–slam impact, in speed for survival and winning, undermines their commitment to endurance, to "hanging in there" and "gutsing it out." Although the tough guy is traditionally supposed to be able to take it, his equally traditional insistence on fast results stimulates low tolerance of frustration. Americans have seldom given much praise to the kind of stoic who simply accepts an adverse situation. Instead they have believed that one can change, and change fast, either the environment or one's place in it.[18]

A get-it-over-with psychology has often colored American military tactics. In World War II and Korea commanders tended to pile their men into all-out assaults rather than careful outflanking movements that reached the objective later but might have saved casualties. (Political consideration sometimes required quick results, but this did not explain all of it.) The same impatience characterized Vietnam tactics, except that firepower was more often substituted for human assaults.[19] In modern athletics too, American runners have tended for a long time to excel at sprints more than at long distances.

The theme of flying, associated with speed, strength, and liberation, is particularly important in America culture; how fitting it is that Tom Wolfe, portrayer of modern America, should abandon irreverence when writing about virile heroes of the air.[20] Superman's gift of flying—originally an extended leap—had a forerunner in the Western hero's mythical jump off a 60-foot cliff into a river, usually the Ohio, to elude pursuers. This was attributed to Daniel Boone, several contemporaries, and Wild Bill Hickok, before reappearing on the movie screen. Flying heroes go back to antiquity, but their flight then was a more minor specialty, the talent of a Hermes, not a Hercules.

The roots of the American attachment to speed-as-strength go back to the rapid but protracted opening up of the country and the twin possibilities of horse and machine. On the one hand, the cowboy's centaur figure coursing the Great Plains; on the other, the riverboat passengers commanding their captain to "go on the fastest" and beat the other boat even if he blew up the boilers (as he sometimes did).[21] In warfare, capital-intensiveness and American aptitudes for technology—without the inuring experience of war in the main population—increasingly favored all-out attack rather than slow attrition. Small wonder that World War II's most famous tough-guy general was a flamboyant, hard-hitting tank commander.[22] Even in warfare, though, mechanization was not the only cause of the stress on speed. Another source was the tradition of the military irregular—the flexible, unregimented fighter who travelled light and moved quickly, be it the Revolutionary backwoodsman or John Mosby's Confederate raider. Such figures never provided the main force of their respective sides, but they presented a link between action and individualism.

Against these tendencies, toughness as endurance had its own American foundations. The expression, "tough it out," which got such a bad reputation in Watergate, goes back to the 1830s frontier if not before.[23] Pioneer and immigrant hardiness; the winter at Valley Forge; Stonewall Jackson at First Bull Run—these and other records remind us that ACT is not just about dash and daring. The Civil War sanctified both kinds of toughness, though postwar myth and reputation made more of rapid movement than solid defense.[24] Inevitably the value attached to endurance has varied with period and section. In the popular antebellum sport of horse racing, long-distance staying power—"bottom"—started out as the main criterion, though the dramatic attractions of speed became more valued in the 1830s and 1840s.[25] Philosophically, endurance received high praise in the Progressive period when popular writers translated into an idiom of toughness the wish to reestablish a moral and productive order upon the quick gains and exploitations of nineteenth–century America. Gilbert Patten, creator of the college hero, Frank Merriwell, made much of the "stayer" who would "persist against all obstacles and succeed in the struggle of life."[26] Urban moralists praised the "dogged industry" of the cowboy, and his endurance of hardship and suffering. Other commentators noted with delight the same qualities, as well as aggressiveness, among American soldiers in the war against Spain.[27]

In our own time the sharpest depictions of solid, punishment-taking endurance have pitted lower-class protagonists against various kinds of exploiters and parasites—thus, Sylvester Stallone in *Rocky* and Marlon Brando in *On the Waterfront*. The heroes of hard-boiled detective fiction were a lower–middle–class variation, their quality a laconic, "mean–streets" persistence against rich marauders. However, the resistance of American society to class consciousness and proletarianism has worked against the idea of a specific lower-class toughness. (*Rocky*, indeed, expressed racial as much as class antagonism: the old stereotype of the stolid, dull-witted immigrant was used to make a white ethnic counterattack on showy, black machismo.)

Of course speed and endurance can go together. The unemployed drifters in the 1880s depression, who "rode the rods" under freight cars and affected to despise "walking bums," combined skill and nerve with all-weather staying power. In its most publicized forms, however, "taking it" in American culture is apt to be intense rather than protracted. This suits the short timespan of movies and action novels but applies to real events also: the famed defenses in American military history—New Orleans, the Alamo, Bastogne, and so on—were short-run affairs. The classic case is American football's mixture of speed and punishment with unlimited substitution and the constant interruption of play. In football, too, the insistence by tough coaches on total willpower for victory works against the stiff upper lip in defeat: hence the spectacle of defeated players weeping in the locker room.[28] Even when toughness *has* required a longer-term endurance, legend and language surround it with images of quick impact and speed. Unlike the British Black Watch, the military corps most famed in America for casualty-taking toughness—the Leathernecks—are associated with amphibious assaults.[29] Again, in World War II, the troops of General "Vinegar Joe" Stilwell, who based his toughness on a stoic infantry tradition, also called him "Galloping Joe" because he liked to go everywhere on foot. Even popular American phrases have linked endurance with fact action: "rough sledding," "he just kept going and going," or—to quote Knute Rockne and Richard Nixon—"when the going gets tough, the tough get going."

The ideal combination lies in Tom Wolfe's account of test pilots and military fliers. To climb the pyramid to the supreme fraternity of astronauts—to survive all the selecting-out along the way—a pilot had to possess

the ability to go up in a hurtling piece of machinery and put his hide on the line and then have the moxie, the reflexes, the experience, the coolness, to pull it back in the last yawning moments—and then to go up again *the next day*, and the next day, and every next day, even if the series should prove infinite. . . . [30]

Speed, short bursts of crisis coolly managed, nerve to go on and on—Wolfe's definition of toughness goes to the heart of ACT. Yet in many other contexts the fusion is not so neat. When presidents take strong, decisive action overseas, they are apt to get widespread support at home, however controversial the issue; but that support swiftly diminishes if the military action becomes protracted and there are weekly casualty lists. Although Americans admire tenacity (and like other people, often practice it in ordinary ways), their historic impatience and their modern affluence work against it.

TOP DOGS AND UNDERDOGS

Despite his praise of independence, the modern tough guy's drive for victory and total effectiveness sometimes makes him an autocratic football coach or the coach's obedient follower. Yet American folklore still praises the gutsy underdog who bucks the organization and gives an old–fashioned comeuppance to institutional bullies.[31] It does so, at least, if the challenger is successful—if he is a Ralph Nader, or a political insurgent who wins his primaries. If he does not win, he is soon tagged as a loser: ineffective, unrealistic, no real tough guy. Aspects of military life illustrate well the dual tendency of American toughness to irreverence and obedience. On the one hand, the back talk to officers and the cults of informality in World War II. On the other, the hazing of plebes at West Point (done in part to mold a heterogeneous intake) and the preference at staff colleges for set book solutions over open-ended problem solving: a production–line rather than a discussive approach to education.[32]

I will not dwell here on the general problem of conformity and compliance versus tough-guy independence (for this see chapter 3). Instead I wish to examine political images and literary devices that have enabled top dogs—leaders and heroes—to exaggerate their brave alignment with underdogs or to benefit from legends that do the exaggerating for them.

The most basic formulas are inherent in the orthodox face of power presented by capitalism and democracy: the economic notion that a competitive market mechanism rather than a ruling class or elite allocates wealth, however imperfectly, to the advantage of all; and the political notion that elected leaders do represent the people—again if not perfectly, at least better than any other kind of leadership. Both ideas encourage the dynamic reformer to attack fat cats and their personal abuses rather than essential structures of power.[33] Whatever their factual merits, these ideas produce their own form of hypocrisy. Western leaders have become adept at justifying almost any policy as an enhancement of life for the unprivileged. Americans got a head start on this early in their history when business classes, old and new, developed their conservative but antiauthoritarian rhetoric of ordered liberty and political equality. The economic doctrines of American conservatism expanded this position when they moved away from the *selective toughness* of a particularly harsh form of social Darwinism in the late nineteenth century (declaring that the strong few must win at the expense of the weak many) to a *distributive toughness* in the twentieth (where tax breaks for the rich were supposed to stimulate the endeavor of most people by expanding the economy).

A more indirect way of posing as the tough champion of underdogs is to exaggerate the power and exploitativeness of adversaries while scorning them individually as soft or useless. This is not confined to Americans. It has characterized political movements that are sharply concerned with strength and weakness—especially those that combine assumptions of superiority with fears of victimization. For example, European fascist attacks on Jews tended to portray them as flabby and decadent but collectively dangerous. In several countries, intellectuals and high officeholders have been viewed the same way. In the United States, however, the conjunction of nativism with antielitism encouraged this dual labelling. Catholic immigrants were portrayed as the brainwashed foot soldiers of the Pope; blacks as inferior but monstrous and the tool of privileged do-gooders. As both examples show, the plain republican fear of servility sometimes included a contempt for the servile, the downtrodden. Muscular Free Soilers of the 1850s, who disliked black slaves no less than their masters, reapplied the old fear of European aristocracy that saw serflike submission as the counterpart of overlord arrogance.

A modern version of this theme occurs in those western movies where the champion liberates a local populace from a predator and his henchmen. Terrorized and impotent, the common folk are initially unable to organize their own defense; it is a matter of implicit debate between different movies as to whether they have the spirit to take on the job or can be trained to do so. Their contemptability is debatable; what is not debatable is the superiority of their savior.

In legends and popular literature there were more superficial devices, too, for combining top–dog and underdog appeals. One tendency in western myth was to exaggerate the physique of real figures, such as Daniel Boone and Kit Carson, while simultaneously exaggerating their opposition—setting them against fantastic numbers of Indians or facing them, gunless, with a bear or lion. A different, twentieth–century tack romanticizes a certain kind of physical smallness, a wiry, mobile leanness. This goes back to the nostalgic celebration of cowboys that started in the 1890s; it became a minor literary convention to contrast their lithe slimness with the heftier, slower physique of farmers and other settlers.[34] Among screen heroes the device caught on in the 1960s when a general shift started from projections of rock-like brawn to catlike nimbleness and sinew. This suited the new era of the sensitive tough.

Some underdog symbols do their work in a negative, "reverse sell" manner. I call them *belying devices*. A belying device is a feature of the hero that superficially contradicts his admired qualities: in this case, his toughness and mastery. It underlines by contrast his possession of those qualities, and it humanizes them. It is less deeply debilitating than a tragic flaw or Achilles' heel, but it can have a psychological dimension. Thus the chief Watergate prosecutor is reported to have said, "I'm one of those little guys who's insecure so I like to get into tournaments with big guys and whip 'em."[35] For individuals pressed into especially demanding roles, a staple belying device is the playful, unheroic posture: it accentuates the protagonist's real toughness in the eyes of others while providing a sense of escape and a release of tension for the protagonist himself.[36] Most belying devices, however, are confined to fiction and myth. American popular novelists rely on them heavily to offset their heroes' tediously extensive competence. They range from the smallness of the late nineteenth century dime–novel hero, Nick Carter—the muscled and multiexpert "Little Giant"—to the dainty coloring and grace of "Dol" Bonner, Rex Stout's thoroughly tough "she-dick."[37] The ultimate in belying devices is physical handicap; it increases the challenge but also represents the humane. Television's Inspector Ironside was impressively mobile in his wheelchair but that was not the main thing. His paralysis conveyed an experienced and wise humanity that put into relief his toughness in cross–examining and his general command.[38]

Belying devices produce their effects by mounting a reverse sort of dare. Telly Savalas's Kojak could afford to suck a lollipop because he was so tough, just as The Flash, the comic-strip hero of fantastic speed, was chronically tardy in everyday life. (As New York's chicken king, Frank Perdue, put it, "It takes a tough man to make a tender chicken.") The same juxtaposition characterized the tough-guy phrase, "I got it, baby," though here the soft element was projected onto another in a slightly dominating way. "He's a tough baby" or "tough cookie" expressed a similar contrast. Occasionally even gentility—mock or real—is pressed into service as a belying device. Wild Bill Hickok used his fancy buckskins as a decoy in several legendary encounters. Mocked as a dude by saloon roughs, he teaches them a violent lesson.[39] On a more searching level in our own times we have the character of Atticus Finch in *To Kill a Mockingbird*. His gentlemanly presence conceals his authority with a rifle, just as it belies his ability to speak out against the violent bigots of a Southern town.[40]

REALISTS AND MORALISTS

The historic duality in American culture between pragmatism and moralism has been much examined by other writers. What they have not explored, however, is the way that admiration of toughness and strength pops up on both sides of the duality.[41]

The society's traditional respect for hard-headed practicality includes a terror of being suckered and of being thought to be a sucker. If American English has a rich range of words for being soft or sissy (from "cream puff" to "yellow-belly"), its number of names for naive victims is even greater when compared with the numbers of equivalent words in British English. "Sap," "pushover," "easy mark," "soft touch," "patsy," "fall guy", expressions such as "I'm not going to lie down and roll over," these are responsible for much of the American tough guy's distinctive idiom.[42] The language speaks not just to the fear of being made a fool of but to the fear of being owned, controlled by forces outside oneself: situations, relationships, even doctrines. One of Joseph McCarthy's skills in deploying the "soft on Communism" smear lay in the way he merged the sucker with the subversive and the sissy: the "fellow-traveller" and "dupe" with the

State Department "cookie-pusher" homosexual. A decade later, a new vogue use of "tough-minded" helped intellectuals to establish their credentials as tough guys too, turning on other, more utopian intellectuals. For such people, wishful thinking and overt idealism were largely synonymous. None of this was wholly new—the threads of intellectual anti-intellectualism run well back into the nineteenth century—but there was now a magnified sense that mental processes themselves could be tough: incisive, fact–devouring, unfooled. The key metaphor of the tough mind was the "analytic tool" (a term largely developed in the 1950s), which would cut through emotive language to the hard realities. Momentarily discredited by the Vietnam war (see David Halberstam's portraits in *The Best and the Brightest*), the tough-minded style was too deeply and broadly based along the political spectrum to succumb to attacks on "technocracy" or yield to the argument that superrealists only saw one kind of reality, the sort represented by quantities, techniques, and tangibles. Obviously, however, the main thrust of tough–mindedness was conservative, a spirit best caught by the boastful cliché, "I see the world as it is, not as I'd like it to be."[43]

Yet the other American style, affirming idealism, hope, and vision, has engaged conservatives as well as liberals. It too has appealed to notions of toughness, suitably dignified as puritan strenuosity and moral dynamism. The rhetorical tradition that produced "Fighting Bob" LaFollette and other champions of righteousness at the turn of the century was not confined to reformers; today, in less combative forms, it is enshrined in the standard rhetoric of presidential inaugurals and other set-piece political addresses. The canon's obligatory references to "renewal," "regeneration," "dedication," and "challenge" articulate within their moral summons an enormous concern with strength and vitality.

Such rhetoric does not coexist with the language of tough-guy realism simply by exalted separation. The meeting of the two is most striking in the acceptance speeches of major party nominees for president, for these speeches must at once set a tone of battle, declare a capability, and promise moral direction and unity in the nation as well as the party. Somehow they must juxtapose the largeness of dreaming dreams with the necessity of hard choices and tough decisions. The line between galvanizing hope and Pollyanaish sentiment becomes thin indeed. The contrary pulls in all of this appeared strikingly in the 1980 acceptance speech of Jimmy Carter. In Democratic party tradition he stressed "justice" and "compassion" as well as the more bipartisan themes of "peace," "vision," and national strength. At the same time he used a series of images to proclaim that he, not his hawkish, hard-money opponent, was the tough realist; that his opponent, not he, merely acted tough in a "world of tinsel and make-believe." Carter's attempt to outflank conservative toughness was the latest version of a Democratic defense against the tag of softness that went back to the 1930s.[44]

In a side-of-the-mouth way, popular writers convey the same tension from an opposite starting point.

A killer's a killer no matter what. I guess it's sadder to look down at the body of a young kid who never said boo to anybody than it is to look down at the body of a guy who spent his life ripping people off, but I'm not paid to be a poet.[45]

The conflict of this remark of Kojak's between humane justice and professional ("I–do–my–job") hardness goes back through hard-boiled writers of the thirties to naturalist writers at the turn of the century, who were caught between a reformist sympathy for victims and a social Darwinist desire to be unsentimental about the realities of power and the survival of the fittest. The tough and tender blend makes it hard for foreigners to re-create the tough-guy hero of modern American fiction and media. The foreign equivalents either seem callous and metallic or just not so quick and dangerous as their American counterparts.[46] The tension between the urge to help others and a self-preserving contempt for sacrificial lambs—sometimes producing the movie hero who reluctantly but knowingly sacrifices himself—is an especially American theme. The tough guy's toughness is all the more vivid because of the underlying sentiment that threatens to break through it.[47]

Historically, the political alignment of moralism with practical toughness has been closer in some eras and events than in others. A high point (or low point) of fusion was the 1840 "Log Cabin" campaign when the Whigs tried to out-democrat the Democrats, successfully stealing and developing a pitch used by Andrew Jackson's supporters to elect him in 1828. Accusing their opponents of monarchical treachery and dissipation, the Whigs claimed for themselves the character of honest, productive farmers and artisans. The Democrats in turn accused the Whigs of being demagogic dandies, insulting the "hard-fisted yeoman" by masquerading as his friends. Thirty years later, in the battle between party spoilsmen and educated reformers, this alignment between images of moral and practical strength was sharply split. To the spoilsmen went the theme of antigenteel, down-to-earth pragmatism; to the reformers the claim of moral strenuosity ("fighting the spoils") and clean, manly virtue against urban corruption. The split was not total; both sides combined moral animus with a concept of governmental effectiveness; but not until the career of Theodore Roosevelt, strenuously combining civil service reform with tough party politicking, was something like the old alignment put together again.[48]

Despite these conjunctions—despite Roosevelt's "applied idealism" and Hoover's "humane efficiency"—people who have written about the dualism have tended to portray it as a sharp dichotomy: cynical dealings on one level, abstract idealism on another, with violent swings between the two. In fact the culture has evolved an array of devices, superficial and deceptive as some of them are, to bridge the gap and provide unified conceptions of moral strength and practical toughness. A widespread method, not especially American, is the expression of self-interest as *dis*interest; another is to say that high ends justify dirty means. A less recognized process works the other way around. In milieus where the primacy of calculating interests has become the norm, moral scruple is distinguished as self-serving pragmatism. This, again, is no monopoly of Americans, but the American wish to be both moral and hard-headed does much to promote it. Eager not to seem naive and squeamish, a government lawyer warns his principals to stay clean merely from the standpoint of not getting caught; a businessman declares that "life is too short" to play crooked games; a football coach tells his team that fouling "won't do you one bit of good; the other team will just foul back." In politics the history of such behavior goes back at least to the eve of the Civil War when moralism was active, yet feared, and entwined with political calculation. The same tendency reemerged in the 1960s when government dissenters on Vietnam felt they had to justify their position in terms of power payoffs and feasibility ("we can't win") rather than morality. The effect, ironically, was to make them look defeatist rather than principled.[49]

The gap, in short, between moralism and practical or material concerns can be bridged in both directions: each may be disguised or enlisted as the other. In one direction, Americans have a special tendency to call upon high purpose and moral energy as a means, a resource, for seeking strength and dynamism (as well as union). The crudest version of this is the popular religionists' promotion of "prayer power" and "God power" as "efficiency methods" for achieving success. More recently we have had the discovery at Harvard of "ethical ideas" as a "powerful" and competitive "tool . . . in resolving management issues and motivating organizations."[50] In the other direction, practical processes and short-run material objectives are sometimes cast as moral and spiritual ends. Much of the popularity of Richard Bach's *Jonathan Livingston Seagull* in the early 1970s surely lay in the spiritualization of sheer technique, as the gull, training for faster, more perfect flight, transcended his physical limits and became immortal.[51] On a more banal plane there is some parallel in the distinctively American use of terms like "goals" and "personal objectives." "I have set new goals for myself" often refers to quite material and short–run plans, but it has the headiness of moral purpose. Here, as in the presidential rhetoric, ideas of vigor and effectiveness are strongly bound up with *motion*: the achieving individual, like the nation, needs a shining locomotive to pull himself on.

DUALITIES IN TOUGHNESS

Dualities in American culture—the pull to opposite attitudes—were noted long before Michael Kammen wrote his book on the subject in the early 1970s.[52] It is not clear in fact that dualism per se is a particularly American tendency. Even if it is, Kammen's account is too diffuse to explain why American notions of toughness and strength can be paired in the way I have set out. Other writers' explanations, too, do not tell us why ACT values themselves seem to be dualistic.[53]

What are the reasons? I suggest two. Each, taken alone, is probably inadequate; but taken together (albeit on different levels) they explain much of the matter. The first is a subjective reason. I have chosen to organize in paradoxical pairs what another writer in another intellectual climate might organize differently. "Muscle and Mind," for instance, might well be presented as a triangular tension between physique, clever competence, and academic or artistic mastery.

The second reason lies in the divisive and destructive tendencies of ACT and a countervailing wish to control and compensate for these tendencies. Ideas of a tough but controlled mental competence curb admiration of the intimidating muscle man; the laconic mode brakes the expansionist; even the celebration of endurance provides a stabilizing antedote to the aggressive connotations of speed (taking it versus making it). The fit of this argument is not simple or easy. Sometimes it applies in reverse: the laconic becomes the isolated self-server; the expansionist the social cooperator. Dual images of toughness can, in this way, suggest two-way control: each side of a pair (top–dog authoritarianism versus underdog revolt, or hard-headed pragmatism versus strenuous moralism) symbolizes a check on the aggressive potential in its opposite. The need for such reassurances lies in the peculiar relationship of ACT values to social order. The very fact of a socially enjoined ideal that stresses self—taking care of oneself, standing up for oneself, fighting for oneself—generates ambiguity. The problem is one for western individualism as a whole, but it is magnified by the historic associations of toughness with contest.

The ambivalence that surrounds American admiration of strength and aggressiveness appears in fictional fantasies of the alienated superhero, stressed and isolated by his destructive potential. "The Incredible Hulk" merely puts into crude formula a development that goes back to *Gladiator*, Philip Wylie's lightly but beautifully written novel of 1930.[54] Again, from Jacksonian times, the democratic humanity of American toughness has always had to compete with the notion that losers are saps, and saps are fair game for exploitation. Barnum's joyful dictum, "there's a sucker born every minute," finds an echo in the coach's slogan, adapted from poolroom hustling: "Don't give a sucker a break."[55] Such pronouncements, however, have an element of bluster. The famous football aphorism, "winning isn't the most important thing, it's the only thing"—versions of which decorated many a corporate office in the 1960s—gets its punch from the fact that others have said it is *not* the most important thing.[56]

The mean guy celebration—the spirit of "nice guys finish last"—draws on three related sources besides the obvious one of commercial and professional competitiveness. The first is the antigenteel tradition. When Harry Hopkins recounted a ploy he used to get more money for his New Deal relief operations, he explained that there were two kinds of administrators, "gentlemen and go-getters . . . [and] I'm no gentleman."[57] Gentlemen played by the rules. Nongentlemen won. The second source goes back to the early nineteenth century and is embedded in traditions of child-rearing. Compared with European traditions, American child-rearing has tended to concern itself with opportunities for natural vigor and expression. Children should be considerate, get along with others, but not be too angelic, too artificially repressed—boys especially should show a bit of the rascal, the hellion. This of course was not a prescription for meanness, but it did provide a sanction for rule-breaking assertiveness. The third source, closely related to this, is the male assumption that authority, in its taming role, is essentially feminine and schoolmarmish. The assumption is not uniquely American, but historical and demographic factors—well identified by others—have magnified its strength in the United States. One result is the inner vulnerability described by John Dean in his account of the Nixon White House: his concern to build a "reputation for toughness" against the charge that he had some "little old lady" in him (that is, scruples).[58]

The striking thing about these ideas, however, is that all of them are contested. Gentility (even in America) has status. Rules and laws are respected, as they have to be in any society. And the belief that moral authority is feminine has had to contend with the ancient equation of manly strength with virtue, honest frankness, and standing up for principle.[59] Small wonder that admiration of "hard ball" toughness in business and politics so often has a furtive quality. Small wonder, too, that contradictory signals, from different groups and institutions within the society, have ensnared several of America's most famous tough guys. The widely divergent careers of George Patton, Joe McCarthy, and Ohio football coach "Woody" Hayes shared one common strand. In all three cases, important institutions (the army, the Senate committee system, Big Ten football) permitted, even encouraged, aggressions that made traditional appeals but ultimately caused outrage. All three figures used the press to project images; all three were finally undone in the press by "ugly" exposure. In each case, different groups were attracted and repelled, but the balance of influence between these groups shifted as it became generally believed that the individuals themselves had gone too far.[60]

LANGUAGE OF RELIEF

In language, as in other spheres, the idea of toughness requires relief. Colloquial language meets the requirements in two senses. It provides symbolic respite and antedote, but it also sharpens the appeal of toughness by throwing it into relief: it provides tough and untough contrasts. The language, thus, supports toughness while offering a sense of control and alternative.

Neil Schmitz has observed that in major American literature the theme of laziness is at least as prevalent as the theme of rugged action.[61] The same is true of modern colloquialisms. Those unhardy perennials— "relax," "take it easy now," "have fun," "have a nice day," "enjoy"—are all distinctively American while standing in opposition to the strenuosity that also pervades American language.[62] Their relationships to toughness are several. If, on one plane, they suggest escape and revolt, they also represent a concern for health and fitness in tanking up for the next bout of energetic output. Their prescription may make better sense than pep pills and foods for quick energy, but in this aspect they are part of the same cultural value. Dependence on activity for a sense of worth and identity (still heard in the phrase, "I keep busy by . . . ") is the other side of the same coin. At the same time relaxation aids the operator whose armory includes relaxed assurance, coolness, timing, and an aura of strength–in–reserve.

A complex psychology governs the long-standing American attraction to pairs of "hard" and "soft" words—from hard sell/soft sell to hard porn/soft porn.[63] The significant thing about these pairs is that they do not simply derogate softness, though the frequent use of these images does suggest a concern with strength and weakness. In some cases, the "soft" term offsets a toughness that may be admired but nonetheless has a connotation of narrowness, callousness, or crude aggression—as in "hard-nosed," "hard-boiled," "hard-sell." In other cases, the "soft" functionally complements the "hard": thus computer "hardware" needs programming "software" (even if sometimes, more esoterically, it also used "firmware"). In these and other instances, the immediate meaning of "soft" is fairly neutral. (The hired gun is, by definition, on soft money!)[64] Symbolically, however, these terms play the joke of the belying device. They represent a technical knowing, the kind of person who understands the most obviously hard approaches but can afford to find another way, sailing in close to an image of weakness but really being strong and effective. The increased prevalence of soft usage along these lines reflects a modern world of sophisticated science: sensitive interviewing techniques, penetrating but wittingly inconclusive ("soft-nosed" research producing "soft" data); nonpolluting production methods ("soft" technology); computer "software" again; and so forth.

Another kind of relief language is that of euphemism and conflict-avoidance. Unlike the genres just described, it is based almost wholly outside ACT values and styles. The reach of euphemism in America is a huge subject in itself. Its functions include the muting of contest (instead of ''opposing'' someone, ''move into an adversary relationship'' with him), the concealment of ambition (say ''ranking member'' for ''senior'' or ''superior''), and the skirting of moral provocation (''positive change'' for ''improvement''). The culture of euphemism goes far beyond tricks of language: it ranges from the old family custom of holding hands at grace to Walt Disney's prettifying of harsh old fairy tales: wolf no longer eats little pig. Anxiety about aggression is not the sole source of euphemism; it is also linked to affluence, commercial servicing, and a complex of values to do with health, moral hygiene and the pursuit of happiness. In a part of their minds many Americans feel that they have both the resources and the duty to clear up, or zone out, all unpleasantness and messiness in their private lives. Social striving encourages euphemism and so does the diversity and geographical movement of the populace. They make individuals less sure of having that common—or at least predictable—background that sustains frank and easy discourse. This brings us back, however, to the fear of aggression. As Florence King has observed, ethnic and cultural pluralism induces Americans to ''zap [one another] with friendliness,'' to neutralize any possible antagonism as fast as possible.[65] ACT and euphemism, therefore, are antedotes for each other. If many Americans sense that the world of euphemism denies part of their identity—a tradition of ruggedness and authenticity—they are also tempted to flee to that world from the more dangerous imperatives of traditional toughness.

2
PRODUCERS AND CONSUMERS

The very style of Ronald Reagan's advent to the presidency contained ambiguity. For years he had called upon Americans to return to an old economic individualism: he had projected simplicity, strength, and puritan rectitude. Toward the Russians he was a man of the West: "It's time for us to straighten up and eyeball them." If most of the time he seemed genial, he stood always for toughness.

In his Inaugural Address, he recognized that the United States faced an "economic affliction of great proportions"—a protracted inflation that penalized alike the thrifty, the "struggling young," and the elderly on fixed incomes. In the standard rhetoric of such occasions, he consecrated the nation to renewed energy and affirmation against its doubts. Yet although his economic policy was to be a brother to Mrs. Thatcher's, he would not emulate her warnings of a painful, rocky ride ahead. Instead he implied that the road would be easy, bought by a kind of inverse dependence on government. Removing the government "roadblocks" would take time but much would then follow, as day follows night—investment would flow, productivity would rise. At the end of the address, when the president had singled out the pledged endeavor of an American soldier killed in World War I, he was swift to add that no such martial sacrifice was relevant to the crisis at hand. What was needed was simply "our best effort, our work" and a state of mind—readiness for "great deeds," belief "in ourselves" as Americans, aided by God.

After the address, there were banquets of great opulence (privately paid for); it was a time of high fashion and long limousines. It became even more evident that many of the president's friends were self-made rich who believed that their own efforts and achievements had earned them the right to enjoy luxury and display it. This in itself was logical, but it sat not quite easily with other forms of toughness that the president had invoked: the physical hardiness, the wood-chopping simplicity, the struggle of ordinary folk in their ordinary lives. The styles of Ronald Reagan paid respect to frontier ruggedness, but they overlaid that respect with symbols of affluence and a glamorizing of consumption. The tension, however, was not simply that of frontier tradition versus consumer capitalism; it lay within business civilization itself.[1]

The historic connections between America's business culture and the theme of toughness are numerous and contradictory. For if the world of "making it" has promoted a tough-guy assertiveness, it has also fostered the opposite, a dependence on organization and its material fruits. American capitalism has in large measure masked this contradiction. It has encouraged people to displace their anxieties: to blame big government rather than big business for their loss of independence.[2] It has also used sales techniques and the thrills of technology to couch its invitations to dependency and self–indulgence within images of individual potency. These patterns are cut deeply into American culture: I will argue at the end of this chapter that neither the movement away from the work ethic depicted by some observers in the 1970s, nor a new awareness of economic limits, has yet dispelled the underlying conflict.

"Just let some of the youngsters I know have a chance and they'll give those gentlemen points." So spoke Woodrow Wilson in declaring battle for what he called "the man on the make" against the restrictive practices of big trust bosses and their henchmen in Congress. His tone declared the traditional equation: constructive entrepreneurship = upward mobility = dynamic toughness. In the 1950s the new upper classes in a typical small city were described to C. Wright Mills in a similar vein:

Boys with a lot of dynamite. . . . They're in there together going places and doing everything that's good for [the city]. . . . They have active investments all over, not just money lying around doing nothing.[3]

As a source of ACT styles and values, the idea of the self–made businessman beating his way upward was all the more important because it lay squarely within urban life even if it also thrived in frontier conditions. Variants of the tough guy were thus able to survive modernization without simply depending on back-to-nature trips and cowboy fantasies. One element, dating from the midnineteenth century, has been the tie-up between business and local political machines. It was not what the civic-minded Wilson had in mind when he praised the "man on the make." Nevertheless it channelled into commercial and political graft the real survival toughness of the immigrant leader, who needed to create some system for himself and his people out of the bewildering urban jungle he found about him.

The more direct, traditional links between commercial business and ACT values can be summarized quite briefly. Inside as well as outside the organization, business competitiveness meant beating out rivals and driving hard bargains; it meant aggressive selling, dynamic growth, and a hard-headed insistence on "results." If manipulation has replaced intimidation in many parts of corporate life, American executives are still more apt to be "canned" for poor performance than their equivalents in most other countries. In 1977 I asked an executive near the top of a large and well–established American financial firm what he meant by "toughness" in business. His very first comment was that you had to be able to fire people—he used this as a way of stressing high standards of performance. In some areas of business, firing has been so common now that it inflicts virtually no disgrace; the fired executive just bobs up elsewhere. In other business areas, bureaucracy has virtually eliminated this pattern; but in politics too the use of firing to demonstrate toughness and mastery could be seen in President Carter's sudden "massacre" of five cabinet officers in July 1979, after public criticism of his competence had become particularly acute. If American business executives, being human, are drawn to the security of price agreements and government help, they are also conditioned by the value, largely a business value, on quantifiable performance. The fact that so many business outcomes are a matter of numbers—dollars and cents— encourages a competitive game attitude, for as in a game you can see precisely who is scoring. Some of this is not intrinsically American: the whole system of stock markets, after all, is tied to the value on quantified growth. On the other hand, the laws that require publication of corporate officers' earnings are by no means widespread outside America. One of their effects is to encourage competitive and mobile-minded comparisons between senior executives. (Here, as elsewhere, there is a chicken-and-egg relationship between capitalism and ACT:

business attitudes promoted and shaped American notions of toughness, but since other factors also produced ACT, it became an influence in its own right, feeding back into business behavior.)

In longer perspective, the American language itself shows how business attitudes have selected and absorbed specific images of toughness. The expression, "I don't buy that," reminds us that the tough guy's stress on not being a sucker has a lot to do historically with a person's need to look out for himself in a bargaining, line-shooting society.[4] Likewise, the "go-aheadativeness of American businessmen"—as the *New York Times* described it in 1855—associated energy, action, and impact, themes that run through the nation's slang, with ambitious "hustle" at work: from old terms like "snap," "zip" and "pep" to "he's a real pistol" or "hit the ground running." The language of money-making enterprise made speed tangible by linking it with acquisition: "get-up-and-get," "go-getting," "get a piece of the action." (It is significant that the more recent phrase, "Can you swing it?" often put into a bureaucratic context the image of action and the idea of pulling off a deal: can you get what you want from a difficult but exploitable organization?) Similar values produced a vocabulary of energetic mastery and competence—what Americans throughout the eighteenth and nineteenth centuries peculiarly called "executive" qualities. The assumption that management is inherently more than custodial, that it requires fast action and impact, goes back to the opening up of the country in the early nineteenth century when American language expanded the use of "run" as a transitive verb: to "run" a bank, and so on.[5] This, of course, has not remained distinctively American, but some other terms for competitive dominance and personal control have: for example, "call the shots" and the small galaxy of phrases containing "put" in a manipulative sense. Long before "put you wise" and "put it over," Americans in the nineteenth century said "put it to," "put it into" and "put the run on" for getting the better of somebody.

The language of business assertiveness and acquisition is not, of course, confined to Americans. Executives in many countries mount sales "campaigns," seek market "penetration," and use various images of strength and dynamism in their public relations. In the United States, however, historical factors gave special assistance to business tough-talk: frontier expansion and the lack of an established aristocracy fostered a business slang that zipped and crackled with plain man color. The tendency remains today. America's corporate managers have been especially attracted to the language of contest and combat: they "run with the ball," add "firepower" to their management teams, talk of "cutting in and zapping" their competitors. Their images have been eclectically borrowed—from warfare and sports, from rural living ("you shot this rabbit, now you skin it"), even from crime ("at a million it's a steal")—but in borrowing, they have amplified and helped perpetuate traditions of talking tough.[6]

The decline in America's industrial and technological competitiveness, so widely discussed in the 1970s and early 1980s, does not mean that business tough talk has become a mere sham. Contrary to some laments, the low (or nonexistent) rate of increase in U.S. productivity and the loss of leadership in applied industrial design to the Japanese and others was *not* due to a management "failure of nerve," nor could it be attributed to a general abandonment of ACT values in the executive suite. The main reasons were "sectoral" and institutional, including the concentration of the economy in relatively unproductive sectors, the difficulty of disinvesting in these, and the deployment of innovation into new products rather than improving ways of making old ones.[7] On the level of attitudes and behavior, some of the recent criticisms of American management performance have pointed, in effect, to an excessive or wrong application of ACT rather than its reverse: too much focus on quick results (next quarter's bottom line) and too much bruising and defensive behavior.[8] Admittedly, the failure in technical innovation and quality control may also reflect a shift of middle-class values in this century away from intrinsic achievement—the desire to create something substantial or strive for excellence against an absolute standard. But this, again, does not entail a general weakening of ACT in business; it says more about focus and application. If the pursuit of substantive achievement has given some ground, the same is not true of organizational gamesmanship: the ethos of getting ahead and winning within corporate structures.[9] The recent vogue of complaining that Americans have lost ambition and the will to win points less to a new passivity than to an old concern about American character and dynamism sharpened by national burdens.[10]

The business tough guy did not emerge as a characteristic American figure until the Jacksonian 1830s and 1840s, when business took on more of the tone of a competitive scramble. Nor, during the rest of the nineteenth century, was there much consistency in the styles and stereotypes of business toughness. At one extreme there was the joyous undertaker in the 1870s who boasted to Mark Twain of how he soaked both rich and poor—"[You] pile it on and sock it to him!"[11] This type, the high-powered huckster, lived on his nerves and was often no physical he-man; indeed, through much of the century, he was largely responsible for giving Americans a reputation abroad for being sallow and dyspeptic. At the other extreme there was the captain of industry, especially as dramatized in social Darwinist terms by magazine biographies in the late 1890s. A man of dignified mien, he was often portrayed as a powerful physical specimen, radiating what one writer called an "intense animal vitality." Competitive, dominating, imbued with vision and driving willpower, he took bold but masterfully judged risks. He had in short a "virile personality," combining a reassuring stateliness with aggressiveness.[12] Even the muckrakers who exposed the tycoons as oppressive and selfish showed an ambivalent fascination with the forcefulness of their characters. (In the hands of publishers like William Randolph Hearst, the very business of "vascular and virile" exposé, as he called it, contained a hard commercial motive.) There also appeared a kind of homily written for managers and their employees that combined Progressive strenuosity with an old–fashioned contempt of welfare-minded social criticism.[13]

By the early twentieth century the image of the successful businessman—a tough man socially as well as physically—was established. Terms like "red-blooded," connoting vigorous masculinity, were frequently applied. As in nearly all periods of American history, reservations about business exploitativeness were largely focused on *big* business, often on behalf of competitive opportunities for the smaller but still successful operator.[14] In the 1920s, soaring productivity in the making of goods (without a commensurate drop in prices) heightened the emphasis on aggressive salesmanship to avoid market saturation. This joined with the new surge in popularized science and psychology, including elements of behaviorism. Sales managers deliberately invoked the spirit of physical combat ("go out there and knock 'em dead") to instill "the right psychology" in their sales force. One manual on salesmanship even urged its young male readers to develop "the faculty of combativeness" by physical exercises each morning.

Combativeness functions through the shoulder and arm muscles as shown by the soldier, prize fighter, athlete, etc. and, well developed, it imparts a feeling of enthusiasm, physical vigor and power of decision that no other faculty can give.[15]

In fiction, Sinclair Lewis did not greatly exaggerate some of the trend's character aspects with his caricature of *Babbitt*, the flabby, would-be tough midwestern realtor, versed in phrases like "gotta hustle," "punchful prosperity," and "real he-stuff."[16]

As much as ever, business values on toughness eddied beyond business itself. Permeating American language, they spanned the gulf between mammon and spirit no less surely than they subsequently spanned the power struggle between corporate enterprise and a New Deal government. In both cases, notions of toughness bonded competing institutions by giving them a common tongue of combat.

Well before the 1920s the styles of sales he-manship had carried over into evangelism, most vividly in the case of Billy Sunday. A former professional baseball player who made much of his hard, rural upbringing, Billy gathered business support and became William A. Sunday, Inc. In punchy, common man slang, he attacked excessive preoccupation with wealth—especially on the part of urban dandies—but he stressed even more that Christianity was "no dough-faced, lick-spittle proposition. . . . Jesus Christ could go like a six-cylinder engine. . . . Jesus was the greatest scrapper that ever lived."[17]

A number of evangelists since Sunday were equally concerned to show that Jesus was no meek-and-mild weakling, that his tenderness and altruism went with toughness and vigor and were highly relevant to business life and practical living in general. (Some Sunday school teachers have carried on the tradition long since and so has Billy Graham.) Bruce Barton's bestseller, *The Man That Nobody Knows*, first published in 1925, epitomizes this concern; it is a landmark depiction of socialized toughness. Barton's Jesus was and remains an all-American archetype hero: a "sociable man," good fun at a party, but in every way "capable of taking care of Himself." The vitality that attracted and commanded both men and women was inseparable from his manly physical vigor. A hard childhood had given him muscles of "iron," as the Temple money-changers (*wrong* types of businessmen) learned to their pain. "Self-control," "nerves of steel," "mastery of the situation," "executive ability," and supreme, selfless courage, all were his. The picture built up by Barton suggests the combined influence of the frontier plain man and business imperatives (Barton himself founded a major advertising firm). One of his chapters is entitled

"The Outdoor Man," and at the end of it Jesus is contrasted with Pilate:

In the face of the Roman were deep unpleasant lines; his cheeks were fatty with self-indulgence; he had the colorless look of indoor living. The straight young man stood inches above him, bronzed and hard and clean as the air of His loved mountain and lake.

Classlessly popular, Jesus' parables spoke in the graphic, simple idiom of ordinary folk; marvelously succinct and sincere, they were "the most powerful advertisements of all time."

More generally too, Barton presented Jesus' effectiveness in business terms: he was a dynamic individualist yet a model especially relevant to the world of organized selling and personnel relations. His "method" warranted the attentive study of any sales manager; indeed, he was "the founder of modern business." "He picked up twelve men from the bottom ranks of business and forged them into an organization that conquered the world. . . . this is the grandest achievement story of all." In telling that story Barton said he hoped "every businessman [would] read it and send it to his partners and salesmen." Yet, though his account semisecularizes Jesus, it is not a crude sellout to materialism. Barton wanted to humanize business, to make it genuinely concerned with service, not just profits. Even this, however, fitted into an American business ethos, part of the "welfare capitalism" of the 1920s, which sought to make the business firm the main citadel of social virtue.[18]

America's "crisis of capitalism" in the 1930s threatened but also illuminated the special relationship between business and American notions of toughness. The crash and depression gave to business rhetoric a defensively shrill quality. Against the expansion of federal officialdom under the New Deal and its recruitment of professors and experts, conservative spokesmen of business asserted their prior claim to the virtues of dynamic self-reliance and hard-headedness. The president, it was said, should recruit men who had "hustled up pay rolls"; his professors should leave Washington and get "more practical ideas" by going into business. In a similar way some old-style politicians deplored the number of New Dealers who had never "worked a precinct." (Among politicians the official whose job depends on vote-getting has the same superiority over appointed bureaucrats that the man who "has to meet a payroll" enjoys in business circles: both have to sell to survive.) Evocations of toughness also enabled the anti-New Dealer to express fears about dictatorship and dependency in the same breadth. "I preach to you," cried Frank Knox, owner of the Chicago *Daily News* and the Republicans' vice presidential candidate in 1936, "the doctrine, not of the soft and spineless kept citizens of a regimented state, but of the self-respecting and self-reliant men who made America."[19]

In fact the Roosevelt administration included a number of businessmen as high-level executives and advisers, and the president and others were at pains to defend the expanded role of government in terms of business vigor and effectiveness. Roosevelt declared that one of the New Deal's main purposes was to "energize private enterprise." General Hugh Johnson ("Old Ironpants"), the gruff and leathery head of the National Recovery Administration, said that his fair trade codes would only "eliminate eye-gouging and knee-groining and ear-chewing in business. Above the belt any man can be just as rugged and just as individual as he pleases."[20] Even some of the administration's more hostile comments about corporate management could be seen as trying to out-business business for the image of tough-minded realism. In a reversal of the usual categories, orthodox business leaders were characterized not only as "economic royalists" (note the court-government connection) but as impractical failures, stuck in the "fuzzy thinking" of old doctrines while the administration was boldly but pragmatically experimenting to end the country's mess. At many levels the New Deal attracted eager-beaver young professionals who prided themselves on their drafting of laws and programs rather than their concern for moral uplift. Humanitarian motives were sometimes hidden behind an unsentimental functionalism that presented the nation as a gigantic business firm. Adolf Berle, one of Roosevelt's economic advisers at the beginning of the New Deal, asserted that neither "social justice" nor "a healthier national life" was the main justification for seeking more equality of incomes. "It remains for the hard-boiled student to work out the simple equation that unless the national income was pretty widely diffused there were not enough customers to keep the plant going."[21]

This is not to say that the subtle effects of business values were the only immediate factor in New Deal styles of toughness. Reform activism combined with moral disillusionment; the sheer atmosphere of national emergency; and, going back into the twenties, the growth of enormous cities with mobster syndicates enhanced by Prohibition bootlegging—these and other factors all helped to produce the New Dealer who sometimes talked either like a logistics-minded war planner or a cleaned-up version of a Chandler detective. The result, however, was not as alien to the respectable business community as the latter's diehards made out. It is not surprising that Thomas Corcoran ("Tommy the Cork"), one of the most tough-guy of the New Deal's political operators yet a widely cultured man beneath his ward-boss mannerisms, should later become a highly successful corporate lawyer and Washington lobbyist, working against the kinds of regulations that he helped to create.[22]

Many New Dealers, their stay in government prolonged by the war, did in fact make it their career. A recurring theme in the class biographies of Harvard graduates who went into government in the depression—those who stayed on as well as those who subsequently left—was surprise that government work should be so demanding and exciting a "ball-game," as one put it. Others, however, said they were glad to leave what was becoming a rut and a source of dependency.[23] Despite the virile images projected by generations of high-level public figures, the New Deal did not end the belief in many sections of the society that government, in particular contrast with private enterprise, tended to attract the indolent and unfit. This attitude goes back to Jefferson, and in modern times it has obtained particularly among the better educated. Well into the 1960s, if not later, there were many American law firms where to leave for a long-term government career—short stints were another matter—was solemnly viewed as a sign of ill health or some other unfitness for the rigors of private competition.

The irony is that elements in American culture have also associated commercialism and its fruits with the very opposite of toughness. These negative associations go far beyond the image of the pink-fleshed, overweight banker. They can be divided into a minor theme and a major theme in American history. The minor theme was strongest in the nineteenth and early twentieth centuries, especially in wartime, when some writers and public figures mounted a romantic yet puritanical attack on excessive commercialism. Their ideal of manhood connected physical and mental vigor not with business competition but with the high purpose of moral and patriotic heroism. Defining strength in these terms, they were able to believe that, as Francis Parkman put it in the 1860s, "a too exclusive pursuit of material success [had] emasculated" and "vitiated" the people and produced a moral and physical "torpor."[24] Three decades later, a number of articulate Americans used a similar position from which to attack business opponents of the Spanish American War. As Theodore Roosevelt, Alfred Mahan, and other imperialists of their ilk saw it, a "scrambling commercialism" caused a narrow, "timid" shrinking from great national tasks.[25] Though neither Parkman nor his main successors really wanted to replace capitalism, their argument hewed to an aristocratic, warrior ethos that stood basically outside capitalism and welcomed war as an uplifting and envigorating call to service.[26]

The more prevalent theme linking commercialism to lack of toughness has been centered on the softening effects of business-produced luxury. It has overlapped the first theme in that American culture inherited assumptions about excessive materialism, luxury-loving, corruption, enervation, and general decadence: they were supposed to reinforce each other. But whereas the minor theme focused on the weakening potential of business activity itself, the major theme has been more bound up with the fact that producers need consumers. The concern here has a basis in reality that amounts to a double bind. The ACT values involved in business enterprise and effort help to produce and sell goods and services that really do encourage physical softness and psychological and social dependence.

The distinction between the two themes remained even when a writer combined them. For example, Francis Parkman, like other upper-class New Englanders of his time, worried about the life of ease, lethargy, and frivolity among scions of the eastern rich. But he saw "commerce" and "luxury" as separate factors in the people's weakening and declared that commerce was the more important of the two. Anxieties about the specific, weakening effects of luxury were more developed among Spanish American War imperialists such as Roosevelt and Mahan. The *Tarzan* books of Edgar Rice Burroughs carried forward both themes by combining primitivism with respect for the wellborn soldier and contempt for the greedy but essentially weak trader. In business civilization there was "cheating, murdering, lying, fighting—[for] money to buy the effeminate pleasures of weaklings."[27]

The worry about business-produced softness goes back to the "cod-God" paradox sensed by the second generation of New England puritans: the feeling that, having come to the New World to seek God strenuously in the wilderness, their very energy had found and developed a vitiating plenty. John Adams put the same concern more broadly in 1819:

Will you tell me how to prevent riches becoming the effects of temperance and industry? Will you tell me how to prevent riches from producing luxury? Will you tell me how to prevent luxury from producing effeminacy, intoxication, extravagence, vice and folly?[28]

Several historians have quoted and commented on Adams's paradox, each putting it into a slightly different context. Neil Harris has linked it to Revolutionary fears of corruption, rooted in European ideas about luxury. John Kasson has discussed it in the light of worries about technology, virtue, and democracy in the early Republic. Daniel Rodgers has related it to continuing anxieties about the effects of the work ethic in nineteenth-century America.[29] Despite this attention, three things remain to be said about Adams's rhetorical riddle. First, the concerns it expresses have recurred, in one section of the country or another, throughout America's cultural history. Secondly, they include anxiety about strength and softness, derived in part from an old belief that luxury made people weak and dependent—physically, morally, and politically. This anxiety, however, did not develop an undercurrent of its own till after Adams wrote. In his time and place it was still an embryonic element in a larger, essentially puritanical concern with moral order and the need for self-restraint against sensual wildness.[30] Thirdly, attacks on the weakening effects of consumer luxury have seldom blamed commerce in the explicit way that political individualists have blamed government programs for vitiating and overwhelming the citizen. This is because American thought and institutions have, from the genesis of the Republic, tended to identify government rather than business or a general business culture as the main potential threat to the individual.[31]

Sometimes, indeed, government has been scapegoated for capitalism's part in consumer passivity and softness. A modern demonstration of this can be found in *The Ugly American* (1958), the semifictional bestseller that helped found the Peace Corps. In their attack on America's Asian diplomacy, the authors—William Lederer and Eugene Burdick—made much of the lavish capital expenditure and commissary consumer goods, which, as they saw it, isolated overseas American officials from native populations and attracted mediocre, freeloading characters into the foreign service. The book's heroes are Americans from diverse walks of life, epitomes of tough, humane wisdom, who go modestly among Asians and give them the kinds of grassroots assistance they need. Against them are ranged various types of toughness gone wrong: manipulated, corrupted, enervated. The array includes a State Department "Babbitt" who uses an old-fashioned, gung-ho tough-talk to tout materialist attractions in his recruiting drives. He shows, in effect, how easily American dynamism can be sidetracked into self-indulgence if it is not balanced by ideals and rational self-control. Yet despite much talk of facing painful realities, nowhere is it even suggested that commercialism or a highpitched consumer society is a root cause of the trouble. The Americans who spoil it all are invariably government officials ("princes of bureaucracy"). When businessmen do appear, they are among the heroes.[32]

Again, in the 1970s, President Nixon expressed the fear that Americans were "becoming soft as they become rich"; but when he talked of causes he seemed to lay the matter solely at the door of a government that had pampered the people. A "leaner" government would give Americans a "new spirit of independence, self-reliance [and] pride."[33] Throughout the attempted cutbacks of the 1970s the terms "lean" and "fat" applied to federal budgets, became favorite expressions of presidents.

These preferences are no monopoly of Americans. When Nixon made his point in 1972, London's *Daily Express* was quick to use it against the British welfare state. "So Soft, So Pampered" ran the article headline, and its animus lay well within some of the traditions of British and European conservatism.[34] Kipling and Baden-Powell, half a century before, had attacked welfare democracy in much the same way for creating softness and dependency. Yet in relative terms there is a difference. The fear of governmental *sapping*, a sense that individual "fiber" is extremely vulnerable to welfare programs, is a larger part of American antigovernmental conservatism than of its British counterpart; whereas the fear of government *restriction* is more equally shared among conservatives on both sides of the ocean, for all the American rhetoric of liberty.[35]

Despite this traditional concentration on government, American expressions of anxiety about softening by amenities and luxuries have sometimes mentioned or implied a commercial factor. We should look at a number of these in their historical setting, for each puts a slightly different cast on the issue. In 1775 the Anglican minister Thomas Coombe of Philadelphia lamented the enervating and unmanly effect of "luxurious customs and fashions." The "decay" of simplicity, lawfulness, and "that strict morality of demeanour, which characterized our plain forefathers" was, he declared, "poorly compensated by all the superfluities of commerce."[36] Coombe's attack, like the cult of wearing homespun, was part of the Revolutionary opposition to imported British luxuries. It represented a nationalist and puritan response to the development in Britain of a consumer society which threatened, morally as well as economically, the plain, hardy independence of Americans. The Boston Tea Party itself, while aimed at British tax and export manipulations, drew support from a belief that tea was unhealthy and enervating. The main target, however, was still government rather than business. The Reverend Coombe et al. echoed dissenting opinion in Britain against corrupt government and the new commercial state. This feeling supercharged the American Revolutionary assault on the mercantile system run by the British government. It carried into Revolutionary America and sustained thereafter much of the country versus court antagonism whose target, again, was principally governmental.

When moralists of the early Republic did blame commerce rather than government for softness and corruption, they found it easiest to do so from the position of martial patriotism. To such people the merchant comforts that followed the Revolution dishonored the hardships endured by the Continental Army (after subsequent wars, too, Americans experienced guilt about civilian ease and fatness). In his introduction to Andrew Jackson's life in 1818, Samuel Putnam Waldo declared that the general rise of commerce, manufacturing, and agriculture had diverted people from the military arts and from patriotism.

Sudden wealth was the result of the exertions of the different classes of Americans. The vuluptuousness and effeminacy usually attendant upon the possession of it, was rapidly diminishing that sense of national glory, for which the *Saxons. . . .* were always celebrated.

Waldo also argued that "the very nature of the American Constitution" was calculated to create "happy *citizens*" rather than "renowned *soldiers* [and] military ardour."[37] Extended to the Declaration of Independence, with its stress on the "pursuit of happiness," and leaving aside its military bias, Waldo's thesis has an enduring relevance. The tension in American culture between producer strenuosity and consumer indulgence mirrors a broader and older tension between puritanism and hedonism.

Another popular biographer of an American hero—John Peck, writing on Daniel Boone in the 1840s—saw the problem in a sectional light. The villains in North Carolina were status-seeking Scottish adventurers who took control of the state's trade, promoted snobbery, extravagance, and "effeminacy," and so despised and disgusted the sober and industrious dirt farmers that they migrated to a new independence in the wilderness beyond the mountains.[38] In this picture, the foreign-born merchant becomes both a high consumer himself and a softener of others; the man of productive hardiness is the frontier farmer. In fact frontier toughness and entrepreneurship have often gone together, but the friction in many areas between debtor farmers and high-interest-charging merchants has been real enough to help perpetuate the notion of the businessman as an exploitative but essentially soft parasite. In American myth, however, it has usually needed the force of a frontier comparison (frontiersman versus businessman) to make the idea stick. Outside the frontier context, tougher images of the businessman have predominated. When Ralph Waldo Emerson decried "reliance on Property" and the atrophying of "civilized man" by mechanical and other devices, he attacked more the fruits of business organization and its recipients than businessmen themselves: "The world is full of fops who never did anything." He later wrote, "Every man is a consumer, and ought to be a producer."[39]

At the turn of the century the concern registered about "overcivilization" echoed Emerson's fear. "Conspicuous consumption" and the establishment of great family wealth caused nearly as much worry about the softness of those who inherited wealth as about the rapacity—the *over*toughness—of the men who were creating it.[40] The spector of a rich, young generation, idle, frivolous, and dandyish, offended the guardians of American conscience. From within the upper class itself, a spate of novels, speeches, and tracts deplored the development and conceived of solutions that ranged from cowpunching to William James's "moral equivalent of war"—a manual labor service corps that would include America's "gilded youth."[41] The problem of "The Second

Generation'' was explicitly presented as a paradox of a business society by the Progressive novelist, David Graham Phillips. Deeply concerned with masculinity and debilitation, he admired the hard-driving industrialist and believed that his son could, if toughly treated, make a man of himself in business too. Unfortunately, both the tycoon and his offspring usually lapsed into the sloth of affluence. Phillips's main hope for the survival of manly strength lay not with businessmen but with the virile political reformer.[42]

In the twentieth century, anxieties about business affluence and softness surfaced again. Politically they found their fullest expression in John F. Kennedy's 1960 presidential campaign. In a *Life* article that epitomized his major campaign themes, Kennedy declared,

The very abundance which our dynamism has created has weaned and wooed us from the tough condition in which, hencetofore, we have approached whatever it is we have had to do. A man who has extra fat will look doubtfully on attempting the four-minute mile; a nation, replete with goods and services, confident that ''there's more where that came from,'' may feel less ardor for questing.[43]

And others echoed the theme.[44] Kennedy avoided explicit attacks on business; on the contrary, his professed policy aims included the stimulation of private industry. At the same time his principal campaign pitch, ''I want to get the country moving again,'' was aimed against the lush privatism of the Eisenhower fifties when survey upon survey had reported that college students were politically apathetic and concerned with economic security. Leading Kennedy figures were proud of their records in World War II, and in that spirit Kennedy called for strenuosity in the nation's service. Over all this loomed the threats of the Cold War and the competitive challenge of Russian communism. Anxieties about the capacity of America to compete arose, in fact, long before 1960. The Soviet launching of Sputnik in 1957 only crystalized a mounting fear that perhaps the Russians were more rigorously motivated and organized for ultimate victory in a global war of ideologies. Would the American people, overfed and materialistic, let their defenses drop?[45]

Even when anxiety about commercialized softness is not articulated, the highly developed production and selling of consumer goods and services put ACT values on the defensive. Take travel, for instance. Think of just a few institutions. Howard Johnson, with its reassuring, standard layout, decor, service. Muzak. The packaged tour. There is in fact no corner of travel that business enterprise has not entered to sell a smoother, easier experience. Even vanning, which began as a form of getaway, expressive individualism, spawned its professional muralists and customizers (not to speak of all those organized rallies).

Some sales promotion fudges the conflict between toughness and consumer self-indulgence by giving the consumer a bogusly tough and masterful image. For if the thrust of commercialism will seek to capitalize on every want and whim, it will also seek to satisfy and use as many of the culture's core values as possible, including those of toughness itself. In the 1970s, the gambit appeared most obviously in cigarette advertisements where a ruggedly determined young man asserted that "Enjoyment's the name of the game," or "I won't settle for anything less than taste."[46] The consumer here was the discriminating nonsucker who knew what he wanted and got it. Another tactic was to make the product a status-symbol associated with athletes and other active achievers ("Do-ers," as the pun in Dewar's whiskey ad put it). A variation on this was to present consumption and sensual enjoyment itself as part of an aggressive, exciting life-style. *Playboy*, its synthetic sex notwithstanding, took a heady trip along this road in its own advertisements.

What sort of man reads Playboy? One who commands every facet of his life. Alive. Active. He experiences life first-hand, savoring each and every moment. No vicarious living for him. He's a doer, not a sit-at-home spectator. And his guide to action is *Playboy.*[47]

From this it was a short step to suggesting that the most unlikely products could expand virility. Even after-shave cologne, packaged as Macho Musk Oil in its phallic bottle, could help men "exercise their natural power," sending whatever signal was specified by the user's "mood-chemistry." Technologically as well as sexually, it all sounds very potent.[48]

This is not to say that commercial promotion alone is responsible for overlaying consumer softness and dependency within the motifs of toughness and mastery. I have referred along these lines to cigarette and liquor advertisements; yet both smoking and drinking have been traditionally associated with virile maturity and not just in America nor just as a result of advertising. There are, however, distinctively American aspects. The ascription of toughness to consumption extends a cultural process observed by David Riesman and Martha Wolfenstein three decades ago, the passage of strenuous work and achievement values into leisure and play.[49] The stance of toughness in consumption is usually more bogus than it is in games and sports, but this does not mean that it is simply the creation of copywriters. It is, rather, the joint product of an evolved language of assertive action and commercially organized temptations to indulge. When someone "breaks out" a thermos or offers to "zap your coffee on the microwave," the language itself make the procedures surrounding consumption seem more violent and active then they otherwise would. (In other areas, too, American jargon and slang has supplied a tough, dramatizing vocabulary for untough activity.)[50]

In 1974 two small scenes near the Grand Canyon illustrated for me the partnership between business selling and popular styles in the shaping of consumer pseudotoughness. Scene one was simply a roadside store sign: "Film. Hit the Rim Loaded!" Scene two took place at the ruin of a large Indian village, officially listed as a "monument." A deluxe camper pulled up; a middle-aged couple got out and moved in different directions. The wife immediately called to her husband, "Where are you shooting it?" No pause for contemplation; just purposeful, piecemeal culture-bagging. Holiday photography is a natural for such attitudes. It provides the idlest vacation moment with a hunting purpose. At amateur levels it is usually more effortless than drawing or painting, yet its very speed and mechanism permits an imagery of energetic action. A handy toy against boredom, the camera substitutes technique and measureable acquisition (snaps of happy faces and pretty scenes) for the more inchoate difficulties of looking and absorbing.

These fragments make a basic point. American capitalism, defined broadly as a sociocultural system, has fostered a close entwining of consumer dependency with aggressive, material acquisitiveness. The great demonstration of this in the 1970s was the enormous expansion in consumer suits against companies and public authorities, not just for obvious negligence but for almost any kind of personal mishap—from injured skiers who sued their ski resorts to the woman who fell and broke her jaw in Chicago's Sears Tower Plaza and sued the building's architect for increasing the wind velocity.[51] On one level these litigants, or their lawyers, were tough, no-sucker individualists sticking up for themselves and trying to get all they could out of the organizations and experts that surrounded them. On another level, however, they were saying that they expected the organizations that provided them with goods and services to take total care of them, even unto responsibility for an accidental fall. There is some parallel in the office-seeking mania that flourished through much of America's administrative history until classified civil services became extensive at the end of the nineteenth century. Despite the supposedly low prestige of most government offices (perhaps supplying a cause of it), hacks and hangers-on would besiege and beseech presidents and other public officials from morn till night. Their behavior, which in many cases became outright addiction, combined aggressive avarice with dependence on job hand-outs, some of which amounted to sinecures.

American capitalism has also given a special twist to the use of luxuries as status symbols. It is not simply that the very command of pleasures and amenities can symbolize their spiritual opposite—a background of rugged achievement that has earned those amenities.[52] It is also that status symbols are believed to help the successful person achieve yet more success, especially by impressing the customer, since American competitiveness plays very much on the psychology of appearance and its effect on confidence and will. The successful person's thirst for luxury is also sanctioned by the great American value on fast and efficient output, a value whose compass extends from labor-saving devices to any amenity that promises a productive nourishment or resting of mind and body. Viewed like this, the electric pencil sharpener, the private plane, the swimming pool, and an evening at the Bunny Club all become tools for the modern tough guy.

All this helps to blur the styles of leisure and work—a process that has inevitably gone further in some milieus than in others. A successful Hollywood private detective told a BBC interviewer that he wore jewelry, expensive flowery shirts, and informal slacks to impress his clients and set himself off from the ordinary, suit-wearing "gumshoe." It "puts you into success." He meant the same thing when he said that being seen with pretty girls put him "into the arena"![53] On a more functional level, executive aircraft are a cinch for combined appeals to comfort and energetic work. Beechcraft has run advertising that simultaneously stresses pleasure and comfort, energy-saving (fuel and personal energy as metaphors of each other), and the competitiveness, swift action, and flexibility required by "your executive role."[54]

The spillover of ACT values into the sphere of material consumption applies further down the economic scale too. There is some evidence that, even allowing for high U.S. standards of living, ordinary American families have spent relatively large proportions of their budgets on "consumer durables"—from sewing machines to cars.[55] Capital-intensiveness, stimulated historically by labor shortage, has permeated the home, and immigrant families often used the acquisition of goods to mark their progress in America ("we got that table there when Bill got his first raise") and to show they have put down tangible roots. For many workers, too, the success ethic, combined with severe limits on promotion at work (few can become foreman), has channelled achievement drives into making more and spending more on tangible items. This in turn helps drive them into second jobs, moonlighting, to keep up with their credit payments.[56] Thus, the drive to work and achieve, the value on material acquisition, and the toughness traditionally associated with these things in America become entangled with the pressure to consume.

Yet none of this can erase uncertainty and unease about the relationship of toughness to the fruits of plenty: It merely sets different images of toughness against each other. In 1889 the editor of *Harper's Monthly* wrote of the "controversy" between an American tradition of expansiveness and spending and a "republican" tradition of frugality: a nonverbal parallel of the expansive versus laconic.[57] The same conflict appears today in the ambivalence of Americans to the many machines and gadgets they buy and use. This is a complicated subject that deserves exploration.

In 1970 a Boston survey of people's attitudes to technology—including television, computers, factories, and machines in general—found that an overwhelming majority (83 percent) approved of technology as a whole. Yet nearly as many (78 percent) agreed that "people today have become too dependent on machines:" This was the commonest criticism.[58] Such ambivalence is not purely American. People in many countries like what machines can do for them, are intrigued with their logic and power, but also fear that technology and its social systems will put them out of work and control, subordinate them, poison their environment, and blow them up. What *is* particularly American is the fear that machines will make life too easy and soft. By threatening self-reliance, machines assault the rugged side of individualism. Yet images of technological prowess, from "Yankee ingenuity" to "harnessing the elements," are a long-established part of American identity.[59] In this spirit Americans tend to promote and sell their technology in the hyped way that they promote much else. Compared with a quieter technological civilization like Switzerland's, American culture romanticizes the machine, however ambiguously, as a source of individual power and even toughness. The culture has engaged with ACT a whole series of overlapping images of the machine and its relationship with people. Ersatz as they mostly are, they offer defenses against the feelings of weakness that technology engenders.

The first such image is that of *servo-assisted virility*: the individual's strength and mastery extended and amplified by the machine. Immortalized in the daydreams of Walter Mitty, servo-assisted virility makes the individual a highly tuned controller possessing not only the skill but the nerve and alertness to use his equipment to maximum effect in a testing situation.[60] Technology here seems to extend the individual's sheer physical potency (via the automobile, for instance) or his control over others (the telephone). Or it may do both, as Steve McGarrett of "Hawaii Five-O" commandingly demonstrated when he used a radio hookup and street map of Honolulu to vector his police cars onto a dangerous fugitive and head off a murder. The telephone and two-way radio have long been associated with tough-talking dynamism and command. They represent the communication power especially valued in a distended and complex society.[61] Computers, for their part, give special support to servo-assisted virility by placing, as one advertisement put it, "hundreds of applications and uses at your fingertips." In fantasy form, television's "Star Trek" program, whose fan club and kits penetrated adult and even college markets, provided a classic development of this appeal. On board "Star Trek's" spaceship, *Enterprise*, Captain Kirk and his lithe crew members crisply and expertly called upon computer memories, automated rocket systems, and instant scientific lab work. This is one of the many places where popular conceptions of technology are essentially magical—any power can be summoned if it is labelled scientific. Yet in real life too, personal computers and desk-side computer links have for many people the attraction of a powerful, high-speed toy.

Another closely related image of the machine is that of the *humanized mechanism*: a projection of traits desired by the individual in himself, but enjoyed vicariously through equipment. The qualities projected can include frontier ruggedness (as we shall see later when we look at off-the-road vehicles); and, if auto manufacturers are right in using all those potent and pugnacious names for their car models, other kinds of toughness and strength can be projected too. The sheer physical hardness of machinery suits it for the symbolism of "hard" masculinity. This factor may help explain why engineering, compared with other professions and not just in America, has till recently recruited extremely few women.[62]

A third image—the *mechanized human*—reverses the second by transferring machine properties onto people. This image, joined with others, has largely replaced the old notion of the strong man who pits himself *against* mechanical power. His death knell was sounded by the legend of John Henry, the Herculean black railroad miner who in an epic contest outdrilled a new-fangled steam drill and then dropped dead from the strain.[63] But long before that legend appeared (around 1870), the tall tales of the southwestern frontier had produced the champion whose mighty frame combined industrial metals with the forces of animals and nature. (The phrase, "greased lightning," coined in the 1830s, is of the same ilk.) Against this background, the comic strips' Superman is a transitional figure. From his first appearance in 1938, he has been pitted against trains, cars, and dams, and followed by planes and other machines—first in competition, then in combat. Yet though Superman's form and emotional reactions are human, his origins are extraterrestial and, more important, his real-life creators have over the years upped his technological powers. His eyesight, for instance, acquired X-ray penetration, then interplanetary vision, and finally a heat-ray that can wreck aircraft, while his skin has toughened from shell-proof to atomic-bomb-proof. He can now even spin off robot replicas of himself. A flesh-and-blood weapons system, Superman is capable of almost infinite technical development.[64]

Some of these transfers from machine to man ride on fairly loose metaphor. There is, for instance, the fiction-hero professional who, deftly commanding a complex of routine procedures, becomes an emergency computer when the routine breaks down: his mind races through myriad options and memories to produce his own solution. Still more loosely, heroes of total prowess, ranging from Inspector Ironside to Rip Kirby, reveal new skills in a Meccano-like process of acquisition. The most academic skill, from knowledge of Sanskrit to musical history, is tacked on to the hero's personality as if it were a mere support system; the skill suddenly appears as a secret weapon, enabling the hero to win by problem-solving. An extension of this is the cultural operator, the tough, intellectual crime-buster or counterinsurgent who can infiltrate any culture or alien group by learning its language and lore in the same way that he masters mechanical techniques and organizational procedures.[65]

On a more explicit level, depictions of man and his mind as a machine range from serious studies to the kind of success manual that claims to be based on "psychocybernetics." Avoid the soft-theorized psychoanalysis; your mind is a "power mechanism" that can be programmed for success and happiness, provided you let it "scan" the right "data." This genre takes the simplest aspects of behavioralism and wraps it in the languages of automated feedback systems and anecdotal tough-talk. Like other "motivational" literature, it is essentially concerned with "psyching" the individual to confidence and peace of mind. Though the use of machine metaphors in success manuals goes back to the nineteenth century, Southern California, especially the Los Angeles area, is a center for this new style of self-help publishing, as it is for other popular business literature with a similar tough-guy informality.[66] The area is also a base for "assertiveness-training." This may reflect southern California's combination of arcadian play, experimentation, and "fast-buck" striving in real estate and new industries. Psychologically as well as geographically, California has been the end of the line for many Americans on the move; and a publishing industry has grown up to appeal to mobile, rootless, yet relatively affluent people with the need and the leisure to seek ready-made systems for finding and improving themselves. The mechanized terrain, with its autos, freeways, and electronics firms, have supported machine-images of the human mind itself.

In the realm of media fantasy, the most literally mechanized human was also the toughest: the "bionic" Steve Austin in television's "Six Million Dollar Man." The series was based on Martin Caidin's novel, *Cyborg*, written in a very tough-guy style for adults as well as adolescents.[67] Almost killed by a plane crash, Austin was mended and fitted with a daringly developed system of metals and electronics, which far more than replaced his destroyed limbs and muscles. The operation made him a devastating secret service weapon, but his story featured human qualities as well as mechanical power. Before the crash, he was a top astronaut and test pilot, superbly trained in mind and body. Only a constitution of enormous stamina could survive the crash and operation, yet despite his toughened ''plastiskin'' (which looked entirely human), he remained vulnerable to some forms of death. Technology found him no pushover: he at first resisted being reconstructed like a ''damn Oldsmobile,'' but he had the ''background'' to understand the medical engineering involved and the resilience to come to terms with it. The success of ''Million Dollar Man,'' and the appeal of all it represents, was not confined to Americans. The series did well in Britain, and several countries have hatched their own man-machine metaphors of toughness. The Japanese nicknamed the ebullient ex-businessman Kakuei Tanaka ''the Computerized Bulldozer'' in his popular heyday as prime minister in the early 1970s; and BMW advertisements used to claim that their cars' ''cockpit''—''control-point for perfect teamwork between man and machine''—was based on the latest in ''biomechanics''![68] Nevertheless, more has been done with the image in America, whose language has established a well-worn route from technics and industry to human traits. ''Vibes'' and ''personal chemistry'' sound tougher and harder than ''feelings'' and ''relationships''; ''broadgauged'' sounds firmer than ''eclectic''; ''cross-reading'' more precise than ''second opinion.''[69]

A fourth way of associating individual toughness with machines lies in *small-scale mechismo*. This contrasts two kinds of technology—compact equipment effectively managed by individuals, and large, impersonal plants. Again, it is not just American. Part of the appeal of the James Bond movies is his role as an adept technological underdog operating a saucy but lethal range of gadgets against the enemy's ''Germanic'' arsenal. *Star Wars* made something of the same division. Small-scale mechismo becomes all the more plausible with electronic miniaturization. A herald of the possibilities was Doc Savage, pulp-fiction hero of the 1930s. Savage's amazing physical and mental prowess was backed by miniature but powerful equipment designed by the hero himself to suit the more strenuous of his travelling methods—jumping between rooftops or padding through the jungle.[70] The association between small-scale technology and individual mobility and flexibility was highlighted in the cult of CB radio among drivers. The very term ''Citizens' Band'' is suggestive. In helping the driver to beat police speed traps, CB enables him to outwit larger-scale, technically assisted authority. This, added to other factors—the trouble-shooting element in CB weather and police warnings, the analogy with pilots talking on their intercoms, the origins of CB use among truck drivers, and the raffish comraderie of CB users—explains the tough-guy overtones in much CB talk: the shorthand jargon, numbers and code names, and the use, albeit spoofishly, of southwestern accents.[71] Small-scale technology is also linked with self-reliance and know-how (from Lindbergh's flight to the do-it-yourselfer's garage filled with gleaming power tools). In some contexts it joins with nostalgia for an older phase in America's technological development: the oily dirt of the B–17 against the disinfected atmosphere of today's large electronic defense systems.[72]

In the 1970s small-scale mechismo provided a meeting point between counterculture and mainstream in combined practical and literary efforts to integrate the natural and primitive with the mechanical. The best-known saga of this was Robert Pirsig's *Zen and the Art of Motorcycle Maintenance*, published in 1974. Pirsig's style was not particularly tough guy, but values of toughness appeared now and again in his book, not least in his cogent argument that people who disdain technology become the most impotently dependent on it: they can't fix things themselves. A more relevant work is John Jerome's *Truck: On Rebuilding a Worn-Out Pickup, and Other Post-Technological Adventures*, (1977). Jerome finds himself between "two futures."

Future A is all that stuff best characterized as "software," post McLuhanistic information bits, maximization, systems analysis. Unacceptable. Future B is Luddite, organic revolution, the land religion. I am circling it nervously. But nuts and bolts have no place here either.[73]

His answer is to get out into a New England barn and there slowly, painfully to learn how to rebuild a rusty but honest Dodge pickup truck, vintage of Truman's presidency. Jerome distances himself contemptuously from the "mechano-constructo-machismo" hunters and others whose needs have turned the modern pickup into a soft consumer salve. He distances himself sympathetically from Elbow, the hippy who sells him the basic truck and gives him practical advice but is too nonverbal for a writer in his forties. Yet he combines elements of both. Working through the deep New Hampshire winter into spring, Jerome invests every tiny, gritty piece of "the process" with psychological and social meaning; he spiritualizes it; he links it with ecology (he is, after all, "recycling" a whole truck!) and the passing seasons. From the counterculture he imbibes an implicit rejection of competition, a positive disdain for mechanical speed, and a self-conscious naturalism. But he also has in him a good deal of the conventional tough guy, try though he may to scrutinize and ridicule some of it. He writes hearty, slangy prose. He dwells with cheerful self-pity on the hardships and ruggedness of his voyage. He is given to sudden alarms lest he sound too sentimental or ideological. He is explicitly concerned with "total competence"; really, with self-reliance and self-testing. His wife is supportive but stays in the background. His essential solution to being "a child of the mechanical age" is to combine earthy antiurban living with small-scale technical know-how, both of which have featured so greatly in the tough-guy imagination.[74]

For most American outdoorsmen, technology offers a more superficial experience of toughness. The equipment industries that have grown up around camping and field sports deploy symbols of heavy duty ruggedness, but each of their products takes the individual a little further from pioneer conditions. In the romanticizing of the West even the Colt 45 caused a problem: the hero's phallic extension was also something he could be accused of hiding behind. A "real man" had to show he could scrap without it. Industrially the problem has caused a cycle of cultural demand and technical response. In the case of the gun, a primitivist reaction has produced a return to archery and "bow-hunting." Industry has responded, and bows are now as sophisticated as shotguns. To complete the cycle, bow-hunters and the industry between them have evolved a technical language of their own, focused more on the equipment than on actually shooting the quarry.

The development of off-the-road vehicles has undergone a fairly similar life cycle. First used as a rugged breakaway from the world of the automobile, they have increasingly been built and marketed with an accent on auto-style ease. Advertisements for pickup trucks in outdoor magazines of the mid-to-late 1970s show what happened. While Ford pickup ads still laid a stress on being "off the road tough, with the muscle to get you there and back," General Motors expanded this appeal to include both rogue primitivism and mechanically supplied comfort. An advertisement from GMC's "Truckin' People," significantly pitched to the whole family and not just the rifle-toting hardhat, star of many pickup ads, put it all together:

There are some kinds of fun that deserve something more than a car. Something tougher. More versatile. Something that doesn't need four lanes of concrete to get you where you're going.

And that's what Truckin' is all about. Climbing in a GMC pickup and getting close to the pleasant things of life. A pine-surrounded cabin. A lonely stretch of beach. Or a fishing hole that only you know about.

You see, we at GMC have been at this truck business for 75 years now. No cars. Trucks.

So, we know what it takes to put together a tough, reliable pickup. One that can be luxurious like the family car. And do things no car ever could.[75]

Ruggedness for independence but also for happy idling. Getting close to nature but staying close to comfort. An advertisement for the ersatz frontiersman who could be tough vicariously, through his machines.[76]

It is ironic that even the extreme "survivalists" of the early 1980s—training their families to shoot Russians and the urban hordes when Armageddon came—depended on, indeed helped develop, an industry of specialists in paramilitary equipment and dehydrated foods. Like the fallout shelter craze of twenty years before, their mountain bunkers and underground caches required substantial investments in material backup. Survivalism was prefabricated self-reliance, a hyper-preparedness born of energetic fear.

Thus, the images of personal potency that surround so much technical equipment perpetuate by their very concealment the tension between ACT and consumer dependence. This can occur in quite surprising places. In the early 1970s I had my first experience of a large professional conference that used closed-circuit television not just to show what was happening in different sessions but to galvanize the whole event with special interviews and news-like commentaries. Conference members, clustered idly around the public TV sets, might wonder where the real conference was taking place. The hearty, urgent manner of the announcers and interviewers masked the fact that technology here offered spoon-feeding in the place of active participation.[77] Ten years later it seems wrily appropriate that the great upsurge of electronic churches should largely overlap the rise of aggressively conservative evangelists. The message may be tough, but the medium is undemanding.

A similar spirit shapes the living patterns of conservative Americans resident overseas. Corporation executives as well as military men and their families often have little frontier spirit when it comes to foreign culture. Backed by lavish American imports and organizations, they tend to form enclaves even in English-speaking countries. The video-tape packaging of American TV programs for such people plays on just this.[78]

Despite these variations, the exemplar of masked conflict between toughness and softness remains the automobile. Styled and advertised as aggressive extensions of a driver's virility, cars have simultaneously become luxurious cocoons with push-buttons placed to economize on almost every body movement. Likewise, for youth under driving age, Trail Finder scooters and mowers shaped like farm tractors have a rugged appeal and offer an initial challenge, but they take the exercise out of hiking or cutting the grass. Though less technological, there was a parallel in the rules requiring American soldiers in World War II—unlike most other troops in the war—to wear helmets even when they were far from the front line; the helmets looked ever so hard and combat-ready, but they also represented the untoughness of excessive protection.

This example is less trivial than it may seem. It was part of the same ambiguity concerning toughness that led American military commanders in Korea and Vietnam to rely on enormous, often indiscriminate firepower to protect their men at the expense of native populations. "You don't fight this fellow rifle to rifle. You locate him and back away. Blow the hell out of him and then police up." This tough-guy statement by a Vietnam commander expressed what had long been the major preference of American military commanders: the affluent reliance on technology rather than irregular warfare and the Ranger tradition.[79] Among the top military policymakers, the toughness/weakness of servo-assisted virility was even more pronounced. When the officials whose advice and decisions devastated Vietnam and Cambodia talked of "calibrated" reprisal, "systematic pressure" and "touches of brass," they were in fact taking an easy way out. For all the talk of "hard choice," they were substituting B–52s and artillery for the unpopular use of American ground troops against people who could not bomb back.[80] The fact that exponents of capital-intensive approaches to the war could themselves be adept and aggressive bureaucrats (from General Depuy in Vietnam to Kissinger in the secret bombing of Cambodia) did not alter the essential cowardice of their policies.

In other realms of politics and policy, too, the spirit of the "neat engineering solution" has produced pseudotoughness. Several American political movements have pinned their colors to the belief that social problems can be solved by introducing or eliminating a tangible substance—silver, gold, alcohol. Many Prohibitionists were intensely concerned with strength and weakness; and in the early 1980s the hard-money gurus of gold showed a special propensity for tough-guy rhetoric.[81] Their relationship to social realities, however, was not so tough. The simplicity of their prescriptions offered a flight from the complex action needed to deal with interrelated difficulties. The same thing was done by Joseph McCarthy. He constructed his arena around a neat engineering solution that looked tough but was in fact an evasion: the winkling of subversives from government and universities. The root trouble was not out there, in foreign power relationships; it was right here, in identifiable individuals who had supported communist policies and passed on atomic secrets. The A-bomb itself was a technological talisman betrayed. McCarthy, of course, presented this in heroic terms, a "win" strategy against the "no-win" of containment. He himself was the skunk-killing farmboy who had become a fearless investigator, taking on well-fixed smoothies and treacherous communists in officialdom. In fact he offered escape, a mirage, an avoidance of internation perplexities, release from a cold war of nerves.

It is well known that there were many cold warriors at the time and more later who saw through all this. The real conflict *was* out there, nor could there be easy respite from what President Kennedy was to call the "long twilight struggle." Some people indeed resented McCarthyism less as a witch-hunt that hurt innocent lives than as a paper-tiger-hunt that distracted Americans from the real communist threats abroad. Supporting various kinds of counterinsurgency overseas, they defined their policy toughness in terms of endurance and shrewdness rather than gimicky, supermanic crusading. Even here, however, the attraction of quick "surgical strike" cures affected foreign policy, from the Bay of Pigs to *Mayaguez*. Here, as elsewhere, the neat engineering solution, with its mix of ostensible hardness and buy-out-the-problems affluence, lived on. More generally too, the conjunction of logistic power with psychological expansiveness has produced the reverse of real toughness. As Garry Wills observes, the sheer ability of the U.S. to influence events halfway around the world makes their leaders all the more afraid of threats far from their shores, and anxious to show that they have the will to deal decisively with them.[82]

The historically rooted tension between toughness and affluence, making it and consuming it, and the strenuosity and reliance on things, has communicated itself in the way children are reared. Indeed, the role of parents in the transmission and reinforcements of ACT is largely to be understood in this context. The claim applies with most force to a wide spectrum of white, middle-class families, but it has some application to Americans as a whole, especially in the childhood years before adolescence challenges domestic authority.

Through the enormous changes in vogues and patterns of American "parenting," a few themes have persisted. One such theme has been the dual tendency of parents to demand and indulge, to push their children to exert and assert themselves while easing their paths with resources and care-giving. From Jacksonian times to our own, foreign travellers have noted the use of democratic tolerance and indulgence itself to encourage and reward aggressiveness and independence in the child.[83]

Against this background we can reappraise the role of "Mom" and "Momism" in shaping American concerns about toughness and independence. In exaggerating this role, social scientists and other writers have been apt to equate advanced material civilization with feminization—an assumption shared with such turn-of-the-century hearties as Theodore Roosevelt and Frank Norris. As Myron Brenton observed in *The American Male*, civilization per se could only be a feminine threat to man caught in restricted concepts of masculinity.[84] That restriction, historically, was largely established by men themselves; the open-ended pursuit of money and success led them to abandon wide realms of culture to women, which increased the danger zone of effeminacy that seemed to surround the young educated male.[85] Having said this, one must add that by mid-twentieth century a kind of "PX-Mom," a cornucopia of middle-class plenty, was reinforcing the tension between toughness and affluence. The tension affected children of both sexes, though probably boys the most. On the one hand, mothers joined with fathers in pressing their children to achieve.[86] On the other, they passed on consumer values and indulged material dependency. Conceptions of motherhood as the fount of all good things are not uniquely American, but they acquired special significance in a giant department-store nation where the main family spender, in an immediate sense, was female. This applied particularly to those suburban mothers who did not have full-time jobs outside the home. The fact that in many suburban neighborhoods the only public place was a supermarket or shopping mall accentuated the spending and providing role of the mother, who was also depended upon as a chauffeur.[87]

As our era of the child develops, fathers add to the ambiguities of toughness by combining new protectiveness with old strenuousness. I am thinking particularly of the sort of father, dynamic in his own life, who unwinds at home by indulging his children or asserts himself by overprotecting them. A few years ago I saw a vivid suggestion of this in a suburban park. A young executive type was with his son, aged about four. The boy was walking along a fallen tree, and at the end of it wanted to jump down. The father said it was too high (which it wasn't) and handed him down. While the boy kept demanding that he be allowed to get up again and ''jump down myself,'' the father did energetic push-ups and then sprinted to another tree and back.

The outcome of all this, again, is *dependent aggression*. American children, more than those of many Western societies, have been pressed not to be crybabies yet permitted to whine for goodies that in turn are used as bribes and rewards.[88] The most striking parallel in adult life is the enormous consumer back-up given to GIs on active service and the shelling out of medals—''nothing is too good for our boys.'' (Of the crewmembers of the U.S. spy ship, *Pueblo*, captured in 1968 by the North Koreans after a brief fight, eighteen were decorated. A British joke in World War II told of three Yanks who went to a war film: one fainted at the sight; the other two got decorated for carrying him out.) It is significant too that mothers have taken a lead in wartime controversies about POWs and demobilization, demanding that Uncle Sam ''bring back our boys.''[89] In psychoanalytic terms, the surrounding of assertiveness with logistical mothering produces aggressive expressions of oral dependency, from hard drinking, cigar-chomping, and gum-working to the mystiques of red-bloodedness that used to surround steak-eating.[90]

We should not assume that trends away from materialism and the work ethic, so oft reported in the 1970s and early 1980s, will swiftly end the conflict between values of toughness and of affluence.[91] Nor should we assume that a growing sense of national economic constraints will easily reduce consumer dependencies. In the first place, as we have already noted, models of competitive toughness in work and in play have survived the work ethic's supposed decline. Secondly, allegations of a shift from ascetic values of work and production to those of leisure and enjoyment are not new. Writing in the 1940s and 1950s, David Riesman and others argued that this was a modern phenomenon, though they did not put a date on it.[92] Half a century before, the conservative sociologist William Graham Sumner had lamented that the ethos of "Work, Save, Study" was becoming "Enjoy, Enjoy, Enjoy." His concern likewise was not new, though the nineteenth century also produced a variety of defenses—psychological as well as economic—for resting and extensive consuming.[93]

It may indeed be that the hedonism of the 1970s tended to be less materialist than its forbears: less concerned with acquisition and physical pleasure than with emotional fulfillment and rich personal relationships. The distinction, however, is tenuous. Consumption in modern America has long been associated with excitement, social relationships, and experience.[94] Conversely, a lot of the self-gratification of the 1970s used a materialist imagery. As Daniel Yankelovitch observed, it posited an array of needs like sections of an ice-cube tray, each to be filled to the brim (in somewhat the same way that "spiritual technologists" talked of filling up from or plugging into Christ).[95] More profoundly, a great deal of the Me Decade's questing for new and flexible life-styles presupposed a bounty of economic resources. Some surveys in the 1970s did indicate that more people wanted to get back to basic essentials, but they also realized that this was not easily done.

Insofar as values have shifted away from self-denial, they have played down an important aspect of toughness. This shift, however, has been exaggerated by social commentators.[96] Stoicism, I have already argued, has never been a major component of the ACT ethos. Although much of the population, for most of the nation's history, has spent its lives laboring to build assets and give the next generation a better start, the bold, expansive operator, who spends rather than scrimps his way to success, has been a more admired model since well back in the last century. At the same time, new life-styles have adopted a traditional and strenuous vocabulary. The pursuit of experience and new and flexible options has appeared as a form of "psychological risk-taking," as indeed it is. Moral obligation corrupted into "I owe it to myself", has been pressed to egocentric purposes, sometimes endorsing cut-throat behavior.[97] Even the search for richer, more spontaneous relationships has sometimes shown an exploitative, "I'll-relate-to-you-on-my-own-terms" quality.

These tendencies should not be exaggerated. Like psychiatrists, theorists of social character are apt to make everyone look sick! As it worked its way through individual lives, much of the 1970s accent on expression and fulfillment produced *un*tough-guy behavior: gentleness, tolerance, sensitivity. But this divergence supports my point. Within the new freedoms of the past decade—leaving aside the traditionalist reactions against them—the claims of toughness have persisted in conflict with those of other values.*

*John McEnroe's behavior at Wimbledon in 1981 brought several of these themes together. The man who could be so generous to other players also showed traditional signs of the tough but self-indulged brat: a self-pity swivelled into competitive determination and rage against authorities; low tolerance of frustration, adapted to all-out effort. To this he added a very modern stress on self and self-expression. "I was talking to *myself*!" he shouted over and over at the umpire who had penalized him for rudeness. The historian Phyllis Palmer has observed to me that much of this spoiled behavior is characteristic of American children of Army people (like McEnroe) and multi-national executives, who are messed up by frequent moves but also pampered by consumer goods and services—an extreme version of the affluent mobility of America's executive and professional classes.

3
ORGANIZED INDIVIDUALS

It's amazing to think that, in the span of a single life-time, the exploration of space has grown from the dreams of very, very few individuals to such a massive cooperative reality.

—Gerald Ford, 1976, on the landing
of the Viking space robot on Mars.

Pettingill hasn't the hard edge I'm looking for. I want a man who knows this business inside out. He's got to be loyal enough to take orders without question and trusted to carry 'em out. On the other hand, he's got to have the guts to talk back—to you or me or anybody else—if he thinks he's right. And he should have a streak of hard-nosed bastard in him.

—Oilman Jim Northcutt, in Jonathan
Black's novel, *Oil,* 1974.

How do the many interpretations of conformity and individualism in America relate to notions of toughness? And how, against this background, have Americans reconciled the individualism of ACT with their modern propensity for "getting organized," associating toughness with efficiency, winning, and systematic preparation?

President Kennedy once remarked that when congressmen came to see him about policies toward the Soviet, they were more rigidly hawkish when they came in a group than when they saw him singly. In this and in other respects, ACT epitomizes the contrary pulls of conformity and individualism. The very insistence on individual assertiveness and capability is often made to satisfy other's definition of toughness. Likewise, the very desire to stand out powerfully from others frequently rides on the wish to impress others. Much of this is not new, and traditional masculinity has reinforced it: toughness in the aggressive male group has to be proved to others, not just oneself.[1]

This does not mean that Americans are, on balance, more conformist than other modern peoples. What is more significant in America is the historic *fear* of conformity, of any falling away from ideals of self-reliance and self-expression. To this is joined the sense that in an organized yet competitive world others may insidiously assault one; that forces not of one's making may capture the inner self.[2]

One way of dealing with these fears is to be a joiner, to help organize society before it gets you, to initiate class suits (a concept little known outside the U.S.) against big interests and maintain a lever on the children's schooling through the PTA. The American penchant for association, noted by Tocqueville and many observers since, is not the same as the conformity also noted by Tocqueville; the two overlap but either can exist without the other. Historically, the American fraternal/sororal tradition has offered diverse associations to choose from and some range of roles within them. Political individualism, moreover, has propelled voluntary and civic group action not just as a way of mobilizing interests but as an alternative to a federal power thought to be simultaneously coercive and distant—divorced from individual action. It is significant that Herbert Hoover, who placed "rugged individualism" in the political lexicon, was not at all a rugged individualist in the nineteenth-century sense. Fanatically worried about the power of big government to sap the individual, he was also fired with the possibilities of social planning and cooperation; through intricate arrangements he sought a balance between collective action and self-reliance.[3]

Some of the tension in Hoover's thought goes back to antebellum America. It was apparent by then that the democracy which was supposed to symbolize and affirm manly personal independence was also a threat to it. Despite their friendship and mutual influence, Ralph Waldo Emerson and Walt Whitman framed two opposite responses to this predicament. For transcendentalists such as Emerson, personal strength required the heeding of inner imperatives. Against the old puritan commitment to social control of natural impulses and individual purpose, Emerson saw society (and not just democratic society) as a threat to self-realization and a maker of cowards:

Society everywhere is in conspiracy against the manhood of everyone of its members. Society is a joint-stock company in which the members agree, for the better sharing of his bread to each shareholder, to surrender the liberty and culture of the eater. The virtue in most request is conformity. Self-reliance is its aversion. . . .

Whoso would be a man must be a nonconformist.[4]

From a modern standpoint, Emerson's writing combined the tough and the untough. His language pushed itself to frequent images of explosion, striving, and firmness against decay; but his "self-directed" man, following his own path, had the courage to stumble and be inwardly uncertain. There was no premium on social competence, on ability in "the popular arts," or on the calculation of passing attitudes to collect public favor. For all the economic and political democracy in many of his reactions, Emerson's concept of the "great man" was basically unaffiliative: the poor and lowly understood his truths but he had no time for the run of ordinary people once he found their limits. Unmoved by social and political events, impervious to the contempt of the conventionally successful, Emersonian man must always be ready for solitude.[5]

In his earthier, more sensuous style, Whitman shared much of Emerson's concern with individual identity and spontaneous power. Yet despite his contempt for placemen and parasites, his individualism was affiliative where Emerson's was not; and because he identified with plain man America, his fear of conformity was much less. If his individualism was imperial, it was embracing too. In *Leaves of Grass*, his vision of an expanded self—himself—absorbed nature and society; it joined sexually with harvests, muscular workers, and lists of vibrant occupations. His very openness was a source of power as well as union.

> Mine is no callous shell,
> I have instant conductors all over me whether I pass or stop,
> They seize every object and lead it harmlessly through me. . . .
>
> Is this than a touch? quivering me to a new identity,
> Flames and ether making a rush for my veins,
> Treacherous tip of me reaching and crowding to help them,
> My flesh and blood playing out lightning to strike what is hardly different from myself. . . . [6]

Whitman's desire for individuality and for union sharpened each other. In a very modern way he believed that "perfect individualism"—the separate dignity of the individual—depended on a "strong . . . aggre-gate" and gave it meaning. The soul's two great balancing qualities were unifying "sympathy" and "that measureless pride which never acknowledges any lesson but its own."[7] Both Emerson and Whitman, then, were concerned with distinctions between individual and society. Both praised a rough-hewn strength that came from within the individual and did so all the more because they felt the pull of democratic affiliation.[8]

According to a familiar view, America's democratic and egalitarian traditions have had dual effects: they have sustained a belief in personal achievement, in standing out through success, but they have also supported the urge to be like others, to conform with common tastes and standards. A complementary line of reasoning is that the achievement value directly promoted the conformist value by impelling a person to strive for higher status and therefore conform to a superior social group.

Another argument, again going back to Tocqueville, is that egalitarian defiance of established classes led to status uncertainties, hence a striving for social distinctions, hence conformity.[9] These formulations stress the ethos of upward mobility, but in other ways, too, great competitiveness encourages conformity since it induces the individual to strive on terms set and judged by others. The mass media (especially color magazines and television), dramatizing achievement and contest and glamorizing standard styles and looks, reinforces this by presenting winners as people who impress audiences (fictional audiences as well as real ones). It accentuates *performance* in both its "engine" and "entertainer" senses: success means *high performance*; it also usually means performing to an audience.

Francis Hsu, the anthropologist, sharpened the paradox in all this and involved it in toughness when he declared that "self-reliance" remained the "core value" of Americans but produced its opposite, group conformity, by stressing the achievement of status.[10] Now if you define self-reliance in purely practical terms—fending for oneself physically and economically—there need be no contradiction here. But ACT has developed strong Emersonian forms in which self-reliance is supposed to be moral and psychological too, including independence of others' opinions. Wherever this view operates, the contradiction remains between being "one's own man" and doing and believing what is socially appropriate.

There is, however, another relationship between individualism and conformity: that of reaction and compensation. Americans have been pulled toward conformity and toward joining as a reaction against the potential for anarchy and isolation in their individualist traditions. This notion supports Richard Hofstadter's idea of compensatory swings in American history between creative individualism and group adjustment, but it lays more stress on the coexistence of the two impulses, even if historical pendulum awards the upper hand first to one and then the other.[11] The coexistence operates within individuals as well as between groups, and it extends several things that were said in chapter 1. The impulse to tough assertion stimulates a controlling group behavior. I have noticed this in the way American children and youth play touch football or informal soccer. Compared with their British equivalents, the Americans tend to talk a lot, and within the talk individual assertion shades into seemingly endless collective planning, commentary, rearrangements.[12] In the culture at large, there is a third stage, a *counter*reaction that admires the tough-guy individualist who "cuts away from the herd" and does not dilute himself in protracted discussion and compromise; he is wrily given credit for his forcefulness and candor.

From this perspective, seeing in ACT a dual anxiety about individual and group, I wish to connect three theories drawn from the past three decades of writing about American middle-class character. Each is concerned with individualism, and each stresses change, yet taken together they show a continuous thread in American models of toughness.

David Riesman et al., *The Lonely Crowd* (1950)

Contrary to the view of many readers and commentators, Riesman's famous theory did *not* hold that Americans had become more conformist; what had changed, it asserted, were their "modes" of conformity, the social psychological mechanisms. These, too, were more complex than usually realized. The predominant mode in the nineteenth century operated on two levels—an "inner-direction" (level 1) derived from social norms internalized via elders at an early age, and (level 2) superficial conformities based largely on the *esteem* of others. This gave way in the twentieth century to a more deeply "other-directed" mode, a flexible radar-tuning to peer-group tastes and media fashions, based largely on the wish to be *liked* and to achieve resonance with others.[13]

When one takes into account other traits that Riesman ascribes to the two types, it is plain that the inner-directed character was more the tough guy (of a moralistic sort). There is some clinical evidence, too, that people who score high on tests of other-direction tend to be less openly aggressive and more dependent on external influences in making judgments.[14] However, as Riesman himself has observed, few people have been purely other-directed or inner-directed, and most Americans would rather be inner-directed. This, again, closely involves concerns about toughness: the laments about conformity that were such a feature of the 1950s and helped make *The Lonely Crowd* a best-seller voiced an anxiety about personal and political passivity. In the early 1970s, Michael Maccoby's study of "high tech" managers found that over half of them worried that they gave in too easily to others. Many, especially the most conformist "company men," expressed conflict between wanting to be a nice guy and the mean-guy element that success in the corporation apparently required.[15]

Again, much of the popular literature that sprang up around the assertiveness training industry in the 1970s was beamed at people's guilt about yielding to others because they needed their approval so desperately. Even *Winning Through Intimidation*, Robert Ringer's bestseller of 1973, was mainly defensive, telling its readers how not to be intimidated and thereby outwitted. The theme of independence versus yielding reappeared in Wayne Dyer's bestseller of 1976, *Your Erroneous Zones*, with chapters entitled "You Don't Need Their Approval" and "Declare Your Independence." A recent article in *Psychology Today* holds forth about the importance to one's identity of saying no—to oneself as well as to others—and declares hopefully that new forces for no-saying versus self-indulgence are abroad upon the land.[16] Among the variants of assertiveness training that sprang up in the 1970s, perhaps the most valid was the feminist version. Many "AT" exponents tried to draw a line between assertiveness seen as good and aggressiveness seen as bad; the aim of women was to overcome traditional modes of submissiveness to men while avoiding excessive, counterproductive aggression.[17] Organized social life, it seems, asks people to be other-directed "glad-handers" (another Riesman term), yet retain an older, competitive toughness, often without allowing for the psychological costs and difficulties of combining the two.

This raises a question about prevalence. Riesman implied in 1950 that other-direction was not yet the predominant mode; and despite the prescience of many of his observations, there are no signs that it has become so. Riesman acknowledged sectional and group differences in other/inner direction but believed that the metropolitan upper-middle classes were leading a long-term trend toward other-direction. Hypothetically, one can see that a consumer society with an economic stress on marketing and services would stimulate other-direction, but this does not foreclose other character responses and trends. Riesman's historical model of long-term shifts may be less apt than one of shorter-term shifts in emphasis and a lot of "pulling and hauling" between the two modes.[18]

David Potter, "American Individualism in the Twentieth Century" (1963)

Whereas Riesman wrote of different kinds of conformity, Potter discussed different kinds of individualism. The predominant definition of individualism, he argued, had shifted from a narrow-culture, frontier and business self-reliance in the nineteenth century to a twentieth-century individuality, stressing nonconformity, self-expression, and dissent. The fact that dissent and nonconformity possessed a long American tradition, and the converse fact that modern dissenters often conformed to their own groups, only qualified this general shift.[19]

Demography supports the first part of Potter's thesis in that most Americans throughout the nineteenth century, and well into the twentieth, lived in very small towns or totally rural settings.[20] His twentieth-century view, on the other hand, is best suited to a trend that had hardly begun at the time he wrote—the splintering of America's educated public into myriad issue groups, professional groups, hobby and leisure groups: a "diaspora," as Lewis Lapham put it, dating from the mid–1960s.[21] The difference from earlier fragmentations of style and belief is that individuals now feel that they can select their affiliation, that they are not bound by class or ethnic group to take on one particular respectability. Since the new splinter groups are not insulated from each other (urban density and the media see to that), Riesman's other-directed consumer acquires an initiative: he or she can choose and switch their reference groups, the collective "others" to which they refer.

As with Riesman's categories, toughness is most obviously involved in Potter's nineteenth-century mode, self-reliance.[22] This does not mean that Potter's notion of twentieth-century individuality leaves no place for the tough guy. We saw in the last chapter that commerce has promoted the image of the unfooled, options-seeking consumer who demands his or her own preference. At the same time, Potter himself conceded that the old rugged values on self-reliance, self-defense, and winning still exerted emotional force in his own time, albeit more defensively. The real trend, surely, lies in a combination of Potter and Francis Hsu's observations. Americans want *both* practical self-reliance and expressive individuality. One result is the kind of business or professional person who is out to "enjoy life," who wants the wary indulgence of "keeping his options open," while being a cool and successful operator, at play as well as at work.[23]

Christopher Lasch, *The Culture of Narcissism* (1979)

Lasch's claim that American middle-class character had shifted from the nineteenth century's strenuous, substantive doer to the twentieth century's narcissistic self-gratifier entailed a corresponding shift in modes of toughness and aggression and their underlying psychology. Directly addressing himself to Riesman's concepts, Lasch accepted that the modern narcissist depended on others for recognition and approval. Beneath this dependency, however, he espied a more selfish and vengeful character than Riesman allowed. For Lasch, the "Me Decade" in which he wrote only confirmed a longer-term trend in capitalist egoism: the result was not a gentle neohippy but a competitive and insecure manipulator.

Lasch's case fits several well-observed trends. Nevertheless, Lasch's way of arguing is hard to take. Amid large organizations it is easy to believe that the modern American, distanced from the end product of what he does, turns in on himself while depending on others for goodies and packaged experience. However, unlike Riesman and Potter, Lasch conceded virtually no qualification and rested his assertions on a narrow psychoanalytic model.[24] Could he really believe that most Americans, even those of the set he knew best, were so sick and nasty? Lasch also overstated his case in suggesting that Americans had become more competitive than they used to be a century ago. There is no evidence that the thirst for winning, the distaste for "taking another's dust," was less widespread or pronounced in the nineteenth century than in the twentieth. Modern organization may make competition more closely interpersonal and more focused on position than substantial achievement—but even that is notably untrue in many fields, from scholarship to entertainment, where competitive craving for rank and visibility is often inseparable from creative drive.

These objections do not make Lasch's work irrelevant to our theme. In becoming a bestseller, *The Culture of Narcissism* tapped some of the yearning, I suspect, that *The Lonely Crowd* had done nearly thirty years before: a wish to return to hardier ways and more productive energies. "We sit fiddling with our psyches," declared a New York *Daily News* reviewer, "while civilization turns soft and runny around us."[25] Yet Lasch's study did show how modern expressiveness and introspection could accommodate an adapted form of tough-guy behavior, whether or not the toughness was genuine. What he depicted was just one of many outcomes, in character and attitude, from America's history.

GETTING ORGANIZED

It remains to be shown *how*—by what administrative and imaginative devices—Americans have meshed their traditional value on self-reliance with the demands and appeals of highly defined organization. In everyday occupational life, as in popular fiction and TV drama, the formulas are largely confined to executives and expert specialists; if they have any relevance to the assembly line, or to typists and sales clerks, little effort has been made to establish it.

One formula is based on the idea of distended organization, decentralized yet centrally monitored. Its key lies in two favorite American words: "assignment" and "mission." The ideal American organization man is so loyal and yet so resourceful that a loose rein suits him. Assigned a clear-cut goal, he can be sent out to operate on his own. In the military sphere the image fits Americans' romantic attachment to irregular soldiering and their association of toughness with speed and flexibility—Merrill's Marauders operating behind the Japanese lines. But it has also influenced the military mainstream. U.S. commanders in World War II explicitly used the notion, "you assign a mission and it's up to the fellow to carry it out," in justifying their system of delegated responsibility. This can be compared with the more centralized British command structure. Even General Patton, for all his controversial high-handedness, kept to his precept: "Never tell people *how* to do things, tell them *what* to do, and they will surprise you with their ingenuity."[26]

In business administration, the underlying concepts of decentralization were developed and implemented by Pierre Du Pont in the 1950s

and then by Alfred Sloan and Peter Drucker. Their ethos was anticipated by two exemplary tales of toughness, Elbert Hubbard's "A Message to Garcia" (1899) and Peter B. Kyne's *The Go-Getter: A Story
That Tells You How to Be One* (1921). Hubbard, a retired soap man-
ufacturer interested in activating rural youth and later in popularizing
the arts, wrote and published "A Message to Garcia" in his magazine
The Philistine. It told, with suitable homilies addressed to business, of
a "fellow by the name of Rowan" who took through the "jungle" an
urgent message from President McKinley to the Cuban insurgent leader
who had to be located somewhere in the mountains. The New York
Central Railroad reprinted over half a million copies for distribution to
its employees and others, and it became one of America's best-known
essays. Its many translations included editions for the Japanese Army
and the Russian railways. In an age that combined imperial adventure
with the crystallization of bureaucracy, it struck a chord. Peter Kyne's
The Go-Getter told a similarly inspirational story of obliging grit and
ingenuity: its hero was a business recruit who passed diabolical tests
secretly set him by his boss. Although the setting was commercial, the
go-getter used the lingo of his World War I days as an artilleryman.

In both stories, thus, a business-oriented writer used a military
backdrop in presenting the obedient but self-reliant hero—a technically
enterprising tough guy who accomplished an almost impossible assignment without asking how to do it. The model suited large-scale business organizations that needed executives, engineers, and salesmen who
could combine initiative and innovation with efficient teamwork. In line
with this, American managements have tended to balance extensive
decentralization with close financial oversight through accounting systems and rigorous specification of jobs and targets. In some firms, too,
operational decentralization and competitiveness has coexisted with a
clublike atmosphere among the executive elite. This is not to say that
corporate decentralization only works well through tough-guy individualism. A comparison of ITT under Harold Geneen with the leading
Japanese electrical appliance firm, Matsushita, has shown how differences of national culture will out, even though Matsushita was relatively Americanized and had followed its own path of divisional decentralization. Matsushita's standards of executive performance were
no less stringent that ITT's, but the latter operated much more through
confrontation and personalized leadership; it produced more feelings
of isolation and more concealment of dependency.[27]

As the ITT case exemplifies, another formula for integrating self-reliant toughness with organization is to accentuate individual and small-group competitiveness within the organization. (It was significant that Geneen used the group meeting—the epitome of corporate life—to make people challenge each other, defend their positions, and produce the hard facts from which he could control policy.) According to this formula, the effective modern tough guy can take the organization's complex demands and pressures while using the organization's resources to achieve his own victories. This often involves the creation of small teams inside the organization to put across a new marketing idea or introduce a technology. The pattern is not confined to business corporations. Ascetic loner though he was, Hyman Rickover's achievement as an engineering innovator fighting Navy bureaucracy rested on welding a close-knit team behind him, using supporters in high places, and playing agencies off against each other. In a very large organization, especially one like the federal government, there are chinks and gaps where a small-group individualist can operate as a sort of guerrilla. Outside bureaucracy, too, many of today's successes are individual or small-group operators who nonetheless live off large-scale organizations: this is true of freelance writers and producers, entertainers, even electoral politicians. It is also true of that proliferating breed, the management consultant, the troubleshooter who rides into town, sells his service, and then rides out again—no dull maintenance work for him.[28]

For those executives who stay within the corporation, notions of gamesmanship give a meaning to work whose end product is out of sight. For the modern gamesman, every plan, every project, can be a win-or-lose test, depending on your homework, timing, and the way you present yourself.[29] At the same time the gamesman will talk of "teams" and "team players," stressing both action and cooperation, while retaining the possibility of being a star player, maybe even coach. Such language adds a twist to the interpenetration of work and play in middle-class life described by David Riesman and others. In Riesman's view, strenuosity flowed from work to leisure whereas the values of entertainment and sociability flowed from leisure to work (as expressed in public relations, the expense account, and office parties). Although both processes have long existed, as corporate life becomes more routine, so the more strenuous images of play are reimported from leisure.

These solutions are not for everyone. For every operator who successfully manipulates the organization, there are those who feel manipulated or circumscribed. In his study of high-technology corporations, Michael Maccoby found that many managers and engineers at middle and lower levels felt powerless and insecure. Over half of those interviewed said they would rather run their own small company than rise high in the big one.[30] The conflict of values and situation must be even greater for routine workers further down the job ladder.

During this century, the nature of work in America has undergone two opposite shifts, one centered near the top of the job ladder, the other reaching up from the bottom. The first is the rise of the professional specialist, either self-employed or enjoying some expert independence within a large organization.[31] The second is the "deskilling" of much of the labor force, from clerks to short-order cooks, as the work becomes routinized and automated.[32] The first trend has done much to preserve models of toughness in modern organizational life. The ideal professional has the authority and certified competence to make crucial decisions, to talk back to his or her clients or employers, while drawing upon a distended community of expert peers. Even the stepped up attack, in the 1970s, on the mystique and guild practices of professionals, recognized their power and prestige. The second trend, the deskilling of many manual and service jobs, is obviously hostile to the values of resourcefulness and independence that shape American notions of toughness. In reducing the physical demands of many jobs, the breaking down and automation of procedures has reduced their mental demand too. For people in such work corporate experiments in self-management and job enrichment mean little. For them, self-expression and achievement in leisure pursuits or moon-lighting as a craftsman or entrepreneur provide the only real means of reclaiming individuality. The main alternative, or supplement, is to follow fictional solutions.

In the 1960s and 1970s, popular writing and the media dealt with the tension between tough individualism and the power of organization in a number of ways. One kind of fictional setup used communications technology to put individual heroes on their own yet make them part of powerfully backed group enterprise. In the TV series "Search Control," the secret service agents out in the field—the men of action confronting danger—were radio-linked to massive computer memories in a central headquarters manned by white-coated scientists. Every so often, as if to double-check that individualism was not forgotten, the communications system broke down, truly throwing the agent onto his own resources. (The same kind of thing, it will be recalled, used to happen at regular intervals to the crew of the good ship *Enterprise* in ''Star Trek.'') The idea of an organization or community distended potently but lightly by technology, found real-life expression in the drivers of campers and dune buggies who sought wilderness solitude yet kept in touch over their CB radios.

The use of multiple heroes, each carrying the action for a spell, is another way of combining personalized action with group organization and spirit. ''Search Control'' did this, making a different agent the hero of each episode. TV Western serials such as ''Bonanza'' largely developed it. An alternative was to retain a constant leading hero but to back him up with a small team of dynamic lieutenants, each of whom might be specially featured in an episode. (In television both formulas were mainly established in the 1960s, along with notions of the more socially sophisticated tough guy; but a forerunner was the multiprofessional team of Doc Savage, Kenneth Robeson's pulp-fiction hero of the 1930s.) In the case of business novels where a corporate organization must be assumed, an old solution is the executive hero who toughmindedly insists on quality—authenticity—of production and service, cutting through the organizational schemers while understanding enough of corporate finance and politics to beat them.[33] Another solution, sometimes combined with the above, is to focus on the rugged owner-president of a large and growing company that commands exciting resources yet is still an underdog outfit, fighting for survival against mammoth oligopolists. Within his own organization, the fighting tycoon may be a loner who gets out into the field to know his company operations at first hand but who works in his headquarters on his own or with a very small staff, removed from his vice presidents, though in touch by telephone and telex.[34]

The ideal modern tough guy, in short, must be adept at *using* social organization without being *of* organization. The formula is not just American: the bestselling British novelist, Frederick Forsyth, has exploited it, and so have some boardroom dramas on British TV. But American writers have mainly shown the way. In some literature the importance of keeping the hero's identity clear of organization and complex social forces is such that it even takes precedence over the win ethic. The hero may win his personal contests yet be let down or betrayed by remote politicians and bureaucrats who are supposed to be on his side.[35] Even when he does win, the victory is sometimes Pyrrhic. Mickey Spillane made this into a philosophy. For him there was no preventing crime. It was too enmeshed with power and social organization (or *dis*organization). Spillane's private eye, Mike Hammer, could not even be sure of protecting his clients and girlfriends. When he could not save them, all he could do was to make their killers pay a bloody price and tell us that the price wiped away the loss. The sense of individual efficacy rested on savored revenge, a barter system.

Not all tough guys, however, can use the private-eye solution. Footballers are a prime example. American football epitomizes the paradox of ACT, supposedly individualist yet flourishing under tight discipline and command. Though largely a game of specialists, football leaves less decision making to the average player than do most team sports. The uniform symbolizes the military regimentation of football: it blows up the player's physique but it depersonalizes him, caging him in equipment till he resembles both a humanoid machine and a mobile component in a larger machine. By learning masses of plays or his bit of each before he goes onto the field, the player is largely programmed to do what the coach and/or quarterback wants him to.[36] How, then, has the modern development of football avoided affront to the individualism involved in ACT? The first answer is that it has not entirely: hence the critiques of the game's authoritarianism and commercial exploitation mounted by several eminent explayers. But for most fans and players there seems to be little contradiction. There are several reasons for this.

First, the sheer physical toughness and speed demanded of players compensates for their loss of autonomy. Authoritarian coaches manipulate the idea of taking punishment so that it includes the capacity to take discipline from the coach. Those players who really feel like rejecting the system usually don't want to be cast as quitters or pass up the chance of making the team.[37] (In the same way there are business executives who count it a mark of toughness to take the heat from a dynamic but bruising boss—these people are eager to stay "in on the action" by pleasing him.) Secondly, the game has its aspects of personal competition and contest. The very standardization of the statistical ratings used to measure a player's contribution to the game—in yardage, tackles, passes, and so on—stresses individual performance by providing stark comparisons with other players. Again, much of the football's violence is self-consciously interpersonal, a feature encouraged by the rule permitting body contact between players even when neither has the ball. All of this is bound up with the element of psychological warfare: the constant effort in football to faze and confuse the opposition. In 1979, the Dallas Cowboys' free safety, Cliff Harris ("Captain Crash") was quoted on the forthcoming Super Bowl game with the Pittsburgh Steelers. "We're going to have to knock Bradshaw [Pittsburgh's quarterback] out early, make him dizzy early." On Pittsburgh's wide receiver: "I'll be looking to hit him, not to hurt him. But that doesn't mean he might not get hurt. . . . I want to make a receiver aware that I'm there. I want him to be looking for me or thinking about me." [38] The very structure of this statement is destabilizing, with its shifts between threat, pretend-decency, and narcissism.

In the third place, the ordinary player's role does require a limited mixture of self-reliance and specialist variety. Self-reliance is involved in the sheer number of plays the footballer has to carry around in his head; in addition, he must improvise and perfect the techniques during the action. Most players, after all, have to have a bit of scope to decide what to go for when. The specialization of players gains enormously from unlimited substitution, which enables the coach to send on expert kickers and field different squads for offense and defense. But, of course, as with much expert professionalism in the larger society, the differentiated roles are largely prescribed: they do not provide great opportunities for spontaneous invention and versatility.

Fourthly, at the expense of most players' autonomy, the game provides a star role for the quarterback and a military commander's scope for the coach. In neither rugby nor soccer is any position so dramatically elevated as that of the quarterback with his crucial passes and his responsibility for calling the plays (if the coach lets him). For his part, the coach, with his telephone linkup to the rooftop spotter and his use of substitutes to carry in orders, can remain the general in charge right through the game.

None of this means that football is unique in the American quest for tough individualism amid organization. Let us go back to one aspect of the game: the idea of controlling the player by having him learn a script—the notes and diagrams in his playbook. This is very American. The emphasis on documentary guidance goes back to the founding of the Republic when diverse and distrustful sections based their new polity on a written constitution. Since then the influence of technology and its kind of rationalism, the rapid intake and movement of population, and general expectations of flux—so that custom and word-of-mouth are felt inadequate for passing on vital precepts—have stimulated the production of manuals for almost everything, from engine-making to love-making. Even "Americanization" classes for immigrants have churned out checklists of patriotic events, holidays, and names, as well as teaching the language.

In many spheres of organization, where the range of activities is very great and the factors cannot all be quantified or precisely anticipated, the American fondness for rationalization by manual and by systematic training merely balances decentralization and autonomy. A pleasant paradigm of this is Marin County's "Vita Course," a woodland route for hikers, joggers, and cyclists—you may follow or ignore the detours, each taking you to a posted prescription of exercises!

In other spheres, though, where the individual is all but replaceable by automation, human programming by manual has gone very far indeed. This does not only apply to factory work. At the time of the U.S.–Soviet space linkup between *Apollo* and *Soyuz* in 1975, the American astronauts took on board far more massive flight plans than their Russian counterparts. For every conceivable mishap there was a procedure to look up. Similar differences were found between British and American military pilots in World War II.[39] The latter were more apt to "fly by the book" rather than the "seat of their pants," though both found scope for personal styles. In the case of football, the relatively small, controllable size of the squads encouraged coaches to take a factory approach to the action, breaking it down into separate but synchronized units.[40]

What football does share with many, more individualistic spheres of American culture is the concept of social organization as a system. A system, in the sense favored by Americans, resembles a complex machine in that it has moving and differentiated but totally interdependent parts. It is in this sense—which includes but goes beyond notions of game and team playing—that Americans like to talk of "roles": "I see myself playing a key role as. . . . " The formula encourages people to exaggerate their individuality without disclaiming loyalty. The essential optimism of it was expressed in 1911 by Frederick Taylor, the pioneer of scientific industrial management:

The time is coming when all great things will be done by that type of co-operation in which each man performs the task for which he is supreme in his particular function, and each man at the same time loses none of his originality and proper personal initiative and yet is controlled by and must work harmoniously with many other men.

This is a lot more plausible in a professional setting than in the time-studied factory methods devised by Taylor. Its essential idea can be found today in the multihero novels of Arthur Hailey, where each main character is a highly individual and resilient specialist, performing vital functions for a dynamic organization or community.[41]

In some conceptions of the system the individual may still pride himself on his irreverence. How many times has one heard even quite conservative people say, "I'm really a bit of an inconoclast," or "I've got to do it *my* way"? But basically they will conform, if only to show that they have the competence to "play the system." For others the notion of a system offers a sense of significance. The Americanism, "plans call for," used in a letter or curriculum vitae, seems to reflect a wish to be programmed for an important purpose while retaining a sense of self-determination. It is in the realm of technology, however, that the concept of system confronts most dramatically the tension between individualism and programming. For if technological organization threatens individual autonomy, its use of expert specialists also affirms it, holding out the possibility that individuals can continue to operate toughly on their own yet be part of a powerful and embracing collective. None put this more graphically than Eugene Burdick and Harvey Wheeler twenty years ago, in their bestselling novel, *Fail-Safe*, where they describe a strategic bomber and its three-man crew. In a way it brings together all I have so far said about American yearnings toward both isolation and community.

The skill and potential danger of the crew's missions made them a "proud and highly qualified lot." If too many of their functions were now automated and preinstructed, not all of them were, and in any emergency they would still have to use resourcefulness and nerve. Each of them sat in a separate burrow surrounded by dials and equipment. Helmets and oxygen masks covered their faces; they could not talk (cursorily) on the intercom; they did not necessarily know each other except by name; they relied on training to work together. Yet:

even in their loneliness they took a pride, for the great glistening smooth-packed machinery they flew also gave them a sense of self. The fact that they were locked into the mechanism, embraced by it, yet in control while at their positions gave them a feeling both of individuality and of being bound tightly to an organization.[42]

4
AMERICANS AND TOUGHNESS

In looking at the wider context of toughness in America, I will use three perspectives. The *sociological* perspective focuses on the relationship between a national ethos of toughness and different groups and classes in America's changing social structure. The *historical* perspective lines up the main causes of ACT and reveals the sequence of its development. The *foreign-comparative* perspective starts with human nature dimensions of ACT and then examines other cults of toughness to show what is particularly American about the tough-guy tradition. None of the three are watertight categories. All of them are to some extent sociological, all deal with historical change, and all refer to foreign cases. But the focus of each is different.

THE SOCIOLOGICAL PERSPECTIVE

Parallel Idiom

The difference between a society's culture and a particular subculture within it depends partly on the distinction between substance and form, values and idiom. This is especially true of toughness and strength where attitudes are implicit in styles of behavior rather than expressly declared.

In 1961 an important essay by David Matza and Gresham Sykes challenged orthodox assumptions about the values and styles of male juvenile delinquents.[1] To Matza and Sykes, these people, who seemed so different, so alienated from the rest of society, were literally rather than fundamentally at odds with their respectable elders. Anticonventional as they were, they still supported and stressed part of the middle-class value system. Beneath the gang's rip-roaring style lay a concern with aggressive toughness as a sign of masculinity and reputation; a thirst for excitement and adventure; and a belief that only suckers tried to advance themselves by steady work. All three values had their counterparts in the larger society, though here they were much more exposed to contradictory attitudes. Even the dislike of steady work corresponded with conventional preferences, since it went with a wish to "make the big score" through smartness, to show off and live it up (a mixture of success and consumer/leisure values).

Subcultural differences, then, are often a matter of style and context (the way and the place in which a value is honored) rather than substantive principle. There is, however, no clearcut line between style or idiom and the value-shadings that it represents. Ulf Hannerz's *Soulside*, another classic study of a deviant group, shows the relevance of this to patterns of toughness. Hannerz studied a black neighborhood in Washington, D.C., in the late 1960s.[2] He found that ghetto male lifestyles, especially those of "street corner men" and "swingers," shared a constellation of interests: sexual exploits; fighting (or boasts of it); sharp dressing; heavy drinking; effective and impressive talking; and winning contests. The strongman and the trickster were both admired, each making his appeal to the downtrodden. Female toughness ranged from the drinking, smoking tough guy to the authoritarian, working mother.

These preoccupations with toughness and mastery had many equivalents in mainstream white culture, though Hannerz chiefly saw the ghetto male constellation as a creative alternative.[3] Economic and social deprivation, joined with black cultural traditions, induced Soulside's residents to express mainstream values in their own way. This rechannelling—usually directed by unemployment into leisure situations—affected the values' substance. The strains of ghetto life encouraged a touchy rather than controlled physical aggressiveness; and the mainstream masculine values of money-making and making it with women found a deviant ghetto connection in pimping. More generally, Soulside bridged past and future tendencies in American society: its macho cult of prowess, sexual boasting, and drinking was well in line with some American male traditions; at the same time it anticipated, indeed helped shape the expressive leisure culture of the 1970s.[4]

Co-Option and Feedback

ACT values and styles construct themselves by co-opting—absorbing and modifying—the symbols of diverse groups. They do so partly through language and personal contact but also via famous representatives of a subculture, especially political and media figures. These representatives adjust the styles and stances of the subculture to general white middle-class values while bringing some influence to bear on these values. The resulting mixture then feeds back to individuals in other groups as a part of a vaguely perceived American ethos. Black subcultures, for example, have provided American language with a stream of pungent ghetto terms; they have also produced public figures, from Eldridge Cleaver to *Shaft* and Muhammed Ali, that have mediated between black and white images of toughness.[5]

In the same way, middle-class politicians and journalists are attracted to underworld and quasi-underworld slang: "bum rap," "hit list," "hush money," and so on. The close connections between city-desk journalists, police and DAs, political machines, and criminal elements have disseminated the language; to use their words and phrases still sounds toughly knowing but their meaning is diluted. One man, Frank Sinatra, illustrates this perfectly, with his mixture of tough-boy behavior, lower-class and underworld film parts, and associations with mobsters, glamorous women, and high politicians. Sinatra and his "Rat Pack" took elements of underworld style, combined them with other subcultures, and forged them into a national stereotype of the tough and successful man.[6]

Class Declassed

The connection between national and subcultural styles can be seen another way. At the heart of the tough-guy tradition lies a difficult relationship between plain man democracy and social class. Cocking a snook at the "posh" and "lah-de-dah"—at what even the British upper-middle classes call "chinless wonders"—is not special to Americans. What is more special is the way this attitude has reached into elite groups themselves, placing them on the defensive against populist notions of toughness. Recent writing on chivalric myth and martial romanticism in America has obscured this process by concentrating on upper-class models of virility.[7]

The key idea here is the "dude," in the old sense, meaning an overdressed or pretentiously mannered easterner or city man.[8] Coined in the early 1880s, the term brought together a number of images and antagonisms which existed before it was used and persisted long after. Blurring class resentment with sectional hostility, it joined the sissy to the sucker, since it usually referred to the eastern gent whose superior traits at home made him a "greenhorn," or a "softhorn," out West.

Versions of the antidude tradition still make professional and upper-class Americans—especially men—feel vulnerable to pressure from below. I do not deny that there are class differences in styles of toughness and mastery nor that some upper-class people form communities of confidence in which their main messages are to each other. In matters to do with toughness, however, these messages are colored and circumscribed by wider-based requirements. Their influence becomes apparent when upper-class people step out of their own milieus. This is particularly so in political campaigns, where "common man" rhetoric still claims so many exponents. In early 1980, when George Bush was running for president, he was "whipsawed" on just this point. *Doonesbury* mocked his preppy pretensions to "Character, Toughness. Neat stuff like that." Ronald Reagan called him a "Preppy, a Yalie, a sissy." Bush duly toughened his image on the stump, just as Nelson Rockefeller (truer to his nature) had developed a folksy yet combative ebullience. It would be hard to imagine an upper-class European equivalent.[9]

Outside politics, two opposite developments have obscured this undertow: first, the international cult of declassé dress, stemming from the "counter-culture" and "radical chic" of the 1960s; and secondly, the big-city stylishness of the late 1970s. The turnover of "in" possessions and phrases, the reign of the three-piece suit, and the popular rediscovery of the preppy look all worked against the old, homogenizing pressures to "be one of the boys."[10] Yet the pressures showed their persistence in the managerial cult of uneducated language, used especially when the accent was on contest, performance, or hard-headed practicality: "you did good," "he warn't mindin' the store," "if it ain't broke, don't fix it." Even Tom Wolfe's essay on speech differences between "Honks and Wonks" noted that St. Grottlesex boys often tried to impose the "ruggedness and virility of various street voices" onto their "honk" intonations. Like upper-class politicians, they sensed that to be too narrowly "honk" was to sound soft as well as snobbish.[11]

Among women, too, the tough-guy swearing done to show equality and liberation has involved "declassiness." Sharon McKern's portraits of Southern women in the 1970s include the "Cosmic Cowgirl," an upper-class type who follows country-music groups and toys with "redneck expletives," and the "Counterfeit Redneck Mother" who wears Big Mac overalls, rolls her own Bull-of-the-Woods cigarettes, and drawls and twangs bad grammer.[12] Like "brown-bagging" and the sales of heavy railroad men's shirts to young professionals in the mid–1970s, this behavior merged traditional declassiness with newer co-options of the counterculture.

From a sociological standpoint, the main factor was a negative one, the historic absence of a ruling class embued with a sense of unity and extending across the whole land. Despite the heartiness and contest developed in prep schools and military academies, elite groups lacked a class-distinctive armory on which to rest their claims to toughness. There was no real equivalent of the links between public school hardship, imperial service, and military officer traditions that enabled Britain's neogentry to feel as tough as anyone *in their own superior way*. We can see this is the overt homosexuality of Britain's male boarding schools (until they became less monastic) and the lack of it in equally male-isolated American boarding schools. Although homosexuality is a natural response to isolation of the sexes, the Americans were unable to include homosexuality within the scope of manly strength when other groups rejected it.[13]

Within these constraints class differences in styles of toughness have varied between sections and over time. In the Deep South, gentility often alternated with more classless forms of toughness, as in hunting, when middle-and upper-class men joined in sweaty fellowship with their white inferiors, and sometimes black inferiors too. Historically, the antidude heydey was the Jacksonian 1830s and 1840s when leading politicians (squires as well as plebeians) adopted a common man ruggedness.[14] They repeated, in tougher idiom, the popular genuflections practiced by Federalists in the declining years of their elitist party. Though much of the repeat was blarney, it removed a political protection from elite stakeouts on strength and virility.

By the turn of the century, however, upper-class easterners were evolving their own culture of manly toughness, exemplified in Ivy League football and boarding-school stories for boys.[15] The urban-industrial separation of classes and the evolution of corporate power and wealth made this more possible; at the same time, exponents of manliness like Walter Camp and Theodore Roosevelt used ideas of gentlemanly fair play to distinguish controlled virility from viciously tough behavior and goody-good sissiness.[16] Their language echoed the "muscular Christianity" propagated by British public school headmasters as they moved into their late Victorian stage of imperialism and organized athletics.[17] Yet Roosevelt—like other young eastern gentlemen—sought to prove himself among lower-class state politicians and western cowboys. He did so, admittedly, from a clearcut class and regional identity; his speech, even his overdone cowboy rigouts, made that plain; but he dramatized the notion that upper-class virility could not be wholly realized within the upper classes. In keeping with this idea the Rough Riders—whose publicity helped elect Roosevelt to the governorship of New York—recruited Ivy League polo players as well as cowboys and Western troublemakers, and not just as officers.[18]

After World War I the widening constituency of football and the rise of the big western teams democratized an upper-class bastion of toughness. In the world of business, managers and professionals began to look more classless, and their styles pervaded the upper classes as salaried executives grew in number and power. Acting like a "regular guy" was now considered an asset in human relations. At the same time the spread of technology and the rise of engineers in business management associated masterfulness with a technical know-how that, again, looked classless.[19] Similar developments occurred in the military. In World War II and after, a combat-ready functionalism and informality made American officers look and sound more like noncommissioned soldiers than did their European counterparts. When General Matthew Ridgway wore his famous paratrooper's grenades in Korea (a reference to the 82nd Airborne Division in which he had made his name), he was exploiting the habit among American generals of wearing helmets, windbreakers, and so on, even when they were miles from the front line.[20] Like their cussing and obscenities, whose rich volume amazed Allied officers in World War II, the classlessness of American officers' headgear—garrison caps, campaign hats, navy "baseball caps"—reflected the conflict between the disciplined hierarchy that all military forces must have and the nation's historic dislike of regimentation and the notion of an officer class.[21]

The epitome of declassé toughness in the 1950s was the crew cut. In source both collegiate and GI, it was championed by the college educated, but its symbolism was classless.[22] The crew cut's hard, bristly edges, exposing the scalp in a simple box, stood for the male technician; it also took ten years off an older man. Youth and age, indeed, have made complex metaphors of strength and status. The declassé pressure on American elites has traditionally identified dynamic toughness with a youthful informality. The connection is *democratic vigor*. The strong leader may be crusty, or "hooded"; in many ways he may hoard his dignity; but he shows that his blood is red and real when he drinks Coke in shirt-sleeves, growls about last night's game to the elevator man, or sports a nickname.[23] (American leaders are more apt than Europeans to have semiofficial nicknames; it makes them sound young and active.)

This does not mean that ACT values have operated a simple bias in favor of youth against old age. In Jacksonian politics, where a profusion of youthful nicknames—"Mill Boy," "Wagon Boy," "*Young* Hickory"—expressed the raw, new democracy, old age was presented in two ways. It could mean feebleness, silliness, being "used up"; or it could mean rugged experience of real life, seasoning, testedness. In the "Log Cabin" campaign of 1840, Democrats who tagged William Harrison as a drunken "Old Granny" included those who hailed Andrew Jackson as "Old Hickory."[24] The ravages of time—especially when joined to a military record—were contrasted with the easy, synthetic shortcuts of privileged youth. This favorable view of age was an ancient one, and folklore carried it into the twentieth century. Yet the ideal American man in terms of toughness and strength has tended since the early nineteenth century to have an age-spanning as well as a class-spanning quality: to be a mature man of youthful vigor or a young man whose prescience and knowledge make him "older than his age" in things that count. This middle ideal, interleaving elements of youthfulness and age, complicates the controversy about American historical attitudes to youth and age—a discussion that has too long assumed a simple polarity between the two.[25]

Class and Toughness in Popular Fiction

Popular action literature of the nineteenth and early twentieth centuries had to work through the difficult relationship betweeen social class and notions of toughness. Despite their seamy reputation at the time, the old dime novels of Beadles Library, and so on, retained a gentility and class consciousness that was far from the political demagogery of the 1830s and 1840s, though both praised the Western hero and shared a studied moralism. At the same time, popular fiction of the period expressed a tension between the attractions of inherited status and of plain man prowess. The fictional hero whose informal dynamism mutes his class background was not fully established until well into the twentieth century, but he was not without precursors.

In *Virgin Land: The American West as Symbol and Myth*, Henry Nash Smith observed that until the late 1870s or 1880s, the western-based dime novel was apt to divide its male roles between a frontier character who spoke in an uneducated dialect and a younger hero from the East whose station suited him for romance with the genteel heroine.[26] The younger man, I might add, did well in western terms; he possessed vigor and courage, but lacking the infinite resourcefulness of the experienced frontiersman, he might need rescue at a dire moment. Even here, then, we have a situation of genteel dependence on a more competent man of earthy background. Smith traced the split in heroic roles back to James Fenimore Cooper's Leatherstocking novels. He argued that the classless young adventure hero, unaided by any grizzled hunter, did not really start to come in until the early 1870s and was not firmly established until Edward Wheeler's series on *Deadwood Dick*. It should be said, however, that even Wheeler tended to a genteel roundedness of style that affected his heroes' dialogue: it is hard to separate literary conventions of the time from qualities of the hero that the author had in mind.[27]

The class and age divisions of the earlier dime novels followed the chivalric model of the young knight or officer with his older retainer or sergeant, a pattern made much of by the English Victorian/Edwardian boys' writer, G. A. Henty, except that the dime novelists created a more equal relationship between their two types of hero. The persistence in America of the heroic split along age and class lines was bound up with the authority and influence of European romantic fiction and drama that commanded many American writers and readers until well into the twentieth century. This, in turn, has to do with residual snobbishness in human character, with American ambivalence to European culture, and with sexual attitudes that sought to idealize women.[28] But there were other tendencies too. From quite early in the nineteenth century we find popular writers trying to establish models of manly vigor, strength, and competence that break out of class types. A pioneer in this is Daniel Thompson's bestseller of 1839, *The Green*

Mountain Boys.[29] Its main hero, the young Captain Warrington, is muscular, cool, resourceful, and commanding. His huntsman's dress is "not rich [but] tastefully arranged." There is some gentility here but no great stress on it; observations about class differences are more focused at the outset on comparisons within his band. Among dime novels themselves, Henry Nash Smith observed that the author sometimes tried to have the class matter both ways by letting the protagonist conceal an upper-class background in a rough local dialect until the right moment came to enlighten the reader and, as often as not, produce a romantic match.[30] Edward Ellis, the leading exponent of this, also experimented with open love affairs between plain man frontiersmen and genteel heroines; but in the end his main solution was to abandon feminine complications and develop the great classless, asexual character of *Deerfoot.*

Atypically for a dime-novel hero, Deerfoot was an Indian: a "good Indian." Perhaps that is why the Deerfoot books have received little attention from writers of the dime novel, despite their great popularity at the time. (Even Smith has no mention of him.) Raised in captivity by white men, Deerfoot has returned to the forest but remains their invincible protector, a total hero in almost every dimension of grace, prowess, and virtue: he even has a mischievous, but of course controlled, sense of humor! A noble renegade against his own savage and treacherous "Shawnoes" (*sic*), he represents the best possible combination of primitive power and civilized morality and control—and of deviance and conformity. On the one hand, he knows his Bible beautifully. On the other, he prefers a bow and arrow to the rifles that the Shawnoes have adopted—he is, of course, an incredible marksman with both. In his slight but athletic person he combines youth and natural dignity, piety and wisdom, superiority in forestcraft and combat yet consideration of human life, all of which make his resemblance to Deerslayer more than a matter of name. His readiness to sacrifice himself for others also links to Deerslayer as well as to Bill Biddon, the "dialect" hero of Ellis's early book, *Nathan Todd.* In *The Lost Trail* (1885), the first of the Deerfoot "Log Cabin" series, Ellis produces his classic formula.[31] Deerfoot befriends and repeatedly saves Jack, a capable but less experienced white frontier youth, and his heavily Germanic companion, Otto. The social character of Jack, like that of Deerfoot, has no intended class connotations of any sort. In fact class and age motifs are replaced by ethnicity. The comic character element of the old frontiersman is transferred onto Otto the German, and the dependent relationship between young gentleman and old, local expert becomes one between a young local hunter and an even more expert Indian, a "matchless youth." The personal status achieved by Deerfoot is so great that he becomes both hero and elder brother figure to the two young whites.

Going beyond dime novels to other kinds of popular fiction in the late nineteenth and early twentieth centuries, we find that the most gentlemanly hero can be implicitly contrasted with the dude and the snob. Even Cedric Errol, the angelic young American who suddenly becomes Lord Fauntleroy, is portrayed as a "manly" little chap, physically sturdy and direct in all his dealings, who humanizes and somewhat democratizes his grandfather, a miserly English earl, and remains true to his New York street-corner friends. The author, Frances Hodgson Burnett, knew just how to appeal to Anglophobic antisnobbery while encouraging more covertly the enjoyment of old-country lineage.[32] Another device used to toughen the edges of the upper-class hero's image is to have him fall on hard times without loss to his strength of character. When Frank Merriwell, that paragon of moral and physical fitness, is forced by family poverty to leave "dear old Yale," he struggles "like a man" to win out over repeated reverses. Long hours and low pay do not daunt him, for he has "courage, push, determination, stick-to-itiveness." He continues, as he has done from his school days, to outface, outfight, and outwit supercilious bullies—the arrogant and vicious Frenchman no less than the overdressed American swell.[33] But it is left to that much more searching story of collegian struggle, Owen Johnson's *Stover at Yale* (1912), to express an eastern upper-class envy of poor boys from the West who have made it the hard way. Quite unusual in American culture, the book has protagonists who express overt guilt about their own inherited money and place—for the ease and lack of testing it permits rather than injustice. *Stover* is more typically American in its solution to this; the implied notion that inherited assets can be justified by hard work and a democratic stance.[34] (Such concerns have surely reinforced the customs that have sent so many rich boys as well as poor ones along newspaper routes and into factory and warehouse jobs during the summer vacations.)

A more extreme, yet common, way of expressing these values and concerns is to make the upper-class hero into an *ex*dude who, temporarily plunged into a rugged western or seafaring environment, endures the taunts of his new fellows, and makes a mightly adjustment. He brings to the new situation an intelligence and, in some cases, an upper-class athleticism that make him a winner once he has learned the ropes. These themes were especially developed around the turn of the century. The leading literary exponents were Frank Norris and Jack London, but the basic exdude theme has survived through the twentieth century in Westerns and other fiction. By usually involving the hero in a shift westward as well as downward—a *diagonal* rather than *vertical* descent—the formula is able to give him a rewardingly rough time without singing too starkly the praises of proletarianism.[35] (The closest British equivalent is Rudyard Kipling's *Captains Courageous* [1898], but Kipling's story is more patronizingly class conscious and less harshly primitivist.)

By the 1920s, however, these devices for coping with the gentlemanly hero became less crucial. By then the protagonist of toughness and competence in American adventure fiction was much less apt to be of clearcut upper-class origins. Now established, especially in Westerns, was the natural gentleman of plain-man background or unclear antecedents.[36] Outside of Westerns, occupation, money, or knowledge might qualify the hero for upper-middle class status, but this would confer no sharp distinctions of style. There was no real equivalent of the British detective and thriller genres that continued to produce heroes whose styles of prowess and physical toughness were inseparable from upper-class qualities.[37]

THE HISTORICAL PERSPECTIVE

Sources

The three main historical sources of ACT—the anticourtier tradition, frontier myths and ambiguities, and the conflicts of consumer capitalism—have a chronological sequence though they overlap in time and their effects interact.

From Revolutionary times, Europe was a negative reference point for American identity. In the patriotic and puritan view, proper American traits were essentially un-European or un-British. Befitting the new nation forged in moral hope amid the wilderness, the true American was vigorous, manly, and direct, not effete and corrupt like the supposed Europeans. He was plain rather than ornamented, rugged rather than luxury-seeking, a liberty-loving common man or natual gentleman rather than an aristocratic oppressor or servile minion. So the stereotypes went, and their charge was not lessened by simultaneous attractions to the refinements, traditions, and rootedness of the Old World. In time, common-man rhetoric became less defensively nationalistic, but the theme of American naturalness versus European artifice remained an important undercurrent. Americans might become great engineers or shrewd politicians, but deep down their strength drew upon the nature within them and about them: they would "harness the elements," not deny or despise them.

The ruling metaphor was ancient in the Western and Mediterranean world: an ordered nature contrasted with the unnatural weakness of the metropolitan. The Roman moralists opposed the integrity, simplicity, and manly directness of the cultivator and small townsman to the duplicity and softness of the city sophisticate. In Elizabethan and Stuart England, a similar stereotype of hardy British provincials versus effete Continentals developed the domestic antagonism between sober country and cosmopolitan court. Entwined with puritanism and nationalism and transferred to America, the country versus court motif became the first great shaper of ACT, expressed ultimately in images of republican simplicity and independence.[38]

What an irony. Country versus court, and puritanism—two major components of the anti-British, republican animus—were imports from Britain. The puritan impulse, with its stress on testing and tempering, struggle and responsibility, had contributed to colonial ideas about strength and weakness long before it was caught up in pre-Revolutionary attacks on the British government's corruption and commercial power. In seventeenth-century New England, as in England under James I and Charles I, puritan moralists inveighed against "effeminacy," evinced among other things in "uncivil and unmanly" long hair. They did not mean to denigrate female qualities so much as to attack men for abandoning sources of strength in their own gender and for abusing natural and social order through "voluptuousness."[39]

In the early Republic, the anticourtier watch became more classless in tone, less associated with gentry leadership than its English ancestors.[40] Although Revolutionary artisan movements paved the way, the literary landmark of the transition was Royall Tyler's comedy of 1787, *The Contrast*. Subtitled *The American Son of Liberty*, it was the first

American play to be successfully performed by a professional company. *The Contrast* attacks snobbish New York fops who slavishly exaggerate European polish and fashions. They are cultural traitors; whereas individual Europeans, true to their own communities, can be respected. Colonel Manly of Massachusetts, the play's hero, is a young Revolutionary veteran. He has "stern virtue," frugal simplicity, practical compassion for the afflicted, and the "candor" and "sincerity" of the true American. He is also a gentleman, in class as well as quality: He dines with an ambassador; he has old-fashioned rectitude. His servant, Jessamy, however, declares that he won't always be a servant. He is a "true blue son of liberty," and his father has as good a farm as the Colonel's! In a significant displacement of class feeling onto race, he affirms that he is no "neger." Though Manly is quick to draw sword for a woman's honor, Jessamy is the more openly pugnacious and dynamic. In the end he receives his share of discomforture from events; but Tyler's point is made: there is more than one model for the American male.[41]

The point at which the Jessamys overtook the Manlys as the main exemplars of American toughness did not arrive till the 1830s, when aggressive entrepreneurship, extensions of political democracy, and a continued fear of European subversion all came together.[42] At the same time Jacksonian political rhetoric deployed pastoral motifs—scenes of peaceful, prosperous husbandry—as an anchor to its own aggressiveness as well as a challenge to Europeanized "pimps" in high places. If John Bull was sometimes portrayed as excessively masculine, an overweight but beefy bully, this did not curtail the traditional association of European politics with drawing rooms, minuets, and feminine entrapment.

In the 1850s and 1860s North-South antagonisms replaced nationalistic ones, though Northerners transferred some European stereotypes (such as idle, aristocratic oppressors) onto the South. In the 1870s, as Northerners turned to their own social and economic problems, the fight over civil service reform revealed the change. Despite the dudish elitism of many reformers, despite indeed their general Anglophilia and their explicit borrowing from British reform, the politicos who attacked them made little reference to their foreign connections. They challenged their manhood, not their Americanness.[43] From the 1880s, Anglo-Saxon racialism, fuelled by the "New Immigration," cut across anti-Europeanism since it aligned Americans with northern Europeans.

Within this realignment one way of distancing Europe was to look for its heroes in the past, among mediaeval knights and fierce Vikings. It still took some juggling to salvage a distinctively American character: to claim, for example, that Americans were the pick of the Nordic race and the next vanguard of Western civilization in a coming race struggle.[44]

Despite these cross-currents, the un-European, anticourtier tradition remained a latent factor in definitions of American toughness. It contributed to other imagery while openly reemerging at particular moments of anti-European feeling. Its predominant version was the polarity between the strength of country-boy virtue and big city/high office plushness, though its effectiveness suffered when our sturdy country-boy got himself tagged as a sappish hayseed, and city living was associated not just with soft living but with *excessive* toughness: exploitation, callousness, selfish hurry.[45] In its purer forms, the anticourtier animus gained from a powerful folk memory. Frank Sullivan played on just this in his ''Weekend at Lady Astor's'' (1938):

All the men wore knee breeches and silk stockings except me. As a virile patriotic Yankee I refused to kowtow to British flummery, but as a concession to international good will I did roll my trousers up to the knee.[46]

Sullivan's timing was good. Churchill's bulldog image and the British fighting record in World War II should not obscure the fact that in the late 1930s many Americans in business and government believed that the British (especially the upper classes) were too effete to go to war or to put up much of a fight when they did.[47] Much later, in a different conflict, Joseph McCarthy tapped the same folklore in his attacks on the State Department's ''lace hankerchief crowd.'' When he declared that ''For twenty years we have allowed dilettante diplomats to do the fighting for us with kid gloves in perfumed drawing rooms,'' the remarkable thing was not his resurrection of old attacks on Foreign Service ''cookie-pushers'' and ''pink tea'' slippers—stereotypes that went back to the turn of the century—but his evocation of basic court imagery.[48] It could have been made in the 1830s or 1840s. In subtler forms, among internationalists and counterinsurgents as well as isolationists, the idea of stout American patriots, vitiated by silken entrapments and smooth-talking parasites, has drawn from the same source.[49]

The second historical factor is more obvious: frontier realism romanticized. The key models were the pioneer, superimitator of the primitive, technically adept but stripped lean by exigency; and the cowboy, mobile, self-reliant, riding across nature's grand canvas. Although much of the underlying reality was not uniquely American, the neighboring experience of Canada suggests that a fine mix of geography and institutions was needed to produce the self-consciously expansive toughness of the American style.[50] A crucial aspect was the speed with which reality blurred into myth, as the frontier interracted with the commercial and intellectual civilization that formed its hinterland. While the West was still being won, politicians, writers, and *frontiersmen themselves* (from the original Captain John Smith to William Cody) were exploiting and exaggerating its events. By mid-nineteenth century there were chains of frontier operators who knew and reinvented each other.[51] Set against the relatively short history of the American people, it was like seeing drama through a telescope—as if in British history a real King Arthur had turned the Round Table into a money-making tournament and, leaping the centuries, had personally sold Sir Thomas Malory and Alfred Tennyson the book rights on Camelot. With one important difference: despite its legends of betrayal, the Arthurian idea was never sullied, whereas the face of the frontier always had a dark side associated with heathenishness, degradation, cruelty, and anarchy.[52] In the long-run, however, the "badlands" quality of the frontier made it all the more fascinating as a testing ground of strength and virtue. At the same time, the idea that frontier violence was "clean" violence has lingered on, aided in the South by the history of duelling. An ex-Marine Texan, removed to Oakland, California, lamented to me in the mid–1960s about the anarchy of northern cities compared with the southern towns of his boyhood. When I mentioned that the South still had high homicide rates, and that Texan boom towns used to have very high rates, he said, "Yes but it was a *gutsy* kind of killing."

The American frontier's depth and variety gave it special force in shaping cultural attitudes. The movement of peoples westward through so much of American history made dynamic expansion a national metaphor for individual qualities. Unlike the imperial adventures of most expansionist nations, frontier experiences reached all the more compellingly into social and personal attitudes because they were not distanced on overseas soil. Below the superstructure of Manifest Destiny, violence and challenging excitement mixed with the mundane, arduous process of domestic settlement; American toughness was both grandeur and grit.

Frontier themes are so familiar to Americans, so studied and discussed, and so woven into this book, that they need not hold us up. Something more must be said, however, about the ambiguities and contradictions in frontier myth that have electrified as well as undercut American perceptions of the tough individual. From the early 1800s the settled population of both the East and West evinced a fascinated horror with frontier folk; they seemed to project their own aggressiveness and revolt onto the wilderness.[53] Since that time the same writers who extolled frontier masculinity and combat prowess have sometimes worried about the destructiveness and personal instability that might contaminate the heroic virtues.[54] The worry has historical basis, but one of its results has been to minimize other frontier characteristics, those of community, neighborly aid, and family endurance against enormous physical hardship. Not till recently, with the rediscovery of women's voices and roles in western settlement, has this communal toughness been properly noticed.

In the nineteenth-century cattle country, peculiar forms of lawlessness emphasized the divided myth. Vigilantism, banditry against railroads and banks, guerrilla terrorism, and the range wars made it hard to establish just who were the good guys and who were the bad. As Kent Steckmesser observed, Great Plainsmen such as Wild Bill Hickok and Wyatt Earp, who murderously worked on both sides of the law, developed dual images. Unlike William Tell or Robin Hood, Hickok, Earp, and Billy the Kid have their satanic as well as saintly legends.[55] Myth, in other words, has dealt with ambiguity by simplifying it into two sharp alternatives, both larger than life. A seemingly different solution, presenting the frontiersman as a balance between the wild and the civilized, does not eliminate ambiguity, for if the frontiersman can draw the best qualities from both, he can also draw the worst.[56]

In the late-nineteenth century, as upper-class easterners sought fitness and fortune in the West and acquired a more favorable view of range life, another source of ambiguity emerged. Frederick Jackson Turner's statement about the closing of the frontier (1893) was followed in the early 1900s by a spate of articles and books lamenting, rather prematurely, the passing of the noble cowboy.[57] A nagging worry to Turner and his successors was that Americans were losing an essential source of their dynamism and distinctive character. The romanticizing of frontier toughness, once associated with expansive optimism, now acquired a second base in pessimism. The optimism did not die, for the imagery of frontier expansion could be transferred to new contexts—industry, science, space, the interior self. But the very sense that the western frontier was declining as a *section* contributed to the nostalgic, eastern belief that frontiersmen were superior as *individuals*. This gave new life to hero worship in popular treatments of the West; more specifically it supported the formula in which the bronzed, virile master of his environment was followed in loving physical detail through the eyes of someone who felt inadequate—a tenderfoot, an eastern woman, a young boy.[58]

We can only touch here on the sexual complexity of western hero worship. Richard Slotkin's work on early frontier myth making provides a nineteenth-century basis for understanding the theme which colors so many twentieth-century Westerns: the preoccupation of two men with each other, in contest as often as in comradeship. It is not just a matter of surmising that "women-starved" men turned to homosexuality. Slotkin argued that the psychology of the hunt dealt with threats (whether animal or human) by making the act of destruction and devouring into one of union and absorption. This argument can be extended. As the dangers of the wilderness receded, the symbolism of the chase and other contests remained useful by stressing the bond between adversaries. Aggression was not just a rupture but a relationship, serving men who could not express mutual affection more openly and vulnerably.[59] All this can be found in western fiction and film; what of course is seldom represented is the darker form of hunt where the male predator is a rapist, seeking in violence a relationship he cannot otherwise achieve.

No account of ambiguities in frontier toughness can get far without recognizing the tangled cruelty of white-Indian relations. Modern scholarship has stressed the guilt in American culture caused by the killing and removal of Indian peoples; more dubiously it has insisted that Indians represented a whole complex of qualities and emotional claims that whites repressed and denied in themselves.[60] In assessing the matter of guilt we must distinguish between nineteenth-century attitudes and more durable legacies. In the nineteenth century the conflicting attitudes of different white groups toward Indians threw assumptions about toughness into question, especially when the different attitudes converged on the same person. Thus, George Custer knew that his reputation for military effectiveness won respect from westerners, many of whom held that consideration for Indian lives was the unmanly and dangerous sentiment of an "Indian-lover." But Custer also felt the weight on his conscience and career from another direction: from vocal segments of eastern opinion and some Indian agents, demanding humane restraint. For many in Custer's position, Indian policies were fraught with competing notions of strength and honor, producing—as in other race relations—the urge to batten down against humanitarian "softness."[61]

Although some of this conflict may have carried over into modern American conceptions of toughness, the effect can be exaggerated. One should not underestimate the power of selective memory and folklore to screen out defensiveness about the past.[62] For most Americans, the predominant picture until the 1960s was one of underdog bravery (the beleaguered wagon train or Simon Kenton running the gauntlet against his captors), not "total war" genocide. Many of the more recent ideas about a complex Indian claim on white psyches and libidos are a back projection of the ethnic and countercultural sensitivies of the 1960s and 1970s. Still, insofar as the frontier is a matter of mind, its effect on modern attitudes becomes what people say it is, if they say it often and frequently enough. And insofar as frontier experience, in some combination of the real and the imagined, suits the projection of one concern (for example, toughness) rather than another, it is a historical force in its own right.[63]

The third historical factor was dealt with more fully in chapter 2 and need only be summarized here. It consists of opposing pressures levied by a highly commercial civilization: the pressure to compete and deliver versus the pressure to consume, be indulged, and amiably follow others—enticements created by the very strenuosity of business endeavors. Americans, as a consequence, have felt soft and dependent when they think they should be rugged and aggressive. Reversing Daniel Bell and others who have stressed the movement of modern consumer/hedonist values away from old producer/ascetic values, I see in American notions of toughness a long-standing reaction against luxury and consumer self-indulgence. Modern selling and technology have both accentuated and masked a conflict that has been going on for centuries.[64]

Paradox and ambivalence have intensified all three historical forces. "Un-European" ruggedness was sought all the more because European culture was seductive. Frontier toughness was romanticized all the more because its seaminess had to be concealed. Business go-getting was praised all the more because its fruits threatened softness. The three factors tied into each other too. In claiming that America's distinctive essence lay in the West, rhetoricians of the frontier were apt to impute European effeteness to the American East. Early resistance to imported European luxuries merged with puritan anxieties about business affluence; and frontier myths, promulgated in part by commercially minded writers and showmen, sharpened the worry that prosperity and urban living would undermine American character. The frontier was on both sides of the matter, for if the struggle and acquisitiveness of western settlement produced sagas of toughness, they also produced abundance.

Tough Guys and Intellectuals

In dwelling on the basic historical sources of ACT, I have stressed continuity rather than change in American attitudes to toughness. In some respects, however, these attitudes shifted as the surrounding society developed. One of the most important shifts was in attitudes toward the mind. Slowly, incompletely, American notions of toughness moved from antiintellectualism to celebrations of performance that included the intellectual and artistic. The life and work of Charles Ives (1874–1954) represented a hinge in this development, a link between old and new. Debunking "sissy" types of music, he used traditional tough-guy themes and concerns in his drive to build new sounds and structures out of popular idiom.[65] Architects and painters, too, starting around the turn of the century, used motifs of toughness—assault, urban realism, earthy vigor—to create distinct American styles.[66] None of this, again, was wholly new. There were precedents in the cultural nationalism of Emerson, Melville, and Whitman: their call for writers who would express the New World's natural grandeur and rough originality rather than make polished imitations of the old.[67] Another and different heritage was the Elizabethan unity of letters with soldiering, statecraft, and business enterprise, which found new forms in puritan New England. The result was an "American Baconianism"—democratized intellect supporting results-minded pragmatism.[68]

In the twentieth century the value placed on sophistication and organizational control brought new forms of intellect and artistry within the scope of toughness. Despite pockets of anti-intellectual resistance, American toughness moved from rejecting complexity as fancy to mastering it as a challenge. This did not, however, preclude admiration of the individual who "got down to basics," that is, cut through unnecessary complexity, fancy talk, "idle speculation." The Cold War, with its systems analyses and multidisciplinary reach, confirmed the new toughness. Images of "orchestration" and "fine-tuning," whether of symphony orchestras or defense systems, fed an aesthetic of mastery and control.[69] Although the disciplines most involved in national security affairs—engineering and the sciences—remained traditionally masculine, the extension of tough styles into the humanities made it easier for intellectual women to be tough guys too. Jews too acquired a tougher public image, not only from Israel's military and frontier successes but from the new connections between toughness and brains.[70]

The Weave of Time

Two other patterns overlay the historical evolution of ACT values and styles. One is a shift back and forth between fusion and diffusion. As diverse images of toughness come together to form a whole, new styles and stances emerge that sooner or later threaten to break up the old unity. In the long run, however—and this is the other pattern—the trend is toward integration. The sophistication of tough-guy values and the way the media has co-opted lower-class and ethnic styles both support this.

Around these patterns we can now summarize the history of ACT and fill in some of its spaces. Distinctively American styles of toughness did not crystallize until the 1820s, but elements were accumulating long before—in puritanism, in the experience of migration and settlement, and in the symbols of Revolution and Republic. It is likely too that early seafaring and whaling provided an infusion of rough masculinity, though this was shared with Britain.[71] From the 1820s, especially in the Jacksonian era, images of toughness became more associated with aggressiveness, democratic informality, and youthful vigor.[72] This was the period when the no-sucker ethic became an important part of ACT. Jacksonian man's great fear of being taken advantage of was partly due to the fluid and grasping world in which he lived: it made him psychologically defensive and apt to project his exploitativeness onto others. But his fear also reflected an opposite trait, a gullibility born of his belief in science-assisted progress and his desire not to lose a business opportunity or be overtaken by events. The attraction of new gimicks and deals sharpened the fear of being suckered. The fear also connected with the paranoia that produced antimasonry and other movements. On a personal plane both anxieties expressed the lack of roots and guidelines felt by the individual in a new country of rapid growth and shifting populations. On a collective level they reflected the nation's military and cultural insecurity.[73]

The nineteenth century produced a multitude of tough styles and models. Coexisting with ''un-tough'' gentility, they ranged from Indian fighters to business hustlers, from politicos and social Darwinists to duellists and southern bullyboys. Before and after the Civil War, moral strenuosity provided some northern intellectuals with a bridge between sentimental compassion and will to achieve. Long after the war was ended, they remembered it as a time of testing, when the youth of an urban, industrial society faced a supposedly more martial South. In their triumph and relief, they neglected the fact that northern cities had their own tested toughness, drawn from the immigrant experience: the trauma and hardship of migration and resettlement, the struggle to find a foothold and defend one's own against other ethnic groups. Although immigrant life and politics fed styles of toughness into the national character, they rarely provided explicit models for the culture as a whole until well into the twentieth century. Even then, racialist and nativist fears maintained the old-stock Nordic type as an ideal hero.

In the late 1890s and early 1900s a new fusion of tough modes supported the various Progressive movements for reform and control of the industrial state. The businessman's drive to build was carried into public life where it was joined by moral enthusiasm and a new regard for training. In adapted form, the tycoon's famous traits of mastery and self-control became part of the national identity. Within the world of business, George Lorimer's *Letters from a Self-Made Merchant* (1902) signalled a new appreciation of the college-trained mind in making ''a fellow's business hum.''

it's simply the difference between jump in, rough-and-tumble, kick-with-the-heels-and-butt-with-the-head nigger fighting, and this grin-and-look-pleasant-dodge-and-save-your-wind-till-you-see-a-chance-to-land-on-the-solar-plexis style of the trained athlete. Both styles win fights, but the fellow with a little science is the better man, providing he's kept his muscle hard.

Lorimer's metaphors recorded a movement in values and styles. Dynamic toughness was adjusting to the new organizations run by professional managers.[74] Among doctors, meanwhile, the association of toughness with professionalism found support in defensive masculinity. Worried about female gains in the profession, medical leaders defined doctoring in frontier and business terms. The ideal doctor was either a penetrating researcher, a frontiersman of knowledge, or a successful crisis-manager who could "mend bullet-holes"—and collect large fees. These attitudes affected other professions too (especially the classroom behavior of law professors who adapted the medical case method to their own combative purposes).[75]

In some spheres of upper-class life, however, the alignment of toughness with professional control ran against the masculine cult of the primitive. For those attracted both to primitivism and control, Theodore Roosevelt had the solution: be moderate and controlled in everyday life; direct violence against targets safely beyond the pale— big game, rebels, criminals, or the Spanish in Cuba.[76] In spite of the high-placed dissent it aroused, the Spanish-American War and its imperialist aftermath provided obvious outlets for aggression and activity, especially among bored and cushioned urbanites. These feelings came to a head in World War I. At the top there was the thrill of helping to organize national resources in a mighty cause. Further down the military ladder, young college men declared what the war meant to them—the chance to employ their energy, prove their manhood, muck in with all sorts, and generally become "finer, straighter, cleaner men," even if it took "dirty work" with the bayonet to do it.[77]

The growth of professional athletics and mass media in the twenties encouraged a more vicarious toughness. Helped by radio, "yellow journalism," and commercialized spectator sports, the athlete became a major American hero.[78] Athletics in turn stimulated an action-hungry, prowess-admiring style in the press. This soon went beyond the sports writer and the purely vicarious. In his monthly magazine, *Physical Culture* (founded back in 1899), Bernarr MacFadden had long been promoting a cult of physical fitness, discipline, and mental alertness; he now took up in a big way the Prohibitionist worry about the sapping effects of alcohol.[79]

The 1920s produced both integration and divergence. In the direction of integration, model toughness both in business and fiction became more classless, and scientific or engineering knowledge a more conspicuous part of virility. A new all-American model was the efficient, dynamic business executive who could sell things, run things, and deal with people.

At the same time there was a divergence between moralistic and amoral conceptions of strength. This was not new, but it became more pronounced with the growth of large metropolitan areas and the sectional and cultural conflicts that followed World War I. On the moral front, religious and business communicators folded ideas of social conscience and responsibility into the ideal traits of the potent organization man. Elsewhere, in the new constituencies of the Ku Klux Klan, concern about strength and weakness underpinned moralistic attacks on polyglot hedonists and heathen. Yet part of its target was the quintessential tough guy, nourished on urban cynicism. Organized, big-city crime developed a language of violence and unsentimentality that found its way into politics, journalism, and the movies.

During the 1930s the pragmatic good guy, from New Dealer to fictional detective, fitted between the cynically tough and the morally strenuous. In the comic strips, the adept and assertive technician could even be a Boy Scout type. This was the heyday of the strong, square-jawed, clean-cut, clean-living hero, from *Dick Tracy* through *Terry and the Pirates* to *Superman*. He became still more appealing when pitted against the technological weapons of organized crime—a fact exploited by the wily J. Edgar Hoover when he deliberately popularized the federal "G-man" detective and his science-backed feats. World War II gave further opportunities for comic-strip supermen, air aces, and other champs battling for America against the twisted forces of evil.[80]

World War II was particularly important in the growth of modern ACT. It lasted longer and involved more of the population than any previous war since the Civil War, yet America was not a war zone, and despite some shortages, most of society enjoyed a relatively high standard of living.[81] This contrast, between the foxholes and civilian and PX comforts, sharpened the significance of combat as a test of manhood. Similarly, the prominence of moms and wives in the main society made stark and challenging the all-male nature of the front-line military group. Long after the war, movies and popular fiction were reworking these themes.[82]

To Americans of the 1950s and 1960s, toughness was more and more bound up with professionalism, intellectual prowess, and the problem of how to use technology without being swamped by it. Politically, the

Cold War theme of "standing up to the Russians" sharpened the value on alertness and endeavor that ran through the nation's leading institutions. Some Americans actually welcomed "the Communist threat" as a way of calling forth effort and a sense of purpose.[83] In the twentieth century, exponents of American business culture had often worried about the motivation of managers and executives. The fear that business dynamism was winding down now joined older concerns about materialism and softness. In view of all this, the Cold War had its uses. It provided a competitive stimulus that sometimes seemed lacking in the nation's suburbs and bureaucracies.

John F. Kennedy and the people and styles he admired represented a high point in the appeal of the expanded, modern tough guy. They offered an exciting, sophisticated virility. Much of Camelot's magic rested on paradox. The Kennedys played touch football; they also wrote books. Their family, with its formidable patriarch, was rich, glamorous, and cohesive; but that drove them to do more on their own. To get elected, they built intricate organizations, yet they eschewed committees, position papers, and bureaucratic flab. They had both style and combativeness, youth and dignity, sex appeal and seriousness. They were ambitious, strenuous, and highly competitive, yet they were liberal, tolerant, quizzical. A cooly controlled suppleness was their key. Since those days, despite all the debunking of President Kennedy's record and the divided feelings aroused by his brother Robert, the kind of toughness they epitomized has continued to command admiration in many circles of government and the professions.[84]

Most of this, of course, was explicitly challenged by countercultural movements of the late 1960s and early 1970s—especially hippies and the youth movement. Their leanings toward androgeny did not simply challenge traditional sex roles and differences; they repudiated the tough guy's whole psychological strategy, with its accent on armor, control, and calculation. In the course of the 1970s, however, pieces of this repudiation gave ground to a modified, emotionally liberated version of ACT. The new tough guy (he or she) was still concerned with toughness, but was more aware of this concern and less afraid of expressing vulnerable feelings. In their different ways, hippies shared with tough guys a yearning for personal authenticity, a wish to "get back to basics," and a respect for candor. From their separate corners they supported the new middle-class search for external simplicity and a richer emotional life. Finding and extending one's limits acquired a new vogue and range; competitiveness became just one way of self-testing.[85]

The possibilities in all of this, from antitough guy to tough guy re-modelled, had parallels in the male gay population, since the butch and sadomasochist crowd did not wipe out their gentler, more androg-ynous brothers. (It is ironical that the macho gays' disdain of one convention should lead them straight back into another: away from the traditional image of the effeminate homosexual to rawhide boots and stevedore gear, traditional emblems of masculinity.)[86] Again, in pop-ular literature and the media, the early-to-mid–1970s produced a caf-eteria of choices from thoroughgoing, countercultural assaults on the tough guy to celebrations of virility that paid the merest lip service to the new critiques. In the middle range, films like *Marathon Man* (with Dustin Hoffman) enabled viewers to have it both ways, to distance themselves from the most obvious tough guys, but to identify with a sensitive, reluctant hero when he stumbled into a tough and exciting role.[87] The women's movement, for its part, supported the new tough-tender mix by celebrating female grit and spirit while honoring the tra-ditionally feminine qualities of expressiveness and caring.

All this seems far from the world of power and statecraft where toughness also became an issue in the 1970s. Yet the criticism of for-eign policymakers who "had to prove their virility" bore the mark of countercultural and feminist ideas, sharpened by the Vietnam War. It is easy to forget now that the Carter administration recruited into for-eign policy a number of younger people who explicitly opposed a "macho presidency"; that Carter himself disliked the chest-thumping interpretation of the *Mayaguez* raid—the view that it signalled strength to allies and adversaries—just as he opposed Kissinger's theory of psychological linkage between crisis areas. It is easy to forget this not just because other foreign policy players in the administration re-mained hawkish, but because the doves never succeeded in making peaceful restraint look tough. Despite a brief attempt to redefine the idea of strength in foreign policy, the powerful association of tough-ness with martial patriotism kept the main levers of tough-guy sym-bolism in the hands of the hawks. (The very terms, "hawk" and "dove," first used together in the Cuba missiles crisis of 1962, biased the issue.) In domestic policy, by contrast, traditional toughness cov-ered a wider range of political stances, from "rugged individualism" to "can-do" government activism, and back via "can-do" budget-cut-ting.

In business and professional life, ideas of toughness during the 1970s became more intricately involved in psychological gamesmanship, in presenting the self and advancing personal projects through the shoals and opportunities of bureaucracy. Among elites a vogue use of the word, "strong"—a "strong program," a "strong management team"—coupled the image of effectiveness with reassurance and stability.[88] At the same time the media exploited lower-class ethnic toughness and the conflict between ordinary individuals and systems—hence the run of television police dramas. Despite the stress on organization and the shift to political conservatism, ACT styles diversified in the 1970s. They became less obvious, more qualified, more penetrated with opposites and experiments.

THE FOREIGN-COMPARATIVE PERSPECTIVE

To what extent has the complex evolution of ACT produced something distinctively American? All the traits of the archetypical American tough guy are valued outside the United States. People recognize that they help individuals to survive and societies to prosper, provided they are balanced by other qualities. In addition, everyone has deep-seated concerns about strength and weakness, derived in large measure from opposing drives for autonomy and dependency, from infantile relationships with powerful figures, and from fear of danger. The "A" in ACT is therefor a matter of emphasis and style rather than absolute difference. Even the energetically personal kind of mastery so beloved of Americans flourishes in other modern societies.

Cultural exports complicate the picture. No part of the American way of life has been more successfully exported than tough-guy styles and accessories. The international appeal of American screen heroes, Westerns and pseudocowboy gear points up the relative nature of the national tough-guy syndrome. The appeal is general enough for styles to be borrowed and imitated by cultures outside the United States. Yet it is the American love affair with toughness that developed those styles in the first place.[89]

The foreign reach of the tough guy is connected to phases of child and adolescent development, especially among boys in Western society, though nobody knows how much of it is biological and how much is socially induced. I have noticed, for example, that British boys of diverse social class, aged between about four and seven, often play out a caricature of the modern American tough guy. They are enthralled by feats of physical strength; muscles and speed; combat skill (even if they don't fight much themselves); and command of technological power. They are addicts of American media superheroes, and it is hard to tell how much of their enthrallment is crosscultural, a primitive stage in their development with technology taking the place of magic, and how much of it is created or at least reinforced by specific American influences. Aspects of this stage reappear in adolescence when the teenager tests himself against adult roles in emulating them, rejecting them, or doing both; he feels anxious about controlling his heightened sexual and aggressive drives. One outcome is a male adolescent syndrome that is not confined to America yet seems to parody ACT. The teenager is narcissistically preoccupied with prowess and physique, while his accent on cool control mediates his dual urge to revolt and to censor.[90] Both these cases—the young boy and the teenager—suggest that American culture has elaborated upon some basic ingredients in human development and sustained them in diverse adult situations.

The irony is that American tough-guy behavior, which is most pronounced among working-class groups, is more distinctively American in its paler, sublimated middle-and upper-class versions. I have observed styles of dominance and physical toughness among Hoboken dockworkers that are not shown so acutely, so personally, by East London dockers, but I would not stress national differences on that social plane. In modern industrial society, manual work fosters a respect for physical prowess and a blunt self-defense against impositions that cut across national boundaries. Among lower-class adolescents, too, the deprivations that encourage "hard-boy" narcissism and tribal swaggering are no monopoly of one country.[91] What I find more remarkable in American society is the subtle persistence of the tough-guy tradition in milieus well removed from physical labor and hardship: among salesmen, academics, preppies. The significance of this applies to society as a whole as well as to classes within that society. Toughness, broadly defined, is no more valued in America than it has been in many warrior nations or in other societies facing acute physical adversity. But America has *not* been such a society for a long time, and its attitudes to toughness reflect it. ACT is largely reactive. Much of it consists of a selective revolt against civilization: a wish to retain primitive vigor and authenticity while mastering the latest techniques of success.

We have, then, to consider ACT as a national, defensive cult. This, however, is not sufficient to define its Americanness, for other cultures, too, have produced cults of toughness and virility and maintained them in urban environments. Let us look at four such cults:

—The values of a past, idealized state, proclaimed by Roman moralists from the second century B.C. to the second century A.D. This, of course, was a much-used source of imagery for American Revolutionaries and republicans.

—The value system surrounding Mexican machismo, including its urban developments in the twentieth century: a magnet to some purveyors and interpreters of American tough-guy values.

—The myth and masculinity of the Australian outback reflecting several conditions closely parallel to those in America's past.

—The development of English Victorian hardiness, and its legacy in upper-class education.

Modern American notions of toughness also bear resemblance to the pre-Fascist Italian cult of *Futurismo*, with its sexual revelling in strength, speed, and technology, including a mystique of numbers and technical data. Futurismo, however, was less controlled, more authoritarian, and more apt to pit images of the machine *against* those of rural nature.

The comparisons that follow are highly generalized and apply at different stages in the development of ACT, but at no point in that development do they simply duplicate American patterns.

Roman Virtue

The moralists who attacked the luxury and immorality of rich young Romans often depicted an earlier Rome whose citizens lived in frugal and modest simplicity. Their distinguishing qualities were a natural but controlled vigor; propriety and honor; soldierly discipline, hardiness and courage; and a readiness to serve the Republic. These stereotypes were sectional as well as historical. A generation of historians, exemplified by Livy, lamented the departure of old virtues from Rome itself while exaggerating their survival in provincial towns.[92] In somewhat the same spirit many of those who decried immorality effected a cult of rustic plainness in their own dress and living styles. Much of the alleged decline in Roman morals was attributed to the attraction of customs imported from Greece and the Near East. Greeks were associated with effeminacy, smooth-tongued duplicity, and exploitation. *Graeculus* ("little Greek") was a term of contempt. We find, thus, in Rome what we noted in the early American Republic: a national identity sought in the strong and simple man of the countryside and his family, whose wisdom and puritan virtue contrasted with the profligacy of rich cosmopolitans. In both societies, the founding, republican virtues were believed to be under subversion by older, excessively cultivated civilizations.

Yet these tendencies and reactions in Roman culture differed in several important respects from the way plain man patriotism developed in America. First, the Roman counterpart attacked immorality much more than softness. There were some attacks on effeminacy and (in the hands of a Juvenal) on effeminate kinds of homosexuality, but sensual excess far overshadowed weakness per se as a target of attack. Even luxury, so castigated by patriot moralists, was associated more with greed and self-indulgence than with dependency or physical debilitation. In the second place, spokesmen for the simple, modest life attacked bourgeois materialism and money-grubbing as much as, if not more than, the wastrel's life of ease. As we have seen, such attacks were by no means foreign to America, but from early days the American plain man ideal gave more place to the upwardly mobile economic striver than did its Roman equivalent. Thirdly, the Roman equivalent did not really posit a classsless hero of lowly background. There were elements in the legend of Cincinnatus that came close to this, but Cincinnatus was of patrician birth and rank. The way that social conflict developed in Rome—especially the establishment of plebeian and patrician interests in different political bodies and offices—helped to prevent notions of classlessness or humble background from taking over the central and traditional images of the ideal Roman.[93] Some vehement antipopulists were idealists of rural frugality, and a number of the very men they feared as demagogues were high-living urbanites. Both have had their parallels in American history and, indeed, in recent politics, but they have not been strong enough to wipe out the broad base and democratic flavor of the American plain man ideal.[94]

Mexican Machismo

The theme of sexual conquest that runs through so many American attitudes of toughness and mastery is more central to Mexican machismo, and the latter makes more of begetting children, especially male one. This is not just a peasant phenomenon: indeed Oscar Lewis suggested in the 1950s that it was stronger in the Mexican city, in association with aggressive urban living styles.[95] Conversely, although machismo has widened into nonsexual aspects of male competence (as it has in other parts of Latin America), this has not developed outside the sexual realm as much as it has in America, where it was always much broader-based. One result is that the fictional fantasies of Mexican culture have given less place to covert avoidance of sexual prowess—exemplified in the American hero who effortlessly (but passively) seduces a luscious, craving woman, or else has no time to satisfy her: duty calls, crisis beckons.

In sexuality, as in other aspects of the subject, it is not easy to allow for two-way attractions and influences between the American and Latin patterns. Generally, however, the sexual emphasis in Mexican machismo has involved more rigid honor codes, including a violent touchiness about dishonor to one's own womenfolk.[96] Standing up to other men is more apt to have a sexual connotation: the Mexicans say *cojones* where Americans are liable to say ''guts'' rather than ''balls.'' Both value systems romanticize the fighting underdog—in Mexico the memory of Pancho Villa and other guerrillas or bandits fighting the Americans and oppressive regimes. However, despite Villa's humble background, the Mexican pattern, with its strongly chivalric overtones, has been less centrally rooted in models of the common man.

Again, both patterns make much of combat and physical prowess. The machete, whose use was traditionally taught to Mexican boys, shares the same word origin (*macho*, ''male'') as *machismo*, and with urban development the term *machetismo* has come to include political and organizational mastery, rather like the American term ''muscle.'' If American language has made much of cutting images, so too, according to Octavio Paz, Mexican usage has produced its own imagery of sadistic ripping—violating women but also exposing one's opponent while remaining guarded oneself.[97] Yet despite the ramifications of this into notions of contest, Mexican machismo puts somewhat more emphasis on sheer stoic stubbornness than does its American equivalent. Passionate, often blithe, yet armored, Mexican machismo does not have the puritan roots of American toughness, and being sensually more free, it has found it easier to treat homosexuality with tolerance.[98]

Outback and Mateship

With the exception of Canada, where American influences are particularly difficult to unravel from the indigenous, the closest resemblance to the American national ethos of toughness is probably to be found in Australia. There, as in the United States, an urban population (more urban indeed) has romanticized a rugged and raucous male life of the frontier (the outback), and found in it the essence of the national character. In keeping with this, there has persisted a common man pride, an ambivalent contempt of old country "swells," and an even greater stress than Americans now put on an unfancy, anti-intellectual kind of practicality. At the same time a great interest in sports and athletic ability has helped keep notions of physical prowess alive in the suburbs. But there are also differences. Australian models of toughness are centered more simply and directly on masculinity than in the United States: sex roles in Australia have for a long time been more separated. Again, though both countries' frontiers have encouraged technical ingenuity, Australians have tended more to stop at the level of rough making-do. The picture is changing with the influx of American business spirit and cybernetics, but the native Australian concept of toughness has been less bound up with images of technological mastery and indeed less dominated by economic dynamism. The causes of this include the arid harshness of the outback, which prevented the rapid opening up of new land. (With the appalling exception of Tasmania, conquest of the Australian bush also involved less violence against the native population.) The sparseness of the outback, its dominance by big farmers, and the convict and radical element in nineteenth-century immigration have made for a more proletarian kind of antielitism in Australia than in America, by and large. It is bound up in the masculine comraderie of Australians "mateship," and it has been more likely to romanticize the travelling sheepshearer and the doomed outlaw than the big self-made man.

Victorian Hardiness

For our last comparison we look more extensively at a development over time. The British case shows how closely a society, lacking a domestic frontier situation, could come to American-style toughness before developments in class structure and related institutions, especially schools, pulled a dominant part of the culture away from business values. Nineteenth-century England inherited a model of John Bull—tough, testy, industrious, and dogged. Its exponents included the self-made factory owner and merchant as well as the squire of "Horseback Hall." Among British Victorians a traveller in time and place from early-twentieth-century America would have found many familiar traits: moral strenuosity, yet also a practical bustling materialism; fascination with engine power; and the enthusiasm for masculine "red blood" voiced by the athlete-intellectual, Leslie Stephen. A general value on energy and strength drew both from commerce and from traditions of field and village sports. They came together in the old nationalist sense of England as a small but doughty people, seafaring islanders who had won many commercial and military successes against the great Continent and were now planting the flag in distant climes.

However, the development of boys' secondary-level boarding schools (public schools) for the upper and upper-middle classes pulled elite notions of toughness and strength away from their potential association with commercial drive and placed them more squarely on the values of gentry and gentleman's club.[99] Later, through schoolboy fiction and other media, public school styles would filter down the social structure, but in the meantime—by mid-nineteenth century—the schools were already taking in and socializing the rising bourgeois. Despite old images of John Bull, in the Crimean War and afterwards upper-class and public school people often saw the bourgeoisie as greedy, physically timid, and soft—even, in the view of Charles Kingsley, effeminate. Similar views flourished in mid- and late-nineteenth-century America, as we have seen, but they were never institutionalized in a way that made them central to ACT values. In Britain, by contrast, the growth and popularity of the public schools, with their spartan living conditions, were in part a response to the industrial prosperity reflected in middle-class consumerism and upper-class, country house comforts. Anxieties about these things were sharpened by military and religious (essentially Pauline) notions of what it took to make a leader, including a paternal belief that a leader should be able to do anything, suffer any hardship, that he asked of his men.

The boarding schools, thus, enabled a ruling gentry class to absorb the rising bourgeoisie without paying a price in consumer softness. This is not to say that a school system alone stood between British culture and a full and enduring manifestation of an American tough-guy type. In the long run broader social and geographical factors surely did make a difference. But the public school element is particularly interesting because it too celebrated a kind of toughness.

As British imperialism flourished in the late nineteenth century, so did public school athleticism and organized games. David Newsome has argued that the concept of manliness entailed by this shifted from antichildishness to antieffeminacy.[100] To that extent, there were similarities with contemporary concerns about manliness in America. (In both countries, social Darwinist tracts on evolution had stressed the importance of sex differences.) However, the longer-term development of public school attitudes in the twentieth century put more weight than did attitudes in equivalent American elites on *grownupness*, as opposed to *maleness*. As the expanded boarding school system matured, its very institutionalizing of sex segregation defused its members' potential fears of being feminized. At the same time, via the prefect system, the public school focus on inculcating leadership, a commanding if light style of authority, created the little gentleman whose ways often made him seem old before his time. The terms of masculine affection, "old chap" and "old boy," and the way that Winchester College traditionally called its teenage pupils "men," attested to this.[101]

Of course, the two notions of manliness overlapped; of course, traditional public school concepts of maturity were quintessentially masculine. Indeed, back in the late nineteenth century, the public school popularity of old words like "mollycoddle" and "milksop" combined the two concepts in the negative image of the babyish fellow ("namby-pamby") who had been pampered by mother or maidservants. Significantly, though, "milksop" was replaced in subsequent decades by "soppy" and "wet," with less antifeminine connotations. The specter of being a mama's boy continued, but it did so mainly in the network of primary-level, boarding "preparatory schools" that developed to serve the public schools. By the time a boy passed into his public school, the specter would have receded: he would be more likely to be taunted for being a childish prep school boy than a mama's boy.[102]

Were British public school conceptions of manliness less individualistic than their American counterparts? Despite its group customs and rituals and its organized team games, British public school culture at the turn of the century made an explicit credo of self-reliance. It did so at least in the eyes of its adult authorities. The scouting movement that extended public school ideals, while imitating such American groups as the Boy Pioneers and the Woodcraft Indians, placed the idea of personal resourcefulness within a paramilitary system of teams, uniforms, and set book training. The historical novels of G.A. Henty, another extension of public school culture, put a similar stress on personal self-reliance as well as flexible organization. The moral overtone of public school self-reliance combined integrity and moral confidence with courage and practical self-sufficiency. It reflected a widespread Western concern for individual character amid urban growth and material temptation. It also suited the demands of imperial conquest and governance, when white men might find themselves isolated among "the natives."

In practice, the public schoolboy's self-reliance mainly meant pratical self-management, not depending on family and womenfolk to pick up for one; it meant organizing one's schedule to fit into the nooks and levies of boarding school life; it meant emotional survival away from home and a confidence in leading others along channels that were largely charted. (On the emotional point, it is significant that in the nineteenth and early-twentieth centuries, American boarding schools used the headmaster and his wife as a surrogate family for the boys much more than their English counterparts did.[103]) Self-reliance, in these senses, was stressed more than tough-guy self-assertion. The legacy was apparent in the mid-twentieth century: compared with English public school culture, American prep school boys in the 1950s made more of individual contest, muscular toughness, a self-centered physicality.[104]

These observations bear on what I have said about the control of aggressiveness in America. Social scientists who have compared modern British and American culture have usually claimed that the British attach more weight to controlling aggressiveness, whereas I have noted its stress in American culture too. The real difference is that, in America, control has had to struggle against powerful traditions of self-assertion; being more embattled, it is in some ways more visible.[105]

AMERICAN TOUGH

We have seen that there are no absolute differences between the American tough-guy tradition and concerns with toughness and strength in other cultures. But we have also seen that ideas of toughness carry different emphases and associations in different societies. Let us put together some of the meanings that have loaded the American tradition. At the outset of this book I noted that these meanings have outstretched formal dictionary definitions of toughness. The "guy who can take care of himself (herself)" stresses dynamic impact as well as mere self-defense—to master a changing environment the tough guy must move fast. American meanings of toughness also combine an unusual concern with self, physical as well as psychological, and a consciousness of others. "Whoop! Look at me," the cry of the "ring-tailed roarer" on the old southwestern frontier, reminds us that narcissism has deeper roots in America than the modern corruptions of capitalism decried by Christopher Lasch. The isolation of frontier life, like the loneliness of individualism, produced a desire to puff out the self while making contact with others; to look good in their eyes while competing against them. Furthermore, having endorsed self-assertion, the society was impelled to build countervailing values of community and control. The fighting reformer and the can-do organizer lifted the values of toughness into a group setting. Yet the tensions remained. Americans find the tough guy both a magnet and threat. Toughness itself is threatened by extreme untoughness—euphemism, "togetherness," self-indulgence.

These frictions reflect the sheer range of American society and the pace of its history. No other country today combines so complex an urban frontier with so large a rural base. A good quarter of Americans still live either in the countryside or in small rural towns. Celebrated by natural monuments, from Niagara Falls to the Grand Canyon, from the Rockies to the deserts, the land tells Americans that their heritage is intensely physical as well as spiritual. (What other modern nation has carved its ancestral leaders into a mountainside?) Despite the fixedness of these symbols, the land stands for action and movement: "mission into the wilderness," "opening up the continent," "staking out new territory." The fear of losing such vigor, of letting the springs of action wind down, is crucial to American identity.

In exalting earthy vigor, American tradition has given the tough guy an unusual relationship to class and status. The tough-guy archetype challenges the upper-classes from below: it commands them to be direct and down-to-earth, not precious, or fancy, or stuck-up. But being tough in America has also meant being a winner and *looking like* a winner, and that increasingly means displaying sophistication and the luxuries of success. Here, as in so much else, the American tradition of toughness is a multiple of opposites. It encourages simplicity and waste, independence and conformity, selfishness and creative teamwork. Its ambiguity is a richness, a range from which Americans must choose, as they move into a new era of constraint and possibility.

APPENDIX
THEORY, FACT, AND FICTION: OBSERVATIONS ON APPROACHES AND METHODS

Full references for authors and works mentioned here are in the Bibliography.

GENRES

This book connects with three kinds of writing:

1. *Works that bear directly and generally on American concerns with toughness, strength and virility, locating them specifically in American culture.* The most striking fact about this genre is that it is practically nonexistent. Edwin Cady's article on "The Strenuous Life" in American cultural history (1966) qualifies for membership and several books discuss the matter while passing on to other things.[1] Some works dealing with American masculinity refer to historical and cultural factors (for example, Geoffrey Gorer on moms and he-men in 1948; Myron Brenton, *The American Male*, 1966; Lucy Komisar and Gloria Steinem on "the masculine mystique" in the early 1970s), but these do not deal with notions of toughness outside their relationship to gender.[2] There has been no general and systematic explanation. Instead, most writing about toughness in America has focused on specific people, periods, and groups: for example, the era and class of Theodore Roosevelt; Hemingway, and hard-boiled detective writers; movie heroes; youth gangs; Tom Wolfe's aviators.[3] Even the antimacho journalism stimulated by the Vietnam war and feminism in the late 1960s and early 1970s usually limited its attack to discrete and allegedly pathological types—especially hawkish policymakers. The effect of all this was to displace onto specific targets something that was more generally American. It is significant that in the 1970s the indirection of humor—movie spoofs, comics, comedy columns—provided some of the shrewdest insights into the culture and psychology of American toughness.

2. *Works on masculinity and male aggressiveness in Western culture (or*

worldwide). Writing of this sort that deals with conceptions of toughness fall into three genres: (1) old theories of male compensation for maternal dominance and other threats (for example, Talcott Parsons, 1947; Jackson Toby, 1966); (2) feminist and men's liberationist writing, especially in the 1970s; (3) nonfeminist or postfeminist writing on masculinity and related aggressiveness (for example, Lionel Tiger, 1969; Peter Stearns, 1979). For our purposes, these analyses are at once too broad and too narrow: they do not pick out the specificallyAmerican elements; and, again, they confine their frame to masculinity. This last point is not so true of Walter Ong's book on "adversativeness" (*Fighting for Life*, 1981), but he too does not deal specifically with American patterns. Some of these studies generalize from American data without explicitly saying what is particularly American and what is not (for example, Parsons, 1947; Marc Fasteau, 1975).

3. *Works on American social character*. I have analyzed elsewhere the different genres that have emerged since the 1940s, the pause in such writing during the "centrifugal sixties," and the resurgence in the 1970s. It seems that the return in the 1970s to general statements about American culture and character absorbed the 1960s stress on conflict and diversity into ideas of contradiction within mainstream values themselves (cf. Michael Kammen's *People of Paradox*, 1972; Daniel Bell's *The Cultural Contradictions of Capitalism*, 1976; and to a lesser extent, Daniel Yankelovich's *New Rules*, 1981). My own work's play with contradictions and ambiguities surrounding toughness bears the same mark.[4]

This brings me to a specific comparison between Bell's *Cultural Contradictions* and my work. There are obvious and close parallels between Bell's thesis and the argument set out in chapter 2 ("Producers and Consumers"). Both of us present a modern, secular version of the "God-cod" paradox: the antithesis between producer values and the consumer hedonism that producers need to sell their goods and services. Both of us allow for economic forces as well as culturally transmitted attitudes that have acquired their own psychological momentum. My study, of course, focuses more specifically on feelings about strength and weakness. (Indeed it departs from most other American social character studies in dealing with *qualities* rather than *relationships*: with the properties of mind and behavior that a people prizes rather than the way they relate to each other and themselves.) Compared with Bell's work, however, my study attaches more weight to continuities and to sources of attitudes that predate capitalism and lie outside what Bell calls "Modernism." Again, it tries to outline what is distinctively American whereas Bell implies that his thesis applies to the "Western world" (though his material is mainly American). Finally, my study, more than Bell's, explores interpenetrations between producer toughness and consumer hedonism; it exposes not just paradox but the devices used to resolve or conceal paradox.

EVIDENCE

Like other studies of American social character—but more than most—this one seeks evidence of attitudes in language and in "projective material" (fiction, screenplays, advertising) as well as in direct behavior. How valid is this?

Language. From the early nineteenth century to the present, the way Americans use language has been marked by an enormous amount of slang in which a rapid turnover of expressions coexists with colloquialisms that stick for decades. Along with this, in modern times, there has emerged a duality between snappy, graphic usage and the verbal megatonnage produced by professional and organizational jargon. Between these two extremes the language runs flotillas of semitechnical, shorthand labels, often using acronyms and numbers. The whole combination suggests a liking for down-to-earth informality, aggressiveness, technical and organizational power, and "inside dopester" mastery. These themes are not smoothly consistent with each other, but they represent major values surrounding American toughness.

In selecting from this language, I do not wish to imply that every time someone uses a strong or aggressive term he or she is expressing a concern with toughness. Overall, however, it is reasonable to suppose social psychological reasons for the persistence of some terms and the catching-on of new ones. The overtones of the language suggest that concern with toughness is one of these social psychological reasons.

Fantasy and vicarious experiences versus direct enactment in everyday life. The heroes and situations featured in popular fiction and the mass media may tell us more about American fantasy models of toughness than about direct, everyday modes of toughness. It may even be that those Americans with the least opportunity to act the tough guy in real life tend to be the ones who like to watch tough-guy action on their television screens. Since we also know from other kinds of evidence that real tough-guy behavior still does exist in America, especially among business leaders and politicians, one may hazard the possibility that America is a society of fantasy-life tough guys led by real-life tough guys, plus another layer of real-life tough guys who work with their hands.[5] But even if material from literature and the media tell us primarily about fantasies, they still have a bearing on American concern with toughness. Nor can a sharp line be drawn between vicarious or projective experience and direct behavior. Media effects have a way of influencing the real scenarios that they are supposed to represent. The marine command, "saddle up!" telling a detachment to move forward, came from John Wayne in *The Sands of Iwo Jima*, though no scriptwriter invented the phrase. Again, in the late 1970s the young manhood of New York's Mulberry Street became more visibly macho, following the success of films like *The Godfather*, *Rocky*, and *The Mean Streets* (which was filmed on the spot). As Clancy Sigal observed, it was hard to know who was copying whom—"probably a little of both."[6]

In politics particularly, projected wishes have real-life effects: voters often support candidates who seem to represent qualities that ordinary people cannot or dare not show themselves; they are attracted both to moralism and to mean guy assertiveness.[7] Politicians themselves blur the line between fantasy and reality. Like fictional writers, they deal in symbols, but their symbol-wielding style and rhetoric must connect with real-life situations.

Then again, the very writers and screenplay directors who provide popular vehicles for tough-guy fantasies have made those vehicles a real and active part of their own lives; for them writing and directing is everyday work, and they draw their themes from the culture about them. Or do they?

This brings us to elite manipulation versus broadly based culture. Some would argue that value themes in popular fiction and the media reflect the preference of corporate elites rather than a genuine folk culture. Through their control of media and intellectual resources, elites largely determine what themes are purveyed and limit the range of options presented authoritatively to the public. A more radical extension of this argument is that elites can influence popular attitudes and preferences themselves, producing a grass-roots "false consciousness."

This line of argument has some plausability but, applied to the question of toughness in American culture, it is one-sided. If corporate control of media themes is so overwhelming, why have bankers and other businessmen in Westerns so often been portrayed in a nasty or contemptible light? Elite members are themselves part of a complex culture of traditional attitudes with which they must deal. As to the argument about false consciousness, even asssuming one can ever distinguish (either theoretically or empirically) between true consciousness and what is falsely imposed, it really makes no difference to the case before us. The fact that cultural manipulators—from the Log Cabin Campaigners of 1840 to cigarette advertisers—have promoted tough-guy attitudes and styles does not contradict the notion of a widely based concern with toughness, whether or not it is a part of false consciousness. In my own view, although the structure of American *economic power* is elitist and concentrated, American *cultural attitudes* reflect a historical pluralism, an interaction between different cultural groups. This is borne out by recent studies which show that television writers and directors hold views to the left of their corporate sponsors and tend to portray business leaders as exploiters and crooks.[8] In a wider sense, corporate influences may well constrain and color the interpretations of the world presented in the media. It might be claimed, furthermore, that elites, in their very espousal of plain man toughness, unconsciously practice a sort of cultural judo. Traditionally threatened from below, by folk conceptions of irreverent toughness, they adopt and adapt some of the styles of that toughness and use it to obscure class differences. In doing this, however, they make concessions to popular attitudes; they do not simply concoct them.

Selection. Much American literature, high and low, has not been very tough. In selecting from the tough-guy traditions in American literature, I have de-emphasized the strands of gentility, sentimentality, and fussy introspection that have also run through it; I have also said little about the attractions and influences of European literature and drama. Such choices, however, do not disqualify the enterprise. Like many other writers who have tried to generalize about American culture and character, I do not purport to show an overarching set of tendencies, accounting for all that is distinctive in American attitudes and behavior. Instead I have picked out one particular concern and explored its ramifications, shaped in friction with other, very different impulses.

NOTES

Full references for works cited are in the Bibliography following the Notes.

INTRODUCTION

1. Syndicated columns: David S. Broder, 28 April 1972; Joseph Kraft, 24 January 1973.

2. This is not meant to imply that projected personality traits solely determined the election, nor that Reagan had the same appeal to different groups. There is some evidence that since the 1950s voter interest in candidates' personal qualities has risen more at the expense of party identification rather than to the detriment of concern with policy issues.

If one looks separately at each of several candidates for the presidency in 1980, the issue of weakness or softness seems idiosyncratic to that candidate. Taken together, however, the raising of so many issues reflects American political culture, and the way each candidate dealt with his issue had political precedents or touched on folklore images. Thus, in meeting the question of his age and stamina, Reagan told audiences that he cut all the firewood that heated his ranch (without an electric saw?). Bush balanced his preppy language and manner by discarding his half-glasses, cultivating a more assertive speaking style, citing his navy flying record, and jogging in visible fellowship with his sons. Kennedy faced Chappaquiddick with a grave listing of the family crises he had weathered. On Lowell Weicker's early candidacy and cultivated image, see Stephen Chapman, "Hard Nose" (1979).

3. The term "can-do" was savored by Lyndon and Lady Bird Johnson but its origins go back to circa 1912 when the U.S. Army 15th Infantry Regiment adopted it as a motto in China: in pidgin English it meant "ability to carry out the mission." The regiment held a can-do week at the end of each training year. See Barbara Tuchman, *Stilwell and the American Experience in China*

(1971), p. 99. The multiple meanings of ''taking care of oneself'' have a longer history. In a dime novel of 1881 Kit Carson declares, ''I was taught by my father, who was as good a woodsman as all Kentucky could boast, how to read the signs of the forest and on the prairie, how to handle weapons and *take care of myself* in any situation.'' (Emphasis added.) Albert W. Aiken, *Kit Carson, King of Guides* (1882), p. 2.

4. On continuities in American child-rearing with regard to assertiveness, see Carl N. Degler, *At Odds* (1980), chap. 5. The history of American comic strips has shown a tendency to split women into browbeaters (shown especially in the humorous strips) and submissive care-givers (shown in the straight ones). The two roles come together in the two-sided behavior of Superman's Lois Lane. Like the comics, American television and popular fiction have had difficulties in producing heroines who are sexually attractive and at the same time thoroughly tough and independent. Here and there the difficulties have been overcome (for example, Angie Dickinson and Cleopatra Jones on television), but no such heroine has been as well established as Britain's Modesty Blaise (created by Peter O'Donnell in 1962). On problems and developments in comic-strip superwomen, see Judy Kalmesrud's interview with Stan Lee of Marvel Comics, *New York Times*, 11 January 1980. On heroines in American and British detective and spy fiction, see Patricia Craig and Mary Cadogan, *The Lady Investigates* (1981). On more universal aspects, see Wolfgang Lederer, *The Fear of Women* (1968).

5. Alexis de Toqueville, *Democracy in America* (1835), vol. 2, book 3, chap. 8. For an earlier perspective on the relative independence of American women, see Roger Thompson, *Women in Stuart England and America* (1974). The twin expectations of women in western myth and reality are explored further by Lillian Schlissel, ''Frontier Families'' (1981) and Shelly Armitage, ''Rawhide Heroines'' (1981).

6. It is significant that over the long American history of women's rights, the West generally led in terms of concrete legislation and support of women's voting and, to a lesser degree, in provisions for independent female ownership of land.

7. This discussion does not take up the fact that today, as at times past, American women have expressed ideas of a feminine strength that are neither male imitations nor gender-neutral. This, however, involves complex issues of feminist ideology and strategy. It includes the choice between stressing especially female qualities and stressing abilities and styles that can and should transcend sex differences. There is also the further complication that militant female *anti*feminists, too, have made recourse to styles of toughness and independence.

8. For more on this see Rupert Wilkinson, ''American Character Revisited'' (1983). By ''social character'' I mean those traits of individual personality and attitude that a population *distinctively* exhibits, that is, tends to show

more than other populations do. In this usage, therefore, social character is relative to the other populations chosen (explicitly or implicitly) for comparison: it may be a foreign population or a native one of a past era. In the case of American social character, my main yardsticks of comparison are the populations of other modern societies, but these measures are not used by all writers on American social character. Also, a given population—of a country, a class, or even a village—may have sharply different or opposing social character traits: it may, for example, have a bimodal tendency to two social character types, two constellations of traits.

Insofar as social character traits are socially conditioned, for example, by training, they are part of culture. By "culture" I mean quite simply a shared way of life: those attitudes and procedures that individuals collectively transmit to each other. In modern society, this anthropological use of "culture" usually refers to the shared values and patterned practices of a nation or larger civilization; "subculture," to those of a smaller group or section.

For other definitions of "social character," see George DeVos, "National Character" (1968), vol. 2, pp. 14–19; and David Riesman et al., *The Lonely Crowd* (1950), chap. 1.

9. Daniel Yankelovich, *New Rules* (1981). The reference to Reagan conservatism is in his preview article, "New Rules in American Life" (1981). Cf. Daniel Bell, *The Cultural Contradictions of Capitalism* (1976, especially the new long foreword, 1978); Tom Wolfe, *Mauve Gloves and Madmen, Clutter and Vine* (1976), essays on "The Me Decade and the Third Great Awakening" and "The Perfect Crime"; Christopher Lasch, *The Culture of Narcissism* (1979); David Riesman, "Egocentrism: Is the American Character Changing?" (1980), pp. 19ff.; Joseph Veroff et al., *The Inner America* (1981). The major work of the 1970s on continuities in American culture was Michael Kammen, *People of Paradox* (1972).

CHAPTER 1

1. Other tough-guy mannerisms include cigar-chomping, jaw-working (especially with gum), and the various grimaces and narrowing of eyes encouraged and permitted by smoking—this last often found among female tough-guys. All these patterns seem to have had their high point a few decades ago, but it is still interesting to compare American tough guys with those of other nationalities when they are put together in a film or television program. In "UFO," a British TV serial of the mid-1970s, a British and an American actor shared roles as the two chief operatives of an electronic security system. Both were meant to be tough, but compared with his granite-faced British colleague, the American was more dynamic, both in what he wanted to do and in the way he grimaced and heaved as he spoke—very stereotyped, American tough-guy mannerisms.

2. John Dizikes has even suggested that early gamesmanship was "in some senses a substitute for physical prowess." Dizikes's archetype gamesman upheld the rules but manipulated them and ignored unwritten codes of sportsmanship. Not uniquely American, he nonetheless thrived in antebellum society where he led a current away from the attractions of British aristocratic sportsmanship. Dizikes, *Sportsmen and Gamesmen* (1981), especially pp. 38–41.

3. Robert J. Ringer, *Looking Out for Number One* (1977), pp. 91–92. Cf. Ringer, *Winning through Intimidation* (1973). Long before this, in his study of a maximum security jail, Gresham Sykes found that prisoners distinguished the "real man" of dignity, fortitude and self-control, who quietly "pulled his own time" and showed that he could "keep his cool" and "take it," from other exponents of toughness and individualism who caused trouble for everyone—the predatory "gorilla," the rebellious "ball–buster," and the touchily pugnacious "tough." Sykes, *The Society of Captives: A Study of a Maximum Security Prison* (1958), chap. 5, "Argot Roles."

4. In early-nineteenth-century America, the word "rugged" came to mean personal vigor, health, and robustness while retaining the older British connotations of hardship, roughness, and rough-edged sturdiness.

5. Manuals on exercise go back through the nineteenth century, but "sportsmedicine" touted equipment as well as theories. On a more frivolous level, the marketing of the "biorhythm" pocket computer in the late 1970s pretended to make a competitive package out of science, physical energy, and self-knowledge. Designed to tell you when your "energy cycle" was at its peak, it would—said its makers, Kosmos, Inc.—"give you a big edge in dealing with another person." Thus could be toughened a tender-minded cult of self-knowledge and physiological harmony.

6. The threat can seem osmotic, as a high business executive suggested when he tried to define to Michael Maccoby the corporate tough guy: "a tough guy genuinely induces fear in others. He has an aura of power, of being right. It is a strength of character, a winning attitude. Most people are backed off by it. You experience his *inner violence.*" Maccoby, *The Gamesman* (1976), p. 114. (Emphasis added). A converse aspect is the use of "he (I) can take care of himself (myself)" as an *under*stated way of claiming good self-defense in a physical fight. In the upper-middle classes, vivid physicality is more acceptable (less threatening, less immature-seeming) in metaphor than as a direct claim.

Violent metaphors in politics have, of course, diverse sources. The historic overlap between boxing and racketeering is one: "he ain't laid a glove on him yet." American political language is more violent than British: Even "bite the bullet," which may have originated with the sepoy uprising in British India, has acquired a distinctively American usage with frontier overtones.

7. "We've got the biggest muscles, the biggest set of muscles on the top C.A.C. (Citizens' Action Commission). . . They're muscular because they control industries, they're muscular because. . . ." This statement, by Mayor

Richard Lee of New Haven about his allies in the 1950s, uses "muscular" five times in four sentences; it projects more clearly than most a fascination with physique onto organization and political power. Quoted by Robert A. Dahl, *Who Governs?* (1961), p. 130; cf. pp. 118–19. Similar projections, aided by cultural nationalism, appear in the fondness of some American writers for anthropomorphizing cities and regions: for example, Carl Sandburg on Chicago—"stormy, husky, brawling, city of the big shoulders."

8. Pecos Bill was the southwestern equivalent of other sectional frontier superheroes that flourished after Appomattox, such as Paul Bunyan, Tony Beaver, and the black John Henry. This phenomenon, then, was not specifically southwestern, unlike the antebellum tall tales and the men-alligators of Kentucky (which was southwest relative to settlement at the time).

9. Linguistically, a fine distinction occurs between the adjective of enthusiasm, "swell" (used from about the 1880s to its high point of popularity in the 1920s), and the less favorable noun referring to a stylish fellow, a "swell." The modern rebirth of the term "dude" crosses the same line.

10. Walter Webb, *The Great Plains* (1931), describes taciturn restraint among range cowboys circa 1900. Roger Mitchel has suggested to me that both taciturnity and talkativeness characterized the farmer who spent much of his time in isolation and behind the plow but then met with other farmers at festive get-togethers. Ray Billington, *The American Frontiersman* (1954), claimed likewise that mountain hunters and trappers of the early nineteenth century were laconic when they met in the forest but expansive in camp.

11. George Horace Lorimer, *Letters from a Self-Made Merchant to His Son* (1902), Letters V and VII.

12. On the cult of curt brevity in marketing organizations, see Marc Feigen Fasteau, *The Male Machine* (1975), p. 124 (in the Dell paperback edition, 1976). Back in the early 1920s Sinclair Lewis's wonderful portrait of the world of the midwestern booster implied that the same men who might wax expansively at conventions also went for slogans within the office like "The Lord Created the World in Six Days—You Can Spiel All You Got to Say in Six Minutes." Lewis, *Babbitt* (1922), p. 128 in the Signet paperback.

13. See Manuel J. Smith, *When I say No, I Feel Guilty* (1975, 10th printing 1977). To a limited extent the book values the laconic by urging the reader not to get into complicating side issues which blur the aggressor's responsibility; the reader (client) has the right not to offer reasons for wanting to do something, changing his or her mind, or even making a mistake. On the level of media stereotypes, Marcus Cunliffe points out to me that the economics and opportunities of movies and television ("a picture says a million words") encouraged the development of the laconic screen hero.

14. Michael Maccoby, *The Gamesman* (1976), p. 102; cf. Hugh O. Menzies, "The Ten Toughest Bosses," *Fortune* (1980). On the opposite kind of behavior see Roger A. Golde, "Are Your Meetings Like This One?" (1972).

15. Richard Barnet, "The Game of Nations" (1971). In the appendix essay I consider more generally the distinction between toughness displayed or projected onto fantasy figures and toughness attempted in real life.

16. Mickey Spillane, *My Gun Is Quick* (1950).

17. Stephen Fender, *Plotting the Golden West* (1982), p. 126.

18. On the level of basic human drives and needs, the connection between strength and speed is more complex and perhaps less obvious than the undramatic, utilitarian connection between strength and endurance. The universal appeal of speed includes its association with surging power; the tension between that sense of power and danger; a bird-on-the-wing feeling of liberation; and even more basic impulses: the desire to reach out and explore, the instinct for hunting, and conversely, for self-protection through escape, and the thrusting and penetrative aspects of male sexuality. By contrast with speed-as-strength, endurance-as-strength is not, sociobiologically, a distinctively male trait; the physical requirements of child-bearing and child-nurture provide a basis for several kinds of stamina that are, if anything, more female than male—thus, the achievements of female long-distance swimmers.

19. On American traits and Vietnam tactics, see Robert Thompson, *No Exit from Vietnam* (1969), pp. 63, 126–27. Chester Wilmot, *The Struggle for Europe* (1952), has a fascinating comparison of the different national approaches to warfare in World War II. He explains the American use of speed and armor with reference to the frontier, mobility, democracy, industrialization and familiarity with machines. See pp. 236–38, 474–77, (in the Reprint Society edition, London, 1954). Stephen E. Ambrose's account of American strategy in World War II generally supports Wilmot's view of American impatience compared with British doggedness and caution, but he shows that in certain situations the roles could be reversed. Ambrose, *Rise to Globalism* (1971), pp. 69–71 and elsewhere. All-out technological power does not necessarily entail speed.

20. See Tom Wolfe, "The Truest Sport" (1976), a warm-up for *The Right Stuff* (1980).

21. Daniel J. Boorstin, *The Americans: The National Experience* (1965), discussed the antebellum background of this: see Chap. 4. Thomas Wentworth Higginson, *Army Life in a Black Regiment* (1870), gives a vivid observation at the time of the Civil War.

22. On George Patton's appeal and World War II achievements, see Charles Whiting, *Patton* (1970), especially pp. 97–99, comparing Patton's record in the Battle of the Bulge with the tough and tactically crucial, defensive fighting of Courtney Hodges's First Army, unsung and even deprecated at the time. On the general trend in American warfare, see Russell F. Weigley, *The American Way of War* (1973), especially pp. xxi–xxii, though Weigley also points out the origins of American "total war" in the extermination of Indians.

23. Writing just before Watergate, James Dickey made a remarkable link between Nixon's usage and the frontier. In his novel, *Deliverance* (1970), Dickey's back-to-the-wilderness protagonists decide to ''tough it out'' rather than confess before a biased local jury their killing of a marauding hillbilly.

The presidencies of both Nixon and Carter were defended, unsuccessfully, in terms of tenacity. ''I'm not a quitter,'' said Nixon near the end. ''A gutsy guy . . . very tenacious,'' said Carter's adviser, Robert Strauss, defending the president in 1977 against charges of (short-run) ineffectiveness.

24. On the Northern side, General George H. Thomas, ''The Rock of Trigamorga,'' was renowned for his devastating success achieved with methodical slowness. ''Old Slow Trot'' the troops called him. On the Southern side, too, ''Stonewall'' Jackson was especially revered. But Jackson in fact got his nickname from one action (First Bull Run) and had at the time a merited reputation for speed. Among Unionists the postwar legends built up Sherman and his ''dashing Yankee boys,'' and Admiral Farragut: ''damn the torpedoes . . . full speed ahead.'' In the Confederacy there was a particular romanticizing of the ingenious raider, John Mosby, and Nathan Bedford Forrest (the calvalryman who got there ''fust with the must'') though the actions of both were in fact based on great physical endurance and fortitude.

25. John Dizikes links this to the development of a popular, thrill-seeking press and the growth of urban amusements: thus cross-country running was largely displaced by the use of tracks and city streets. In ship-building, however, speed (versus durability) had long been a special feature of the American industry, for economic and military reasons that went back to colonial times. Dizikes, *Sportsmen and Gamesmen* (1981).

26. Cf. *Frank Merriwell's Grit* quoted by Russell B. Nye, ''The Juvenile Approach to American Culture, 1870–1930'' (1966). In a later story by Patten (Patten used the pseudonym, Burt L. Standish), about motor racing, the hero, Roger Bollwood, concentrated on ''endurance,'' knowing that ''through speed alone . . . he could not hope to triumph'' over the leading car. He aimed for second place, hoping that the leader would break down, and in the process goaded the leading driver with his calm steadiness (''On College Battlefields,'' 1917). This stance jibes with the pro-underdog elements in ACT but the eschewing of all-out speed is not distinctively American: it has a universal hare and tortoise theme and was sometimes featured in the Victorian-Edwardian boys' novels of G.A. Henty.

27. Quotation by Gerald F. Roberts, ''The Strenuous Life'' (1970), chap. 6, from John Baumann, ''Experiences of a Cowboy,'' *Lippincott's Magazine* (1886).

28. Described as early as 1893 by Richard Harding Davis (''The Thanksgiving-Day Game,'' *Harper's Weekly*, 9 December). On the subject of speed and impact, the former coach of Ohio State enunciated ''three principles'' in tell-

ing his players to "take it to them": The team that wins "hits the hardest," "starts the fastest," and is "too damn smart" not to win. (TV film on "Woody" Hayes in the BBC series, "Americans," 10 April 1978).

29. Marine commandos and paratroopers tend everywhere to have special reputations for toughness; this aside, it is only in the past decade that a highly mobile unit in the British forces—the Special Air Service—has established a preeminent renown for tough effectiveness.

30. Tom Wolfe, *The Right Stuff* (1979), p. 24 (emphasis Wolfe's). Elsewhere in the book Wolfe's conception of toughness includes "stand-up" qualities too, though they have an uneasy relationship with passing the organization's tests.

31. For universal aspects of this, see Orrin E. Klapp, "The Clever Hero," (1954); Klapp, "The Folk Hero" (1949), pp. 17–25.

32. Cf. Correlli Barnett, "The Education of Military Elites" (1969). Also William H. Whyte's devastating study of attitudes to Herman Wouk's *The Caine Mutiny*. Whyte, *The Organization Man* (1956), chap. 2. In 1980 a humanities professor at a large midwestern university confided to me that he found seminars and discussion groups "unsatisfactory"; he preferred to lecture. With no apparent sense of contradiction he explained that his university's teaching system was based on "frontier individualism": It let him do whatever *he* wanted to do in the classroom.

33. Karl Marx's argument that capitalism, more than other systems, conceals group domination is cogently presented by Robert L. Heilbroner, *Marxism: For and Against* (1980), p. 117.

34. "Cowboys," Theodore Roosevelt declared, "[are] smaller and less muscular than the wielders of axe and pick but they are as hardy and self-reliant as any men who ever breathed—with bronzed, set faces and keen eyes that look all the world straight in the face as they flash out from under their broad-brimmed hats." Quoted by Gerald F. Roberts, "The Strenuous Life" (1970), chap. 6. A fictional precursor in the 1880s was Edward Ellis's dime novel hero, Deerfoot. A modern version is Jack Schaefer's Western classic, *Shane* (1949).

35. John Dean, *Blind Ambition* (1976), caption following p. 256.

36. Cf. Tom Wolfe's portrait of the astronaut, Alan Shepard, before becoming the first American in space. Wolfe, *The Right Stuff* (1979), pp. 233–34, 250.

37. See Rex Stout, *The Hand in the Glove* (1937).

38. In somewhat the same way the round bulk and ethnic swarthiness of "Cannon," the 1970s television detective, helped create a persona of tolerance and compassion that could be soft but in fact make all the more impressive his command, speed, and crispness in emergency. Other examples of more outright handicaps like Ironside's include the TV series, "Longstreet," featuring a blind but highly competent and tough-talking police detective; and the

psychologically commanding cripple in Max Brand's *Larramee's Ranch* (1924, 1966). In television a fall in the popularity of detective films stimulated an increased use of belying devices and other gimmicks in the late 1960s and early 1970s.

39. The dress appears to have been a reality; the encounters fiction or semifiction. See Kent Ladd Steckmesser, *The Western Hero in History and Legend* (1965), pp. 127–29, 137–38. In at least one reported encounter, Hickok was ridiculed not as a dandy but as a frontiersman who looked like an Indian, by an offensive English snob. Ibid. p. 129.

40. Harper Lee, *To Kill a Mockingbird* (1960). This, however, is a sectional variation, imaginable mainly in the South or rural upper-class New England. The use of gentlemanly understatement as a belying device—softer-toned than American laconic—is more a British feature. Cf. Geoffrey Household, *Rouge Male* (1939), an exemplary British tale of survival.

41. A particularly relevant discussion of America's dualism, applied to foreign policy, is in Stanley Hoffman, *Gulliver's Troubles* (1968), pp. 176–94. In a recent variation on the theme, Stephen Fender's study of Gold Rush travel accounts finds that the male writers were more apt than the females to oscillate between romantic exaltation and technical classifying—the women, for reasons of background and role, found a middle ground of writing. Fender, *Plotting the Golden West* (1982), pp. 13, 88ff. Cf. Leo Marx, "Noble Shit" (1973), pp. 709ff.

42. Surviving slang originating in British English (or English English) has a fair number of sissy-softy terms though several of these have at some point been widely used in America too; for example, "cry-baby," "lah-de-dah," "pansy." The equivalent native American list is much longer, but Americans probably use and coin more colloquialisms in general. By contrast the British have produced very few colloquialisms for being exploited or "made a monkey of." The key American word, "sucker," goes back to about 1835, but the noun did not develop its full modern connotations till later in the century. John Russell Bartlett's *Dictionary of Americanisms* (1848), gave it as a Western term for "greenhorn" or "awkward country fellow." Nearer to the modern sense was Bartlett's definition of "suck in": to cheat or sponge on, as the water is sucked out of a sponge.

43. Cf. David Halberstam, *The Best and the Brightest* (1972). On historical antecedents, see Irving Babbitt, *Literature and the American College* (1908), chap. 5; Peter Shaw, "The Tough Guy Intellectual," (1966); the essay, "Paleface and Redskin," in Phillip Rahv, *Literature and the Sixth Sense* (1969), pp. 1–5; Rupert Wilkinson, "Connections with Toughness: The Novels of Eugene Burdick" (1977), pp. 223–39. William James published his original concept of "tough-minded" versus "tender-minded," denoting temperamental as well as ideological types, in 1907 (*Pragmatism*, pp. 19–23 in the Meridian paperback). Even more than James's work, Jack London's *The Iron*

Heel—also published in 1907—portrayed intellect itself as an instrument of aggressive toughness; and he demonstrated that it could be wielded on the left, though he showed some ambivalence about the use of theories in attacking capitalism. London's socialist hero, Ernest Everhard, as "strong-minded" as he was muscular, mercilessly flayed self-serving abstractions; his arguments "bristled with facts"; he revelled in verbal and mental "in-fighting." See also Frank Norris, *The Octopus* (1901), whose character, Annixter, supports a remarkably modern depiction of combined intellectual and anti-intellectual virility: pp. 24–25 in the Signet paperback. On the wider issues concerning American pragmatism, intellectuals, and ideology, see the articles by Jill Conway, Martin Malia and (an opposing view) S. M. Lipset in *Daedelus* (1972), issue on "Intellectuals and Change." At a popular level, Robert J. Ringer's self-help book, *Looking Out for Number One* (1977), provides a lexicon for the conservative uses of tough-guy realism. Making much of "the reality hurdle," "the goody-two-shoes of unreality," and "shattering myths," he scorns alike do-gooders and government regulators. "A realist is a person who believes in basing his life on facts and who dislikes anything that seems imaginary, impractical, theoretical or utopian." This does not deter him from presenting his own "theory"—in fact, numerous theories and categories of behavior.

44. On New Deal imagery and rhetoric, see the next chapter. Adlai Stevenson's acceptance speech of 1956 (17 August, Chicago) is a model of conventional idealism and Cold War concern to sound tough, for all its reputation for eloquence. A study of the many drafts and memos that contributed to Carter's speech of 1980 (14 August, New York) shows both a toughening of style ("rebuilding" becomes "hard but necessary investments") and advice to stress "vision" as the president was said to lack it. I am grateful to Rick Hertzberg, Carter's chief speechwriter of the time, for my access to these documents and his own observations.

45. Victor B. Miller, *Take-Over* (1976), p. 6. Based on the "Kojak" television series.

46. Consider, for instance, the British heroes of Frederick Forsyth and Len Deighton, or British tough-guy TVseries such as "The Professionals"; or again, spaghetti Westerns. A mythic American description occurs at the beginning of Louis L'Amour's *Hondo* (1953): "He was a big man, wide shouldered, with the lean, hard-boned face of the desert rider. There was no softness in him. His toughness was ingrained and deep, without cruelty, yet quick, hard and dangerous. Whatever gentleness that might lie within him was guarded and deep."

47. This produces a nice line in the *Rip Kirby* strip (syndicated, June 15, 1977). As Rip goes to rescue a dangerous thug lying in the desert, he muses: "I hope I live to regret this."

48. In the controversy over civil service reform, proreform cartoons deployed naturalistic and rural motifs against the urban darkness of the ma-

chines—the hero a Hercules or slightly military-looking country youth standing against paunchy, crabby bosses and plutocrats. Cf. Allan Nevins and Frank Weitenkampf, eds., *A Century of Political Cartoons* (1944), pp. 130, 144, 150, 152, 162. Called "hermaphrodites" for disdaining party loyalty, some reformers in turn questioned the manhood of those who wore party yokes—Edwin Godkin called them "political eunuchs."

49. This applied especially to Senator William Fulbright and to George Ball. In other areas of foreign policy, Richard Rosecrance has observed to me similar pressures on academics recruited by the State Department's Policy Planning office in the late 1960s. In a superb article on party politics just before the Civil War, Bruce Collins argued that the Republicans' economic argument for Free Soil cloaked and advanced an underlying "moral impulse" against slavery, rather than vice versa. Collins, "The Ideology of the Ante-bellum Northern Democrats" (1977), especially pp. 115–18. A similar suggestion, applied to Radical Republicans after the Civil War, was made by John and LaWanda Cox, "Negro Suffrage and Republican Politics" (1967), pp. 303 ff.

50. Mark Moore, of the Kennedy School of Government, at a Duke University conference, quoted by David Broder, syndicated column, 13 April 1981. For images in popular religion, see Norman Vincent Peale,*The Power of Positive Thinking* (1952), pp. 63–4; cf. D. W. Brogan, *The American Character* (1962), p. 81n (in the Vintage paperback); Louis Schneider and Sanford Dornbusch, *Popular Religion* 1958), p. 92 and elsewhere.

51. Richard Bach, *Jonathan Livingston Seagull* (1970).

52. Michael Kammen, *People of Paradox* (1972); cf. Kammen, ed., *The Contrapuntal Civilization* (1971); and Thomas L. Hartshorne, *The Distorted Image* (1968), especially on writing in the 1930s and 1940s. See also Marcus Cunliffe, "American Watersheds" (1961), p. 493; and Leo Marx "Two Kingdoms of Force" (1959).

53. Walter J. Ong suggests that basic human attractions to contest include the uses of opposites and "againstness" in establishing identity. Ong, *Fighting for Life* (1981), pp. 15–16; Cf. Gregory Bateson, "Morale and National Character" (1942), a more qualified view. Michael Kammen's list of specifically American causes does not clearly separate causes of pluralism from dualism. See Kammen, *People of Paradox* (1972), chap. 4. A brilliant essay on American and modern western dualism is Michael Zuckerman, "The Fabrication of Identity in Early America" (1977). Among these and earlier explanations of American dualism, several focus on aggressive individualism and thus involve notions of toughness; but the dualism they perceive is not internal to tough aggressiveness. Cf. Robert S. Lynd, *Knowledge for What* (1939); Franz Alexander, *Our Age of Unreason* (1942).

54. Variations appeared in the *King Kong* movie of 1932, in some *Superman* strips of the 1950s and 1960s, and *Tigerman* strips in the 1960s–70s era. The composite formula of "The Incredible Hulk" accommodates several tradi-

tional images: the sensitive but courageous loner, forever on the move; the man who would be both ordinary and stupendous; the isolation of over-achievement. Like *Superman*, its use of the alter ego (the hero as an ordinary non-superman) makes it easier for the ordinary person to identify with the su-perhero—the alter ego, like Batman's boy-apprentice, Robin, provides an in-termediate step to identification with the superhero himself.

55. Or the original, "Don't give a sucker an even break." The impact of professional sports on American language is obvious. It includes the projection of mean-guy labels onto equipment; for example, the "Ugly Stik" fishing rod of the 1970s (note how dropping the *c* harshens and visually sharpens the word). On the inculcation of hostile aggressiveness in professional and college sports, see Paul Gardner, *Nice Guys Finish Last* (1974), especially pp. 59–61, 112–15.

The attitudes that sanction abuse of suckers merge, at one end, into the stance of contemptuous rescue already mentioned. In a *Buzz Sawyer* strip (syndicated, 24 January 1974) the detective seizes a young sap by the coat lapels and roughly tells him off, in order to save him from being framed a second time by his friend."

56. Likewise, the Green Berets' "When you've got 'em by the balls their hearts and minds will follow" plays against the kinder-sounding talk about "winning hearts and minds" by civilian counterinsurgents in the Kennedy era. In a different way, ambivalence toward aggressive toughness appears in the parody following of "Dallas's" J.R., and in the use of language to associate with harsher toughness than one in fact shows: for example, reference to "frank and brutal" discussions of "hired-gun" consultants. In this connection I like especially the alternative high-tech slang for an effective process: "quick and dirty," or "clean"!

57. Quoted by Arthur M. Schlesinger, Jr., *The Age of Roosevelt*, vol. 3 (1960), p. 352 in the Sentinel paperback.

58. John Dean, *Blind Ambition* (1976), pp. 47–48.

59. These equations were strongly articulated in America into the early twentieth century and remained in populist and Southern rhetoric for much longer. Their roots go back to the Roman term, *virtus*, denoting courage mixed with wisdom, or glorious service to the state. *Vir*, the Latin for man, could also mean a man of honor, of courage, or of physical prowess in war. Like *vis* (strength), it derived from the Greek for strength or force, *is*. In Europe, well into the sixteenth century, "virtue," the derivative of *virtus*, could refer to divine or superhuman potency as well as to good conduct. The supreme repository of goodness was divine power whose image, in a male-dominated society, was male.

The notion of manliness as "upstanding" may have had a phallic element; it also drew on the relative social independence of men, compared with the dependence of women on guile to defend their interests "behind the scenes."

Male dominance also promoted the assumption that men, more than women, had the strength and largeness of mind to hold to abstract principles.

60. The World War II "face-slapping incident," when Patton struck a shell-shocked soldier in a hospital, was not dissimilar to the incident that finally got Hayes fired: his striking of a player in a football game. At another game he had attacked a cameraman. In Patton's case, however, Gallup surveys indicated that most Americans did not want him removed from his post.

61. Unpublished paper given at University of Sussex (1975).

62. Though these are twentieth-century terms, there was some anxiety in parts of late-nineteenth-century America about the depleting effects of hyperactivity. Cf. George Beard, *American Nervousness* (1881); Daniel Rodgers, *The Work Ethic in Industrial America, 1850–1920* (1974), chap. 4.

63. From the early nineteenth century to the present, Americans coined "hard" terms which then enjoyed wide usage: for example, "hard cider," "hard money," "a hard John" (FBI agent), "hard-eyed," "the hard choice" ("hard options"), "hard hat." "British English," however, contains an enormous backlog of combinations like "hard and fast," "hard-bitten," "hard as nails," "hard-pressed," "hard-driving," and so on. It is evident that the polar imagery of hard and soft is basic, universal, and capable of many meanings. On gender aspects applied to the sciences, see Liam Hudson, *The Cult of the Fact*, London (1972). What is still significant about American usage is the frequent coining of hard and soft *pairs*. Further back in history, Americans substituted hard terms for quite different British terms ("hard liquor" for "spirits," "hardware store" for "ironmonger") and made a hard term more favorable (moving *hard-fisted* from meaning stinginess to productive sinew).

64. It will be noted that "hard money" now has two meanings: the old one of tight credit, and the newer, bureaucratic meaning of secure, in-house salary as opposed to less secure but more entrepreneurial dependence on short-term grants and so on. "Firmware" consists of programs built inerasably into physical equipment, for example, the plastic programming disks inserted in some kinds of washing machines.

For a survey of different kinds of euphemism not confined to America, see Hugh Rauson, *A Dictionary of Euphemisms and Other Double Talk* (1981).

65. Florence King, "The Niceness Factor: Good Guyism in America" (1981). Identifying herself as a tough-minded conservative who admires aristocratic clarity, King associates American "niceness" with a growing but deeply rooted feminizing of society. She underestimates the commercial and organizational incentives to administer soothing, unaccompanied by any literary vernacular. The air-sickness bags marked "For Your Motion Discomfort" have little to do with feminization. Nor, in personal relationships, is it due to feminization when the male adult, meeting family friends, finds relief from the solemn or joshing hardness he must show to the other men by expressing a sweety-sweetness to the women and children. However, King's phrase about zapping

with friendliness applies with remarkable literalness to a family friend in California who recently *hired* a "cupid" to shoot her husband with a surprise "love arrow" on his forty-seventh birthday. What a paradigm of innovation and convention, distance and affiliation. Like the remarriage ceremonies at silver and golden weddings, the event declared that modern American marriage, no less than the American polity, required extreme and energetic affirmation.

CHAPTER 2

1. A year later, according to a *New York Times*-CBS News Poll in January 1982, a plurality of Americans believed that the Reagan's "style of living" was too "extravagant": 48 percent for, 43 percent against, 11 percent unsure. Women, the poor, blacks, and Democrats were particularly apt to take this position, which was evenly supported and opposed by respondents in the $20,000-$30,000 income bracket. One element in the relatively equal balance of opinion generally may have been the dual nature of the presidency itself: its ceremonial as well as executive function.

2. Opinion surveys in the past two decades have revealed widespread distrust of big corporations, but not for undermining the individual with too much welfare and personal control. Public opinion has tended to praise corporations for the goods and services they bring, but to question their honesty and resent their general power.

3. C. Wright Mills, *The Power Elite* (1956), p. 43.

4. This may help explain the place of poker in American culture, from its spread up the Mississippi in the 1820s and 1830s. The great importance of bluff in the game stresses realism in a negative way, since the player does not know a crucial part of reality—his opponents' hands. Bluff coupled with risk-taking investment ("upping the ante") suited a society of business gambling and frontier morality where often you did not know a trader's background or his assets or what price he would really settle for, and where you could likewise conceal your own hand. The game is all about strength and weakness (in concealing the strength or weakness of a hand) and the mastery needed to have and convey confidence. There are striking parallels here with the bachelor world of pool, especially poolroom hustling, which has generated a lot of toughness and speed-related slang. More generally, there is a connection with the importance attached in American culture to detecting and exposing "phoneys" (the very term is much more common than its equivalents in British English).

5. The earliest use I have found for "run" as transitive is political—to run a ticket (Maryland, 1789). Candidates were run for office as well as (intransitively) running. Democracy contributed to this usage, against the "standing" for office, which British candidates still prefer: a posture that appears more dignified, less supplicatory, but thereby less dynamic.

6. Tough-guy language seems particularly prevalent in highly competitive industries such as computer products, where competitive selling and presentation comes together with engineering innovation. Tracy Kidder, "Flying Upside Down" (1981), p. 56, gives a nice vocabulary of this. See also Michael Maccoby, *The Gamesman* (1976), p. 102.

7. For an analysis of various factors, see Lester Thurow, *The Zero-Sum Society* (1980), chap. 4. One factor not discussed by Thurow is the impact of defense spending, especially on basic industrial investment. He does show, however, that the 1965 downturn in U.S. productivity *preceded* the downturn in expenditures for "research and development": this suggests that a general decline in American inventiveness is not to blame. Thurow's distinction between "product" and "process" innovation points less to a drying-up of "American know-how" than its misdirection compared with leading foreign competition. Presumably it reflects oligopoly market structures and the lack of domestic price competition; this leads to competition in products and styling, encourages fancier consumer tastes, and so back to the problem of toughness—its ambiguous position—in a business society.

8. The "quick results" charge has been made on the political right as well as the left. See General Alton D. Slay, "The Air Force Systems Command Statement on Defense Industrial Base Issues," (1980), pp. iv–17ff. The argument here links short-term focus to poor quality control. Such arguments, however, go against earlier analyses of American corporations which often concluded that they sought long-term market position rather than short-term profit.

On tough-guy corporate behavior, see the U.S.-Japanese comparisons in Richard Tanner Pascale and Anthony G. Athos, *The Art of Japanese Management* (1981).

9. A study of children's readers found that the incidence of (substantive) achievement themes in their pages rose from 1800 to 1900 and then declined and correlated with the number of patents issued in proportion to population when the data was analyzed in twenty-year periods. Richard DeCharms and Gerald H. Moeller, "Values Expressed in American Children's Readers: 1800–1950" (1962), pp. 136–42. The same article reports other historical studies of achievement values. Cf. Christopher Lasch, *The Culture of Narcissism* (1979), especially chap. 3.

10. See for example William Gaddis, "The Rush for Second Place" (1981), pp. 31–39: a piece marked by non sequiturs, confusion of cause and effect, and muddle about national ends. Or again Paul Blumberg's lengthy analysis of America's economic decline, which he claimed to be "paralleled by a subjective loss of confidence and failure of nerve at high levels." His main evidence for this was a number of articles by business writers and leaders critical of the nation's economic performance and pessimistic about the trends. Searching

criticism by an academic like Blumberg is apparently cowardice when practiced by business people. Blumberg, *Inequality in an Age of Decline* (1980), chaps. 3 and 4, especially pp. 171–73.

Much of the debate assumes too easily that loss of confidence in *America* leads to loss of confidence in self and loss of will to achieve. Carl Everett Ladd has questioned in fact that Americans have lost confidence in the national future. Cf. international Gallup poll finding high levels of American national pride: reported by Marjorie Hyer, *Washington Post Service*, 20 May 1982. Joseph Epstein, *Ambition* (1980), argues engagingly that a lot of ambition— drive for money, power, or status—is still around but has become, during this century, more challenged, more rivalled by alternatives, and more defensive (either furtive or crassly promoted). He underestimates, however, new forms and sectors of ambition. Epstein's position is broadly supported by David Riesman et al., *The Lonely Crowd* (1950); and, quite recently by Ann Hulbert, ''Friends for Now'' (1982), on the rewriting of Dale Carnegie. It is opposed by Tom Wolfe, *Mauve Gloves and Madmen, Clutter and Vine* (1976), essay on ''The Perfect Crime''; and Christopher Lasch, *The Culture of Narcissism* (1979).

11. Mark Twain, *Life on the Mississippi* (1883), chap. 43. Cf. Twain's *A Connecticut Yankee in King Arthur's Court* (1889), which illustrates beautifully the convergence of business hustle, engineering, and ''plain man'' democracy in a language of toughness.

12. See Theodore P. Greene, *America's Heroes* (1970), chap. 4., ''The Hero as Napoleon'', especially pp. 127–31. Francis Galton represented the British influence in fusing strength-worship with eugenics and social Darwinism but the latter did not necessarily support capitalist laissez-faire. It was used to do so particularly in America. See Thomas F. Gossett, *Race: The History of an Idea* (1965), chap. 7; Gertrude Himmelfarb, *Victorian Minds* (1968), chap. 12; Richard Hofstadter, *Social Darwinism in American Thought* (1944), especially pp. 174–75. With regard to risk-taking and toughness, Chicago's International Monetary Market has run an advertisement, ''My motive is profit. My style is aggressive. I know trading on the IMM is risky, but I like it.'' (*Economist*, 2–8 August 1975).

13. Cf. S. DeWitt Clough's anthology of inspirational business toughness, *Backbone Hints for the Prevention of Jelly-Spine Curvature and Mental Squint* (1908), especially Charles Eugene Banks's poem, ''Make Way for the Man,'' and Elbert Hubbard's famous essay, ''A Message to Garcia.'' Clough's collection went through several editions including one published by an Australian business journal in 1936.

14. Cf. William Letwin, ''The Past and Future of the American Businessman'' (1969), pp. 1–22. This is not to deny that, from Progressivism through the New Deal, reformers have been divided about the acceptable scale of business units and the kind of competition wanted.

15. Quoted by Clarence Darrow, "Salesmanship" (1925).

16. Sinclair Lewis, *Babbitt* (1922). The depression, too, stimulated aggressive salesmanship to move merchandise. Two great documentary novels of the 1930s contain vignettes of the tough-guy sales manager or dealer, willing his target to be a contemptible sucker: James T. Farrell, *Studs Lonigan* (1936), vol. 3, pp. 744–49 in the Signet paperback; and John Steinbeck, *The Grapes of Wrath* (1939), chap. 7. Each is a small study in the psychology of tough talk.

17. Quoted by Richard Hofstadter, *Anti-Intellectualism in American Life* (1963), p. 116, in the Vintage paperback. Sunday's career as an evangelist ran from 1905 to his death in 1935.

18. *The Man Nobody Knows* was still being printed in the mid–1970s, though later editions have omitted the cruder business references. Peter Marshall's writing was very similar in its portraits of a tough, outdoor Christ. Billy Graham, an outstanding salesman of Fuller Brushes before he turned to evangelism, has at various times stressed that Jesus was not a "sissy"; he has even claimed that Jesus was an "avid sports fan" and had the body of a great athlete.

19. Quoted by Arthur M. Schlesinger, Jr., *The Age of Roosevelt*, vol. 3 (1960), in the Sentinel paperback. Before becoming a Hearst executive, Knox had been a Rough Rider with Theodore Roosevelt. His declaration copies the style, not the exact content, of a sentence in TR's famous speech, "The Strenuous Life" made before Chicago's Hamilton Club in 1889. See Roosevelt, *The Strenuous Life* (1900).

20. Hugh Johnson, *The Blue Eagle from Egg to Earth* (1935), p. 208. Johnson's general speech was splendidly vivid and used a lot of frontier and combat metaphor.

21. A. A. Berle, Jr., "The Social Economics of the New Deal" (1933). His argument made economic sense, but its tone was all of a piece with other New Deal statements. At other times, however, he did argue that government should be the moral leader of business.

22. David Lilienthal's *Journals*, vol. 1, *The TVA Years* (1964), gives a sharp personal observation of Corcoran's tough-guy development through the 1940s. See entries for June 12, 1933, and October 4, 1949. Cf. William Shannon, *The American Irish* (1963), chap. 16. William E. Leuchtenberg, *Franklin D. Roosevelt and the New Deal* (1963), pp. 337–46 describes some of the social context of the New Deal antisentimentalism, including the link with gangster and private-eye stereotypes. With regard to war metaphors, this aspect of the New Deal involved businessmen-planner types from World War I. In policy terms generally, there was no one New Deal stance toward business: positions varied according to sector, agency, and date.

23. Based on my own study of *Harvard Class Reports*, for Harvard College classes graduating in the 1920s and 1930s.

24. See especially Parkman's letters to the *Boston Advertiser*, 17 October 1962 and 30 June 1963: Wilbur R. Jacobs, ed. *Letters of Francis Parkman* vol. 1 (1960). On others of his view, see George M. Fredrickson, *The Inner Civil War* (1965), chap. 10.

25. Theodore Roosevelt, "The Strenuous Life," speech given before the Hamilton Club, Chicago, spring 1899, and reprinted in his book of the same name (1900); and Roosevelt, *An Autobiography* (1913), p. 224; also quotations in John P. Mallan, "Roosevelt, Brooks Adams, and Lea" (1956), pp. 216–30.

26. In the later group, Homer Lea came the closet to envisaging an alternative society to commercial civilization; he was not much appreciated in America and was too extreme for Roosevelt. Cf. Mallan, "Roosevelt, Brooks Adams, and Lea" (1956).

27. Edgar Rice Burroughs, *The Return of Tarzan* (1915).

28. Letter to Thomas Jefferson, 21 December 1819; see Lester J. Cappon, ed., *The Adams-Jefferson Letters* (1959), vol. 2, p. 549.

29. Neil Harris, *The Artist in American Society* (1966), pp. 31ff; John F. Kasson, *Civilizing the Machine* (1976), pp. 36ff in the Penguin paperback; Daniel T. Rodgers, *The Work Ethic in Industrial America, 1850–1920* (1978), pp. 103ff. On a longer time-span, there are some similarities with the arguments of Daniel Bell and Christopher Lasch: see Appendix.

30. Elsewhere in his letter Adams mocks the predeterminism of Calvinists; but his attack on "effeminacy" goes back to the seventeenth-century uses of the word by Massachusetts clergy. This is discussed further in chapter 4.

Another source lay in Florentine thought and its Atlantic ramifications. P.G.A. Pocock, *The Machiavellian Moment* (1975), shows that this tradition made links in the direction of luxury-effeminacy-dependence-corruption, but his treatment does not suggest that specific concerns with effeminacy, weakness, or softness were very salient.

31. Adams's conundrum was put in reply to a letter from Jefferson about the venal corruption that had made the Romans an "unenlightened and *vitiated* people" (emphasis added: see note 28 above). Jefferson placed the blame for this on Rome's political leaders, especially Caesar, not on commerce. Adams himself offered no answer to either problem, Rome's or America's, beyond that of personal, exemplary *exertion*.

32. William J. Lederer and Eugene Burdick, *The Ugly American* (1958). A series of loosely-connected cautionary tales allegedly based on real episodes, with a nonfictional epilogue, *The Ugly American* was made into a movie and found favor at the Kennedy White House. It prompted a congressional investigation of foreign aid and formed part of the climate that shaped the Kennedy's interest in counterinsurgency as well as the Peace Corps. On the book's historical resonances, see Rupert Wilkinson, "Connections with Toughness: The Novels of Eugene Burdick" (1977). Lederer's own writing put more blame

on the consumer softness and weakness of the American civilian per se which he contrasted with the rugged but flexible military man. See Lederer, *Ensign O'Toole and Me* (1957), which rehearsed much of *The Ugly American, A Nation of Sheep* (1961), and *Our Own Worst Enemy* (1968).

33. Interviews with Nixon reported by Garnett D. Horner in *Washington Star-News*, 9 November 1972, and by James Kilpatrick, *Washington Star-News*, 16 May 1974. Nixon's speech accepting the 1960 Republican nomination showed he was prepared to blame commerce when it could be associated with the enemy government. He warned against the Russian "economic offensive that softens the nation," just as, more elaborately, Henry Ford's *Dearborn Independent* in 1920 accused Jews of undermining Americans with "luxuries" and overpriced "gew-gaws."

34. Peter Grieg, "So Soft, So Pampered," *Daily Express*, 11 November 1972.

35. The two concepts overlap: freedom is seen to require and create a stout independence of character. American political rhetoric, from the Revolution to modern convention speeches and presidential inaugurals, has been especially apt to equate individual freedom with collective and personal strength. But this supports my point about relative emphasis. President Hoover's persistently articulated fear that government welfare would undermine individual character was particularly American. So, more harshly today, is George Gilder's male-entrepreneurial-tough-guy attack on feminism and the welfare state. (Gilder's book, *Wealth and Poverty* [1981], spent several weeks on the *New York Times* list of the fifteen nonfictional bestsellers.) Margaret Thatcher, on the other hand, who has demonstrated and projected toughness more than any other contemporary British conservative, has usually made more of freedom and "incentives" than of general strength and character in her assault on "wet" public spending (despite the stress on self-reliance in her "think-tank's" report on the family and the welfare state).

36. From quotations by Perry Miller, "From Government to Revival" (1961). Such sentiment was not peculiar to divines. In 1775 John Hancock, the prominent Boston merchant and public figure, warned Bostonians against a moral undermining which would lead to extravagance, "effeminacy" (*sic*) and ruin by the "glare of wealth." Hezekiah Niles, ed., *Centennial Offering Republication of the Principles and Acts of the Revolution in America* (1876), pp. 39, 42.

37. Waldo, *Memoirs of Andrew Jackson* (1818), p. 16 (his emphasis). Cf. Howard Mumford Jones, *The Pursuit of Happiness* (1953). Note also the Roman tone of Andrew Jackson's address to the "Embodied Militia" before the Battle of New Orleans, December 28, 1814: "Inhabitants of an opulent and commercial town, you have by a spontaneous effort, shaken off the habits, which are created by wealth, and shewn that you are resolved to deserve the blessings of fortune by bravely defending them." John Spencer Bassett, ed., *Correspondence of Andrew Jackson* (1926–35), vol. 2, p. 118.

38. John M. Peck, "The Life of Daniel Boone" (1847).

39. Emerson, "Self Reliance" (1841) and "Wealth" (1860). In "Self-Reliance," the attack on amenities—physical "crutches"—is secondary to the theme of "smooth" overconformity and social dependence. The essay on "Wealth" accepts the test of commerce for both skill and honesty. Elsewhere Emerson does scorn the marketplace for making people conformists and synthetic, and implicitly, therefore, weak.

40. On "conspicuous consumptions," see Thorstein Veblen, *The Theory of the Leisure Clas* (1899), chap. 4. The term "overcivilization" is Larzer Ziff's. See Ziff, *The American 1890s* (1966).

41. James, "The Moral Equivalent of War" (1910). The essay inspired the William James Camp in Vermont and other youth organizations for physical labor and public service.

42. See especially Phillips, *The Second Generation* (1907). Cf. James R. McGovern, "David Graham Phillips and the Virility Impulse of Progressives" (1966); Kenneth S. Lynn, *The Dream of Success* (1955), an ungenerous but illuminating book, especially p. 158. Women also joined in the argument that "idleness and luxury [were] making men flabby," sometimes to the point of welcoming a war: for example, Sara Grand, "The Man of the Moment" (1894), pp. 626–27.

For different perspectives on concerns with vigor and physical action at the turn of the century, see Thorstein Veblen, *The Theory of the Leisure Class* (1899), chap. 10; John Higham, "The Reorientation of American Culture in the 1890s" (1970); Gerald F. Roberts, "The Strenuous Life" (1970); and T. J. Jackson Lears, *No Place of Grace* (1981), chaps. 3, 4.

43. Kennedy, "We Must Climb to the Hilltop" (1960). The very style of this passage has an Emersonian ring. The mood was strong among Kennedy's friends and supporters at Harvard, but the Cold War factor helped extend it beyond a narrow elite. Kennedy himself declared that "our increasing lack of physical fitness is a menace to our security," and he set up the President's Council on Youth Fitness under Oklahoma's football coach, Bud Wilkinson. Cf. Kennedy, "The Soft American" (1960).

44. See quotations by Henry Fairlie, *The Kennedy Promise* (1973), p. 20.

45. Particular disquiet was caused in the early 1930s by apparent findings that American POWs in Korea had collaborated with their captors much more readily than had Turkish and other prisoners. Subsequent corrections never quite caught up with the myth. Cf. Albert Biderman, *March to Calumny* (1963); H. H. Wubben, "American Prisoners of War in Korea" (1970), pp. 3ff. On the symbolic importance of wartime experience to the middle-aged, civilian "Kennedy type," see Wilkinson, "Connections with Toughness" (1977), especially pp. 227–28, 238.

46. Quoted from Salem and Winston cigarette advertisements in 1978. A

Tareyton ad, "Us Tareyton smokers would rather light than switch," spoofed its own famous spoof of the tough-guy appeal.

47. Quoted in November 1971 issue. This kind of advertisement ran regularly in the early 1970s.

48. Faberge advertisement, quoted in *Playboy*, November 1978.

49. David Riesman, "Some Observations on Changes in Leisure Attitudes" (1952); Martha Wolfenstein, "Fun-Morality" (1951). This trend has remained more specifically American than Riesman anticipated, for if the extension of leisure has been a general Western phenomenon, the dualism of strenuosity and hedonism has been particularly entrenched in America.

50. On presidential use of tough talk to conceal weak policies and records, see Rupert Wilkinson, "On the Toughness of the Tough Guy" (1976). As early as the 1840s, a person wishing to take back or modify what he said could "bite in" his words. Later, instead of "quitting" (itself a sharp and snappy word) he could "cut and run," "cut away" or "cut his losses," or stage a "pull-out." Today, loafers can still "bat" or "hack around." If you need a rest, "take ten" or "take a break"; if you need to slow down, "pace yourself." Failure in the early nineteenth century could be dramatized as a "bust"; now as a "bomb." Leave difficult problems on the "back burner"; leave difficult customers on "hold" or in a "holding pattern." (Mechanical images add potency: ejector seats enable pilots to say "punch out" instead of "bale out.") If you have to make a compromise, give it the hard bargaining status of a "trade-off." Never comply with another's policy: "go with it" or "swing with it." Even to "back off," especially if said in a certain way, sounds tougher than simply to abandon a position or renege. For a people as a whole, nonexpansion can be called "zero population growth," for universities and economies, "steady state." Are we "getting nowhere fast?"—that marvellous Americanism, unlike the other phrases, has at least a self-mocking quality.

51. A survey of insured architect and engineering concerns found that 30 percent of them were sued in one year alone, 1976. The study is by Schinnerer and Co., reported by Paul Godberger in the *New York Times*, 16 February 1978. I do not mean to obscure the convergence of several factors in this trend: the political organization and group awareness of consumers; the reaction against the power of professional experts, the contingency fee (high legal fees if you win a suit; none if you don't) and an American tradition of litigiousness.

52. Cf. Jonathan Black's popular novel, *Oil* (1974), especially the opening pages. The whole book is in tune with the Watergate era, including the Nixon White House's cult of technological luxury as an extension of power.

53. Series on "Americans," BBC television, 6 March 1978.

54. Beechcraft advertisement, "Mobile executives have an immediate advantage," *National Geographical Magazine*, May 1981.

55. John Myerscough has shown this historically in comparison with Britain,

in an unpublished study at the University of Sussex. The comparison probably holds for France and Germany too, going by what we know of their family spending patterns. Cf. Harold Lydall and John B. Lansing, "A Comparison of Personal Income and Wealth in the United States and Great Britain," *American Economic Review* (1959).

56. The levelling off in real wages from 1969 stimulated but did not create this process. Cf. Ely Chinoy, *Auto Workers and the American Dream* (1955); R. E. Lane, "The Fear of Equality" (1959), pp. 35ff; Robert Coles, *The Middle Americans* (1971). The point about immigrant families was made to me by the economic and demographic historian, Jim Potter.

57. "The Editor's Easy Chair" (1889), pp. 147ff.

58. Irene Taviss, "A Survey of Popular Attitudes toward Technology" (1972). Based on three, greater Boston towns, the sample covered different social strata fairly equally. The most popular single belief polled was that machines "made life easier." Higher up the social scale people tended more to favor technology and to say they did not feel too dependent on it. "Yea saying" (the tendency to agree with questionnaire statements, especially among the least educated and skilled) may have exaggerated the amount of ambivalence reported, but seems to have accounted for only part of it. Surveys of California's population in 1972 and 1974 produced similar findings: Todd LaPorte and Daniel Metlay, *They Watch and Wonder* (1975). By contrast, survey questions which lump science and technology together have obtained more uniformly favorable answers.

59. Thomas Dewey's speech accepting the Republican nomination for president in 1948 (June 24, Philadelphia)—a complete statement of traditional beliefs and hopes—provided a stock, ambiguous version of the "harnessing" theme: Technological achievement is necessary and laudable but not enough; it must be matched by spiritual endeavor. It remains, however, an indispensable part of America's publicly defined self-esteem: witness the press treatment of the desert failure of U.S. helicopters in the attempted rescue of Iran's hostages. According to a National Science Foundation survey in 1981, more Americans attributed U.S. world influence to "our technological know-how" than to any other factor.

60. James Thurber, "The Secret Life of Walter Mitty" (1942).

61. On the telephone's association with power and assertiveness, cf. Mark Twain, *A Connecticut Yankee in King Arthur's Court* (1889), where "Hello Central" becomes a desperate catch phrase for the dynamic engineer-businessman Yankee; and Theodore H. White, *The Making of the President, 1960* (1961), pp. 445ff in the Pocket Books paperback. The incorporation of the telephone and two-way radio into personal power needs was most famously demonstrated by Lyndon Johnson, who installed phones all over the place and on his ranch set up elaborate radio communications with his operatives.

62. Why some occupations are statistically more male than others is a prob-

lem beyond the scope of this book. The more human sciences—for examples, biology and social sciences—have tended to be more female, but so has mathematics. Engineering is particularly associated with business and industry and is closer to the toys and games traditionally thought suitable for boys. Again, this is not just American. After all, in most countries, when a couple is out in a car, it is the man who usually drives.

63. Lawrence W. Levine has noted that black equivalents of the white John Bunyans did not emerge until after slavery—before then, the underdog trickster hero predominated. Levine, *Black Culture and Black Consciousness* (1977), pp. 104, 400–401.

64. Batman, starting two years after Superman in a nation rearming against the possibility of war, represented a different use of science and technology for physical strength. Whereas Superman inherited his strength from extraterrestrial origins, Batman made himself strong and effective through scientific training and knowledge backed by equipment.

65. I have developed the notion of the "cultural operator" in my article, "Connections with Toughness: The Novels of Eugene Burdick" (1977). Some of it goes back through Nick Carter, dime-novel hero of the 1880s, to aspects of the Indian fighter and mountain man. The mechanical side absorbs American industrial approaches to knowledge (the unit approach to college learning, and so on). The concept is not entirely American—there are elements in James Bond.

66. Cf. U. S. Andersen, *Success Cybernetics* (1966).

67. Caidin, *Cyborg* (1972). The author, a pilot, was involved in aviation medicine. The book is more right wing and brutal than the TV series. A pessimistic precursor is Bernard Wolfe, *Limbo '90* (1953). Written in a much less tough-guy style, it uses the theme as an appalling cautionary tale against the excessive mechanization of life.

68. The BMW advertisement ran in the *Economist*, London, 21–27 May 1977. Significantly, Tanaka has been quoted on his blunt, "un-Japanese" manner: "I think like an American." (*Time*, 2 October 1972, p. 15.)

69. This connects with the American language of numbers that deserves its own study. The American fondness for scores, indexes, and numerical phrases connotes many things associated with toughness: high-performance machines; hard-headed empiricism; scientific authority; a precision to "zero in on." Unlike other technological usage, it provides a whipcrack slang ("ten-spot," "six-pack," "hanging-ten"). Digital handles on legislation ("Title IV," "clause 7a") enable diverse people to feel that they are securely in the know—esoterically yet in common with others. Scores like grade point averages objectify and clarify achievement in a distended society. Numbers language suits business calculation and factory timekeeping, and America, of course, is not alone in this; but "I figure" for "I think" is a characteristic, sense-toughening Americanism. For a historical perspective, see Robert Middlekauf on patriotic

numerology at a time of national trial: "The Ritualization of the American Revolution" (1970), pp. 31–34.

70. Kenneth Robeson's Doc Savage stories were first published in pulp magazine form in 1934 (Philadelphia).

71. Also, the in-group belligerence of some bumper stickers: "You Can Bet Your Sweet Ass I'm a CB-er." It is remarkable that truck drivers have not been more romanticized as tough-guy heroes. Perhaps the proletarian routine of their assignments inhibited it. A new tendency to feature them appeared in some films in the 1970s. CB radio was involved in several of these. The song hit, "Convoy," which told of truckers organizing a convoy to foil the police, invoked a lot of toughness in their radio exchanges.

Long before the CB cult, a relaxed and cool southwestern drawl became part of the radio voice of military and airline pilots all over the United States. Tom Wolfe attributed it to the Appalachian accent and "uphollow" syntax of one man: the fighter ace and record-breaking test pilot, Chuck Yeager (who became a USAF general). See Wolfe, *The Right Stuff* (1979), pp. 44ff.

72. I have said more about these and other attitudes to technology in my article on Eugene Burdick, "Connections with Toughness" (1977), especially pp. 233–35. The imagery and influence of machines and industrial production in American attitudes is a big subject. Cf. Mark Twain, *A Connecticut Yankee in King Arthur's Court* (1889); Leo Marx, *The Machine in the Garden* (1964); John Kasson, *Civilizing the Machine* (1976); Dixon Wecter, *The Hero in America* (1941), chap. 16; Geoffrey Gorer, *The American People* (1948), chaps. 5, 6.

73. Jerome, *Truck* (1977), p. 4.

74. The few friends mentioned in the book do include a semihippy male trio who move between subsistence farming and odd-job carpentering. On one level *Truck* is a charming account of adventures in mechanical problem-solving, with lots of detail and homemade diagrams. The author joins the spiritualizing of technique, seen in Richard Bach's *Jonathan Livingston Seagull* (1974), to the "craftsman" type of engineering executive depicted by Michael Maccoby *The Gamesman* (1976), chap. 2.

75. The GMC and Ford advertisements ran in *Outdoor Life*, July 1977 (published in New York). The Ford ad explicitly mentions toughness four times. The same issue has an article on long range chuck-shooting in which ruggedly clad hunters sit on chairs and use a special rifle and binoculars clamped to table and tripod.

76. The modern tension between aggressive, outdoor gadgeteers, who use nature to give their equipment (guns, snowmobiles, dune-buggies) greater play, and ecological, leave-no-trace primitivists, who use nature to build character, has some parallel in the conflict earlier this century between utilitarian conservationists (such as dam builders) and wilderness preservers. Both invoked images of toughness and strength, including practical antisentimentalism on one side and a mystique of natural regeneration on the other. One source of the

conflict was that mastery, success, and "go-ahead" dynamism required Americans to admire technical innovation. This, however, threatened old-fashioned craftsmanship, simple hardiness, and the wilderness. John Philip Sousa's blast against the phonograph (pictured ludicrously on a canoe trip) was a response to just this.

77. The conference, on alcoholism, took place in Washington, D.C., in June 1974 and was sponsored by a U.S. public health agency. About 4,000 people attended from across the country. A latent antipathy was revealed when I started my own talk at a panel session. A television set in the wings suddenly started competing, with a loud soundtrack and picture from another session. I murmured something about free competition, and there was applause: I then confessed that I was "preelectronic man," and there was even greater, indeed very great, applause. I sensed that the rogue set and I between us had released something more than sympathy for the speaker and his minor wit. Watergate was much in the news, especially in the Washington air, and with it the misuse of electronic devices such as tape recorders and bugging devices. I think this magnified the audience's wish to support an individual speaker against technological intrusion.

78. Cf. advertisement for Ponte Culture Television, *International Herald Tribune* (Paris), 16 January 1981.

79. Brig. Gen. Glenn D. Walker, quoted by Robert Kleiman, "The Air War in Indochina," *New York Times*, 28 August 1972. A host of military rules, officially designed to limit civilian casualties, did exist but their impact was limited.

The use of the singular to describe enemy forces ("he is hurting badly") is not itself confined to Americans: Churchill, Montgomery, and others used it in World War II. The usage has two opposite effects: it creates an overtone of chivalrous single-combat between national representatives, and it provides an impersonal euphemism for killing ordinary people.

80. The substitution became most overt with President Nixon's "Vietnamization" policy, in which massive bombing was supposed to ease the withdrawal of American troops. An ex-State Department dean of a foreign affairs graduate school likened this to the western movie gunman who backs out of a saloon, pistols blazing! (Edmund Gullion, of Tufts University's Fletcher School, interviewed on Boston television, 13 February 1971.)

81. Cf. Tom Bethell, "Hard-Money Men" (1981), pp. 33–40, which also described the links between "goldbugs" and survivalists.

82. Garry Wills, "The Kennedy Imprisonment" (February 1982), developed this argument with special reference to Truman and Kennedy.

83. Cf. Seymour Martin Lipset, *The First New Nation* (1963), chap. 2; Richard L. Rapson, "The American Child as Seen by British Travellers, 1845–1935" (1965). These observations held for both sexes in comparison with Europeans, but this is not to deny the special pressures for religious and domestic submis-

sion that feminine independence had to negotiate. Cf. for the 1820s, Kathryn Kish Sklar, *Catherine Beecher* (1973), pp. 31–32 in the Norton paperback.

84. Myron Brenton, *The American Male* (1966). Exaggerated critiques of Momism and feminization do not necessarily posit an aggressive reaction: Cf. Hans D. Sebald, *Momism* (1976); Patricia Cayo Sexton, *The Feminized Male* (1969). E. E. LeMasters, *Parents in Modern America* (1970; rev. ed., 1977) notes the bias in research attributing psychological disorders to mothers but makes the same absolute equation between feminizing and material civilization: see pp. 55–56; cf. chap. 8. David Graham Phillips, the Progressive novelist, was an early synthesizer of fears of affluence and luxury with fears of feminization and female consuming.

85. Feminist opinions themselves have differed about the extent of female initiative in bringing this about. Cf. Kathryn Kish Sklar, *Catherine Beecher* (1973); Ann Douglas, *The Feminization of American Culture* (1977); and William Leach, *True Love and Perfect Union* (1980).

86. Some studies have found that, on the level of explicit injunctions, white middle-class parents were as likely to require independence, competitiveness, and self-defense from girls as from boys. Others have disagreed and have found that parents played with their boys more roughly and confined them more to sex-typed toys and clothes. However, the father who makes special tough-guy demands on his son seems more and more to have become a lower-class phenomenon. Cf. David D. Aberle and K. D. Nagaele, "Middle-Class Fathers' Occupational Role and Attitudes towards Children" (1952); Leigh Minturn and William W. Lambert, *Mothers of Six Cultures* (1964), chap. 11 (based on a suburban New England town in the early 1950s); Eleanor Emmons Maccoby and Carol Nagy Jacklin, *The Psychology of Sex Differences* (1974); E. E. LeMasters, *Blue-Collar Aristocrats* (1975), chap. 7. In drawing from these works, I must repeat that I am generalizing across ethnic differences. Thus some famous kinds of Jewish mothers may be seen as an extreme version of the "PX-Mom" alluded to above.

87. I do not wish to imply that momism/antimomism was confined to middle-class suburbia. The longevity of "son-of-a-bitch" and the umpteen versions of "mother fucker" show the range of concern about mother power and maternal dependency. Neither term has a real equivalent in British English.

88. Teachers who have taught young American and European children in London and Paris have noted to me the special tendency of American parents to be concerned about crying. The use of bribes and rewards was observed as early as the 1830s and 1840s. See Edward Pessen, *Jacksonian America* (1969), pp. 90–92; Richard L. Rapson, "The American Child" (1965). A small recent endorsement is *The Super Sitter*, issued by the U.S. Government Printing Office in 1977. A guide for teenage babysitters, it included, in the words of the catalog, ideas for assembling "a surprise box to help the sitter make friends with the child and to minimize the child's fear when parents leave."

89. Eric John Dingwall, *The American Woman* (1956), illustrates in several places the prominence of mothering themes in World War II and just after and the way men both liked and resented this. The demands of motherhood erupted in especially strident form during the squabble of September 1972 over prisoners-of-war returning from Vietnam: Were they to come straight home or to go to military hospital?

90. A development and synthesis of some noted interpretations in the 1940s and 1950s would postulate this. A residual puritanism inhibited mothers from tactile sensuality with their infants. Mindful of hygiene and efficiency, they weaned early, then tried to make up with conscious love and provision, sometimes a semiflirting (if the child was male), sometimes rewards that were conditional on the child's achievements. The result for the child was that sensuality, not fully developed or directly expressed in early relations with the mother, was channelled into an acquisitive and showy self-gratification. Cf. Geoffrey Gorer, *The American People* (1948, rev. ed. 1964); Margaret Mead, *Male and Female* (1949), Part IV; and Erik Erikson, *Childhood and Society* (1950), chap. 8. Some of this may be confined to a mid-twentieth-century period; but the substitution of sexual prowess and show for sensuality lived on in some parts of American life. Cf. Dan Jenkins's best-selling football novel, *Semi-Tough* (1972), which was made into a movie. Big on female breasts and male asses, the book contained little sexual activity despite its raunchy reputation.

91. Various opinion polls found that Americans in the 1970s said more and more that they wanted to turn away from making and getting more (both as a national and personal goal) and from putting work at the center of their lives in favor of such things as personal development, self-expression, capacity to enjoy life, and better human relationships. Even if survey respondents exaggerated their virtuous nonmaterialism and "laid back" attitudes, the data suggested at least a change in what Americans thought they *ought* to want. See William Watts and Lloyd Free, eds., *State of the Nation* (1973), pp. 257, 259: Harris poll surveys circa August 1977; Yankelovich, Skelly, and White survey for American Newspaper Publishers Assoc., reported by Charles B. Seth, *Washington Post*, 1 June 1979; Daniel Yankelovich, *New Rules* (1981). Yankelovich's information indicated that the trends were led by college graduates and white-collar groups but were by no means confined to them. Among other things, he found that a declining proportion of Americans—86 percent in 1968, 67 percent in 1978—defined a "real men" primarily as a good provider for his family. This related, however, to increased acceptance of dual husband-and-wife careers outside the home: it did not necessarily signify a rejection of occupational prowess. It is significant that his case examples of professional-class people who had turned away from the rat race to a fuller and more natural-seeming life-style claimed that they had first won success at their jobs. And how many others turn aside to avoid failure?

92. David Riesman et al., *The Lonely Crowd* (1950). Martha Wolfenstein, "Fun-Morality" (1951) suggested a shorter-term shift between the 1920s and 1950s. Riesman's argument that the focus of the culture changed in the twentieth century from production to consumption is more generally accepted than his associated thesis about changes in types of conformity, but it has not gone unchallenged. See Marshall Graney, "Role Models in Children's Readers" (1977). My own and others' calculations show no great increase in leisure consumption as a proportion of personal income in the first half of this century.

93. Cf. Daniel T. Rodgers, *The Work Ethic in Industrial America* (1978), especially chap. 4.

94. Cf. Riesman et al., *The Lonely Crowd* (1950), on the consumer who seeks "experiences rather than things": p. 143 in the Doubleday Anchor paperback. Riesman saw in this a trend away from materialist acquisition; I am more persuaded that the two attractions coexist.

95. Yankelovich, "New Rules in American Life" (1981), p. 50; Louis Schneider and Sanford M. Dornbusch, *Popular Religion* (1958).

96. "Self-denial" means many things. Yes, American morality has become less concerned with restricting sensual impulse. No, Americans have not moved radically toward an ethos of high-spending and material gratification: That ethos has been strong, if contested, since colonial times. Cf. Carl N. Degler, "The Sociologist as Historian" (1963), p. 492, on nonasceticism in nineteenth-century business classes. There have also been shorter-term cycles: hence, the shifting success of prohibitionism in nineteenth-and twentieth-century America.

97. Cf. David Riesman "Egocentrism: Is the American Character Changing?" (1980), pp. 19–28.

CHAPTER 3

1. On American versions, cf. James C. Thomson, "How Could Vietnam Happen: An Autopsy" (1968); John Dean, *Blind Ambition* (1976); Philip A. Cusick, *Inside High School* (1973). Lionel Tiger, *Men in Groups* (1969), shows the cross-cultural dimensions of group pressure in male toughness, whether or not his stress on the sociobiology of hunting is correct.

2. I think this partially explains the special prevalence of anal language in American tough-guy slang. The sense of vulnerability and self-defense appears most obviously in such terms as "protect ass," "taking care of my own ass," or "hanging your hide out." Other terms, like "shaft" and "kiss my ass," suggest an abhorrent fascination with homosexuality, but this may sharpen general feelings of vulnerability; as Erich Fromm has noted, the sexual expresses the social as well as vice versa. This does not preclude simpler reasons for such language: its suitability for demeaning aggression ("knock him on his

ass," you're "full of shit," he got "canned") and its handiness in making ordinary actions sound rough and dirty "'haul ass," I've "busted my ass"). The sheer focus on anal anatomy is still remarkable; other kinds of "dirty," sexually violent language are less distinctively American.

3. A nice case study of this is B. A. Lohoff, "Herbert Hoover, Spokesman of Humane Efficiency: The Mississippi Flood of 1927" (1970). Hoover's famous reference to "rugged individualism" was made in a conventionally conservative campaign speech that nonetheless eschewed laissez-faire: 22 October 1928 in New York. Six years later he declared that the term had been "used by American leaders for over half a century." William Safire, *Safire's Political Dictionary* (1978), p. 621.

4. Emerson, "Self-Reliance" (1841). Just before this statement, he praises the superior independence of babes and boys, as yet uncowed by society; and he starts his essay with images of cosmic independence and "wintered" animal power.

5. See especially Emerson's essays, "The American Scholar" (1837), "Self-Reliance" (1841), and "Circles" (1841). Emerson did not reject success per se or American exertions for it; he combined disdain for the cheap values of the "multitudes" in recognizing success and for their hopes of an easy route to success, with the belief that everyone had superior talents that their own awareness and sense of excellence could develop. See Emerson, "Success" (1870).

6. "Song of Myself" (1855, rev. ed. 1881), verses 27, 28, in *Leaves of Grass*.

7. Quotations from "Democratic Vistas" (1867, rev. ed., 1881) and Preface to 1855 edition of *Leaves of Grass*. Cf. Whitman's Preface to the 1956 edition (open letter to Emerson, August 1856, no day given). I am indebted to an unpublished paper by Karen Putnam, observing that Whitman's "pride" and "sympathy" were metaphors for individualism and equality.

8. Though Whitman is better received in modern times than he was in his own, his social extension of individualism bore some resemblance to the ideas fragilely pursued in Brook Farm and other communitarian experiments before the Civil War. John L. Thomas, "Romantic Reform in America, 1815–1865" (1965), pp. 656ff, deals acutely with the dimensions of individualism in these communities, including the use of family models and the opposition to established institutions.

9. Cf. Seymour Martin Lipset, *The First New Nation* (1963), chap. 3.

10. Francis L. K. Hsu, "American Core Value and National Character" (1961). The idea of an American "core value" makes sense if one thinks of it as the central element of what is distinctive in the national culture rather than the center of *all* American values, many of which are shared equally with other peoples.

11. Hofstadter indeed attributed his historical model to Freud's concept of

"reaction-formation." Richard Hofstadter, "Commentary: Have There Been Discernable Shifts in American Values during the Past Generation?" (1958).

12. David McClelland found that both American and Japanese school children, compared with some other foreign children, were more involved in group activities and referred more to the opinions of others, yet also put more value on the development of their own capacities as opposed to interpersonal obligations and relationships. Though the number of nationalities compared was very small, he suggested tentatively that "the value on self-realization [was] checked and disciplined" by learning sensitivity to others through group activities. McClelland, *The Achieving Society* (1961), pp. 197ff in the Free Press paperback.

13. David Riesman et al., *The Lonely Crowd* (1950), with major new prefaces in 1961 and 1969). Riesman and his associates also postulated a prior, "tradition-directed" mode entailing direct, external conformity to detailed and static rules and roles . All three modes were connected to economic and, more dubiously, demographic stages. These causal ideas, like the psychological modes themselves, have been much discussed elsewhere, including Riesman's subsequent prefaces. On the confusion of other-direction with conformity per se, see Charles Hartshorne, *The Distorted Image* (1968), chap. 9. Even David Potter made this mistake: Potter, "The Quest for the National Character" (1962).

14. Elaine Graham Sofer, "Inner-Direction, Other-Direction, and Autonomy" (1961). Cf. William H. Whyte, *The Organization Man* (1956).

15. Michael Maccoby, *The Gamesman* (1976), pp. 93, 190. Maccoby did not stress this finding himself. Fifty-nine percent of the managers reported fear about giving in too easily. This was one of the most frequently checked of eighteen worries, fears, and related "difficulties" reported in Maccoby's questionnaire. The interviewed managers consisted of two hundred and fifty executives from twelve—especially two—high technology corporations. Since these were highly innovative firms in electronics, weapon systems, and the like, it might be that they were atypically stressful and competitive. On the other hand, as Maccoby himself argued, they were at the forefront of industrial trends in the United States.

16. Anthony Brandt, "What It Means to Say No" (1981).

17. Cf. Stanlee Phelps and Nancy Austin, *The Assertive Woman* (1975).

18. Sanford M. Dornbusch and Lauren C. Hickman, "Other-Directedness in Consumer-Goods Advertising" (1959), found a trend, one interpretation of which was that other-direction reached a high point in the 1920s. *The Lonely Crowd* was unclear about periods: it implied that inner-direction seemed to be emerging "in very recent years" (p. 19 in the Yale University Press paperback) but it mainly located inner-direction in the nineteenth century. It did envisage an alternative response in the "autonomous" person who could choose whether or not to conform. See also Riesman and Glazer's companion work, *Faces in*

the Crowd (1952), in which the supposed case studies of other-direction are susceptible to very different interpretations.

The idea of shorter term shifts adds a new dimension to the argument about continuity versus change that runs through many of the criticisms and defenses of *The Lonely Crowd*. Cf. Seymour Martin Lipset and Leo Lowenthal, eds., *Culture and Social Character* (1961); Carl Degler, "The Sociologist as Historian" (1963); Cushing Strout, "A Note on Degler, Riesman and Tocqueville" (1964). A charming perspective on section, other-direction, and toughness is in Gregory Stone, "Halloween and the Mass Child" (1959). Riesman et al. argued that the modern trends to other-direction were America-led but international rather than America-unique; but some of the commentators above have pointed out the resistances and variations in other modern societies.

19. Potter's essay of 1963(revised 1965) is not to be confused with his book, *People of Plenty* (1954), which is more diffuse but stresses continuities. His revised essay did not use the word "individuality" but, I believe, it best summarizes his notion of individualism in the twentieth century. His lectures on the same subject at Stanford in the early 1960s used the term "individuation."

20. The year 1920 was the first decennial census year that showed more than half the population living in incorporated towns and cities of 2,500 or more. I do not imply by this that rural and small-town settings guaranteed conformity. Of the 1830s and 1840s, the period in which Tocqueville and other visitors found much conformity, Michael Fellman has argued that "each man" had a "wide latitude" of forms in which to seek truth, from moral authoritarianism to libertarian anarchism. Hence the flowering of experimental communities. Fellman, *The Unbounded Frame* (1973), p. xv. I doubt, however, that most middle-class people felt they had such latitude.

21. Lewis H. Lapham, "Intimations of Morality" (1980): a memorable essay on the temporary surcease of *Harper's* magazine and the response of its readers. See also Lapham, "Gilding the News" (1981).

22. Cf. Clyde Kluckholn's summary of various studies, suggesting a trend to "individuality" versus "rugged individualism." Kluckholn, "Have There Been Discernable Shifts in American Values during the Past Generation?" (1958).

23. Maurice Farber's comparison at mid-century of lower-middle class British and American parents favored Potter's conception over Hsu's. Farber found that the American parents stressed individuality, liveliness, *and* getting on with others as qualities that child-rearing should instill, whereas the British parents placed a higher value on self-reliance and self-control. The American parents were mainly concerned with developing social skills without squelching natural spontaneity and imagination. The traditional values of self-reliance and self-defense were left, it seems, to other sources in the culture. On the British pattern, see the Appendix. Farber's samples consisted of insurance clerks, 44

percent male in the British group; 51 percent in the American. See Farber, "English and Americans" (1953); cf. Farber, "English and Americans" (1951).

24. The American interest in the psychology of self, demonstrated in Lasch's own predilections, have wider and more varied sources in American culture and institutions than he suggests. Cf. Marie Jahoda, "The Migration of Psycho-analysis" (1968); Rupert Wilkinson, "American Character Revisited" (1983).

25. The *Daily News* comment was quoted in the front advertising pages of the Warner paperback edition (1979). Lasch's subsequent comment, "Politics and Social Theory" (1979) reiterated his own concern for "self-help and self-discipline," which he believed capitalism had eroded.

26. Quoted with other generals by Chester Wilmot, *The Struggle for Europe* (1952), pp. 515ff (in the Reprint Society edition). The quotation about assigning missions is from an interview with Gen. Omar Bradley reported by A. J. Liebling in the *New Yorker*, 10 March 1951. Wilmot implied that MacArthur's autocracy was an exception, and he shows how American decentralization came to affect the whole Allied command. He also notes that Patton discussed plans more democratically with his staff than did Montgomery, whose ascetic, solitary style was in some ways more individualist than the Americans'.

27. Richard Tanner Pascale and Anthony G. Athos, *The Art of Japanese Management* (1981). The authors acknowledge that Geneen's style of management was by no means the only American pattern, but they make a cogent case for its influence. See especially chap. 6.

28. These observations put their own perspective on the antibureaucratic, organizational guerrilla style of the JFK White House decried by Garry Wills in "The Kennedy Imprisonment" (January 1982). What Wills sees as a personal macho innovation of the Kennedys is just one of many attempts to wrest flexibility and efficacy from large-scale organization while accepting that scale. A more institutional version applied to business corporation is Gifford Pinchot III's concept of "intrapreneurship," which goes beyond decentralization, beyond the establishment of "semi-independent departments run by hard-driving yes-men" (in the words of Norman Macrae). Under Pinchot's scheme, a business or technological innovator might join his own personal investment to that of the corporation. On this and some far-reaching developments of the idea, see Norman Macrae, "Intrapreneurial Now" (1982).

29. Cf. the attitudes of corporation "comers" reported in Walter Guzzardi's series of articles, "The Young Executives" (1964). Also, Eugene Emerson Jennings, *Routes to the Executive Suite* (1971); Michael Maccoby, *The Gamesman* (1976); and Tracy Kidder, *The Soul of a New Machine* (1981). Jennings's book features the "anti-organizational posture" of the "mobility-bright" executive who gets to the top largely by projecting a winner's image.

30. Maccoby, *The Gamesman* (1976), pp. 38–39, cf. pp. 108–9, 36–37. A major source of anxiety was the "competition and uncertainty" of corporate

life. In some ways, it seems, the big company was *too* tough without giving its executives a sense of being able to control and predict threats. With regard to top managers, Michael Maccoby argued that gamesmen came into their own in the post–1950s, when they succeeded less innovative and irreverent leaders. Maccoby attributed this to the demands of competition (including international competition) and the development and marketing of new products by expert but interdependent teams. I think he overstated the newness of all this. The drive to compete and win was more *written about* in the 1960s and 1970s, as compared with William Whyte's relatively compliant *Organization Man* (1956), but much of the behavior—including the use of athletic metaphors—was not new.

31. Through this century the fastest growing part of the labor force has been what the U.S. Census calls "professional, technical and kindred" workers. Before the 1950s the fastest growing section was engineers, accountants, and chemists. After 1950, the fastest growing section was a miscellaneous group of semiprofessional workers, ranging from nurses and airline pilots to morticians, primary schoolteachers, and laboratory assistants (groups that often aspired to more professionalism, credential systems, and so on). Between 1960 and 1970, however, an even faster-growing group consisted of college academics and natural and social scientists. (The above is based on my analysis of U.S. Census data.)

32. Harry Braverman, *Labor and Monopoly Capital* (1974), gives a powerful account of this trend, but ascribes it too easily to capitalist profit-seeking as opposed to more general trends in industrial rationalization and urban consumer demand.

33. Especially Cameron Hawley, *Executive Suite* (1954), made into a film with William Holden and Barbara Stanwyck.

34. Jonathan Black's novel, *Oil* (1974) uses all these themes, pitting a successful exwildcatter and several secondary heroes against Ivy League bureaucrats of the major oil companies. Earlier in the century magazine biographies went through three phases in adjusting their heroic models to organization. In the early 1900s the dynamic political reformer largely replaced the tycoon hero while retaining much of his forceful individualism and powerful physique. Then, in World War I the emergency cooperation of government and industry helped to produce a new magazine hero, the master of organization, either business or governmental. Sometimes he had the old-style physique, but his forcefulness usually joined a drive for rational efficiency to fitness, patience, and tact. Cf. Theodore P. Greene, *America's Heroes* (1970), chaps. 6 and 8. Greene's analysis ends with Word War I. Since then the fluidity of the New Deal agencies and the establishment of "in-outers" who move at a high level between government and private occupations have supported new images of organizational individualism.

35. I explore this further and relate it to the sacrificial hero in my article,

"Connections with Toughness: The Novels of Eugene Burdick" (1977), p. 236. Cf. H. J. Friedsan, "Bureaucrats as Heroes" (1954).

36. In "The American Nature of Football" (1972) John L. Finlay argued that baseball, with its individualistic, high-risk action, reflected an earlier stage of American capitalism than football, which was a sport of "corporateness." Baseball too, however, has become more organized: it has even been argued that "the game is now controlled more from the dugout than from the field" (John Dizikes, *Sportsmen and Gamesmen* (1981). Basketball, on the other hand, retains free and fast-flowing patterns that give a lot of scope to each player. So does soccer, though some of its jargon and planning is getting more like American football both within and without the United States. To be fair, some intellectual defenders of American football would argue that fluidity of play and autonomy of the individual are not necessarily the same thing; especially for certain positions such as "free safety" (the very term is significant), I still think that the playbook restricts the average player's autonomy.

37. Cf. interview with George Sauer reported by Jack Scott, *Intellectual Digest* (December 1971), p. 53.

38. Quoted by Dave Anderson, *New York Times*, 17 January 1979.

39. A study by Professor Tom Patterson of the University of Glasgow (now Strathclyde).

40. The fit between developments in football and American "industrial folkways" is explored by David Riesman and Reuel Denney, "Football in America: A Study in Culture Diffusion" (1951, 1954). But technology need not be very present for the programming of method. As a college student in 1959, trying out as a summer salesman of encyclopedias, I found that the sales manager, distrustful of such raw material, wanted me to learn word-for-word his doorstep pattern and know the psychological steps it represented.

41. The quotation above is from Frederick Winslow Taylor, *The Principles of Scientific Management* (1911), chap. 2, pp. 140–41, (in Taylor, *Scientific Management*, Harper edition, New York, 1947). In keeping with his exaggeration of factory individualism, Taylor used analogies from baseball rather than football.

Without reference to specialism, the most strenuous assertions of corporate team-playing individualism can sound vague and contradictory. Cf. John William Ward, *Red, White and Blue* (1969), chap. 5, "The Ideal of Individualism and Reality of Organization," especially Ward's discussion of a 1951 *Fortune* editorial. Ward omits the saving possibilities in specialism, and he misquotes Taylor.

42. Eugene Burdick and Harvey Wheeler, *Fail-Safe* (1962), chap. 9. The whole book is more pessimistic about individual autonomy, though it offers some chinks of light. Much of Tom Wolfe's book about astronauts, *The Right Stuff* (1979), concerns the same subject. NASA treated its astronauts as computer-led automatons and medical guinea pigs, yet, to attain the astronauts'

pinnacle, a flier had to show "single combat" qualities of courage and competence. It was these, according to Wolfe, that excited a special male admiration in the public at large. Wolfe probably exaggerated this, but he did identify a tension among astronauts themselves involving different notions of toughness and organizational efficiency. It included the clash between standing up to the bureaucrats—thereby running the risk of being selected out—and taking without complaint their demeaning demands.

CHAPTER 4

1. David Matza and Gresham M. Sykes, "Juvenile Delinquency and Subterranean Values" (1961). In generalizing about gangs, the authors drew on a wide number of studies. Their article represented a concern with notions of deviance that flourished in the early 1960s. It also connected with continuing debate about the extent to which working-class groups have different value systems from those of middle-class groups.

2. Ulf Hannerz, *Soulside* (1969). I have singled this out from many studies of black American ghettos because it was particularly concerned with the relationship of subculture to the wider culture and society and discused aspects of toughness and gender within this framework. However, much of the interpretation given here is mine.

3. Hannerz identified what he called "mainstream . . . life styles" within the ghetto too. Also, drawing on Matza and Sykes, he briefly noted that even the "ghetto-specific" male pattern overlapped a "lively but slightly subterranean masculine tradition in mainstream culture." He did not assign importance to African traditions above the level of "microcultural" details of style. *Soulside*, pp. 78, 198–99.

4. I don't wish to imply that all subcultures of toughness in America are based on a rechannelling of mainstream norms due to deprivation. Like black subcultures they have their own past and interpretations of that past, which affect their conceptions of toughness. Nonetheless even an advantaged subculture is shaped by geographic and economic barriers and opportunities as well as by its mental heritage—for rich Texans, aridity and oil as well as the Alamo.

5. Though less applicable to racial ghettos, Herbert Gans's idea of a trend from communal to "*symbolic* ethnicity" complements this theory of co-option and feedback. See Gans, "Symbolic Ethnicity" (1979).

6. See especially Sinatra's private detective role in *Tony Rome* (1967). By adopting underworld slang the detective helps make it semirespectable. Sinatra's Hoboken Italian background (less deprived than he claimed), his progress from scrawny, "hungry" singer to Hollywood power, and his merging of public and private roles all come out clearly in Tony Scaduto, *Frank Sinatra* (1976).

7. Cf. T. J. Jackson Lears, *No Place of Grace* (1981), Preface, Chap. 2; John Fraser, *America and the Patterns of Chivalry* (1982).

8. "The new coined word 'dude'. . . has travelled over the country with a good deal of rapidity since but two months ago it grew into general use in New York." *North Adams Transcript* (Mass.), 24 June 1883. The reason, perhaps, was that upper-class easterners started seeking the West in large numbers in the 1880s, for health, identity, and adventure as well as invest-ment. Early derivations in the 1880s included "dudish," "dudism," "dudi-ness," and the female "dudine." The term may have come from "duds," meaning clothes, brought over by English colonists. The development of "dude ranches" produced "dude-wranglers" and "dude-punchers," hands appointed to look after the new animals. The term also came to mean a railroad conduc-tor (because of his uniform and east-west travelling?), and in World War II it sometimes referred to an army recruit. The term could be relative: in Zane Grey's *Dude Ranger* (1931) a solid, young Iowan farmer becomes a "dude" when he signs on as a cowhand in the Southwest. In the mid-twentieth century the black ghetto development of "dude" as a sharply dressed hipster, a master of city street life, gave the term a more favorable meaning and led to its mod-ern, neutral use as an alternative to "guy." Cf. chapter 1 on the two-edged relationship between American toughness and showiness.

9. Cf. *Doonesbury* by Garry Trudeau (syndicated strip), 10–11 May 1980 and several earlier strips in the same month, questioning whether preppy toughness was tough at all. *Doonesbury*'s subsequent play with the Maryland Audubon Society in 1981 was a more frontal attack on American upper-class gentility and its efforts at being masterful.

10. Trimly cut to show male physique, the waistcoat reaffirmed traditional maleness against the unisex tendencies of the late 1960s. In America, how-ever, its connotations are less upper-class than in Britain, due to all those Western and pool-hall versions in the movies. What John Brooks called "parody dis-play" largely developed out of the declassé cult of the 1960s. It is less spe-cifically American than he makes out, though affluence and older democratic traditions have extended it in the United States. Cf. John Brooks, "The New Snobbery" (1981); Brooks, *Showing Off in America* (1981).

11. Tom Wolfe, *Mauve Gloves and Madmen, Clutter and Vine* (1976): "Honks and Wonks." Wolfe notes (I think exaggerates) the containment of class prej-udice within geographical labels.

12. Sharon McKern, *Redneck Mothers, Good Ol' Girls, and Other Southern Belles* (1979), pp. 16, 24–25.

13. For more of this comparison, cf. T.J.H. Bishop and Rupert Wilkinson, *Winchester and the Public School Elite* (1967), pp. 29, 33 n. 47; and James McLachlan, *American Boarding Schools* (1970), pp. 328–29.

14. Robert Gray Gunderson, *The Log-Cabin Campaign* (1957), gives some excellent descriptions of this.

15. A study of boys' fiction in the Victorian and Progressive eras finds a shift in focus after about 1895 from self-made youth starting in poor circumstances to well-to-do boys in private schools. This was not, however, just a class shift; it also placed individual striving within a team or other peer group and thus suited the onset of government bureaucracy and corporate organization. Christopher Gerry, "Becoming Adult" (1982). Cf. Daniel T. Rodgers, *The Work Ethic in Industrial America, 1850–1920* (1974), pp. 143–44. John Fraser, *America and the Patterns of Chivalry* (1982), argues that the democratic contests staged in prep schools and Ivy League colleges of the period provided a training for business and so bridged gentlemanly and capitalist values.

16. Cf. Walter Camp's *Book of College Sports* (1893), Introduction; Theodore Roosevelt, "The American Boy" quoted by Gerald F. Roberts, "The Strenuous Life" (1970). Also "An Ideal Boy," *Choate School Brief*, June 1906, quoted by James McLachlan, *American Boarding Schools* (1970), p. 272. The difficulty of line-drawing was exemplified later in Owen Johnson's prep school story, *The Varmint* (1910), where "Tough" McCarty, a basically decent friend of the hero, Carl Stover, is admired but considered rather *too* bad.

17. Cf. David Newsome, *Godliness and Good Learning* (1961), chap. 4; McLachlan, *American Boarding Schools* (1970), chap. 9.

18. Theodore Roosevelt was unusual for his eastern class in that he plunged into both the worlds of lower-class eastern politics and western cow-punching. I do not deny that he acted on particular needs to prove his toughness; also, he did an unusual amount of cultural bridging—between East and West, gentleman and politico, reform and organization, intellect and action. In doing all these things, however, he was, as Richard Hofstadter said, "master therapist of the middle classes." See Hofstadter, *The American Political Tradition and the Men Who Made It* (1948), p. 231, in the Vintage paperback edition. Theodore Roosevelt himself gives a classic statement on class, politics, and self-proving in his *Autobiography* (1913), p. 63.

19. Irving Babbitt had already noted that in the large midwestern universities "the really virile thing to be was an electrical engineer." Babbitt, *Literature and the American College* (1908), pp. 118–119.

20. Noncommissioned Americans' uniforms were, conversely, smarter than their European equivalents, again making for less rank distinction. Since the late 1960s British army officers in the field have adopted a classless (rankless) military sweater with cotton shoulder sections. (In the 1970s it became popular among civilian youth in smaller towns and village.) Officers usually wear these sweaters, however, with the officer's distinctive peaked cap.

21. It is significant that two of America's most profane-speaking and tough-behaving generals in World War II— "Vinegar Joe" Stilwell and George Patton ("Old Blood and Guts")—came from old-stock, upper-class families. Each

reacted differently to plain man pressures. Stilwell detested anything that smacked of snobbery, from British officers with canes to regimental balls; he liked to wear ordinary GI outfit without insignia; and in 1942 he slogged his way out of Burma on foot with his men when he could have flown. He *concealed* his upper-class background and his excellent mind in a rough and aggressive informality. Patton, by contrast, played polo and wore immaculate uniforms; but his ivory-handled revolver had a classless, if fancy, cowboy toughness, though it took a general's rank to get away with wearing it. Dramatizing a tradition that expected the American calvary leader to be hard-driving, bold and independent, Patton *combined* an upper-class swank with a more classless roughness.

22. Crew cuts started, at least in name, with Ivy League rowing crews in the late 1930s and in some quarters they continued to have collegiate and graduate connotations after the war. But it was the use of the crew cut under helmets in World War II that made it catch on widely in the postwar period. My study of Harvard Yearbook photographs from the early 1920s found that among the top athletic teams in the late 1930s and early 1940s the rowing crews usually had the shortest haircuts, but most of the haircuts then were not really crew cuts.

23. These messages are for each other as well as those beneath. The annual booklet containing the biographies of candidates for Harvard's Board of Overseers has two photographs for each: a formal picture in business clothes and an informal picture in shirtsleeves or overalls or ruggedly clad for the outdoors.

24. In the 1844 election, "Old Dick," Kentucky's fighting Irish Richard Johnson, was also known as "Old Tecumseh" for reputedly killing the great Indian chief. If General Winfield Scott came to be known disrespectfully as "Old Fuss and Feathers," Zachary Taylor was known more respectfully as "Old Zack" and "Old Rough and Ready"—names which, like "Old Hickory," originated with the troops. "Old," of course, could connote familiarity. "Young Hickory" was applied to two Democrats, James Polk and then Franklin Pierce ("Young Hickory of the Granite Hill").

25. Cf. David Fischer, *Growing Old in America* (1977); Lawrence Stone,"Walking over Grandma" (1977); and Fischer and Stone, "Growing Old: An Exchange" (1977). Also, C. Vann Woodward, "The Aging of America" (1977), p. 583ff, with commentary by others.

The term, "young veteran" (a contradiction in other countries where military veterans are long-service "old soldiers") reflects the ideal perfectly. So did John F. Kennedy's Inaugural Address, invoking both experience and youth: "the torch has been passed to a new generation of Americans, born in this century, tempered by war, disciplined by a hard and bitter peace, proud of our ancient heritage. . . ."

26. Henry Nash Smith, *Virgin Land* (1950), chaps. 6, 9, and 10. See also

the roughly parallel variations in fictional and semifictional depictions of Kit Carson recounted by Kent Ladd Steckmesser, *The Western Hero in History and Legend* (1965), pp. 27–8, 36–40; also Leslie A. Fiedler, *Love and Death in the American Novel* (1960).

27. The first of the series was *Deadwood Dick, the Prince of the Road* (1877). A striking precursor is Duke Darrell, hero of W. J. Hamilton's *Old Avoirdupois: Or, Steel Coat, the Apache Terror* (1872).

The *Old Cap Collier* series—of varied and uncertain authorship—that began in 1883 has a terser style, both in description of action and the words spoken by the hero. It is notable too that "Old Cap" is, despite his nickname, a *young* detective of "Herculean strength" whose image thereby combines the advantages of age and youth. Edmund Wilson argues that from the Civil War American prose styles, both in fiction and nonfiction, became simpler and faster-paced, "more what was later called 'efficient.' " He traces this in part to the influence of the Western plain man and southwestern humorists, as well as the urgency of war and the mechanical "speeding-up" of American life, but his examples focus on speeches, memoirs, and leading prose writers. Although the dialect characters in dime novels have also been said to reflect the southwestern "cracker-barrel" humorists, it still remains that the dime novels' kind of popular writing lagged behind the development depicted by Wilson. See Edmund Wilson, *Patriotic Gore* (1962), pp. 635–54.

28. Marcus Cunliffe reminds me that as late as the 1930s American movie heroines spoke with more genteel accents than their male opposite numbers—not surprising when so often they were taught English elocution.

29. Daniel P. Thompson, *The Green Mountain Boys: A Historical Tale of the Early Settlement of Vermont* (1839). (Thompson's original story was published c. 1823.) Ethan Allen, who in real life organized the Green Mountain Boys against New York and later led them into the Revolution—a man reputed for physical strength—had fancier tastes than Warrington, but in other respects he was a combination of several characters in the novel.

John Dizikes, *Sportsmen and Gamesmen* (1981), chap. 4, shows the declassing effects of American sporting and frontier society on the heroes depicted in the 1840s by the emigré and aristocratic, British sportswriter, Henry William Herbert. Herbert's ultimate amalgam was Harry Archer, who united elements of sports and science, European and American, white and Indian.

30. The classic example is Edward Ellis's hero, Seth Jones, but there are elements in Ellis's Nathan Todd and a variation in Edward Wheeler's Calamity Jane. See Henry Nash Smith, *Virgin Land* (1950) on Cooper's efforts to create a young classless hero, though the result is less fighting-tough.

31. Edward S. Ellis, *The Lost Trail* (1885); cf. Ellis, *Nathan Todd: Or, the Fate of the Sioux Captive* (1860).

32. Frances Hodgson Burnett, *Little Lord Fauntleroy* (1886), following serialization in *St. Nicholas* magazine.

33. Burt L. Standish, "Frank Merriwell's Nobility: Or the Tragedy of the Ocean Tramp," (1899); Standish, *Frank Merriwell's School Days* (1901). *Little Lord Fauntleroy*, too, has an element of "fallen on hard times" in the situation of Cedric's widowed mother; but the converse theme is more salient: Cedric's retention of character when he moves to better circumstances.

34. Owen Johnson, *Stover at Yale* (1912), especially chaps. 6, 15, and 27. For examples of this in more recent popular fiction, see the character of Fowler Kean in Louis Auchincloss, *Venus in Sparta* (1958), chaps. 1 and 11; and of Warren Black in Eugene Burdick and Harvey Wheeler, *Fail-Safe* (1962). American writers have often depicted the rich man's son as weak in contrast with the self-made man, but only rarely has there been an Andrew Carnegie who would abandon the system of inheritance. Most critics of the inheritor believed he could redeem himself.

35. See especially Frank Norris, *Moran of the Lady Letty* (1898); and Jack London, *The Sea-Wolf* (1904); also elements of London's character, Vance Corliss, in *A Daughter of the Snows* (1902). The racialist uses of this formula by Norris, Owen Wister, and others are explored in Thomas Gossett, *Race* (1965), pp. 214–47, in the Schocken paperback. Conversely, however, Norris was also concerned with hereditary weakness that made class descent and reversion to the primitive into an awful degeneration. See Norris, *Vandover and the Brute* (1914), and *McTeague* (1899). For variations of the exdude theme, see Larzer Ziff's discussion of the stories of Richard Harding Davies and others, in Ziff, *The American 1890s* (1966), chap. 12; and Zane Grey, *The Dude Ranger* (1931).

36. An important landmark in this development was Owen Wister, *The Virginian* (1902). See also Zane Grey, *The Last Trail* (1909).

37. If comic strips count as fiction, then *Rip Kirby* (started just after World War II) represents the most striking breach of the convention in modern American popular fiction that requires the tough hero to be not too obviously upper-class. It may be recalled that Kirby, a thoughtful, bespectacled, pipe-smoking private eye, has as an assistant a most respectful manservant, Desmond, who even calls him "sir." Kirby exercises his fine physique in a gym club, commands an extraordinary range of physical and scientific skills, and in a pinch is as quick with a gun as with his fists or a karate chop. To fit all this into the usual stereotypes, it is not enough to note Kirby's inseparable nickname or to point out that he and Desmond really enjoy a comraderie, nor that Desmond once had to remind an old-fashioned foreign rustic that he had an "employer," not a "master." The fact remains that Desmond is a *belying device* of a class-linked kind that is more usual in British detective and adventure fiction (where even Sapper's ultratough Jim Maitland can wear a monocle). It is true that the American detective writer Rex Stout contrasted Nero Wolfe's detective ability and interpersonal toughness with an upper-class collection of

attributes: high connections, formal suits, intellectual and gourmet tastes, and a wonderful, well-fed fatness. Nero's physical immobility is also contrasted with the tough, bustling qualities of his legman, Archie Goodwin. But the risks of this are safely limited by splitting the hero roles between Wolfe and the classless Goodwin, who often occupies more space in the book. In the case of the TV series' Inspector "Ironside," another relatively upper-class detective, the belying device represented by his confinement to a wheelchair *offsets*, as an underdog trait, his gentlemanly manner.

A more trivial, recent version of the Desmond paradox in Rip Kirby is the role of the factotum, Max, in the TV series, "Hart to Hart." He is familiar with the rich detective couple who employ him and patronize him.

38. In modern Britain, country versus court became North country versus the South. Northerners and midlanders were seen on both sides as blunt but friendly, canny but honest, taciturn and rugged. Southerners (especially of London and the surrounding home counties) were effusive but unfriendly, parasitic and soft-living. Since the North was and is more working-class, these stereotypes were partly based on class; but they did not honor the rural over the urban, for the North was associated with industrial grime and the South with lawns and rhododendrons.

In *The Road to Wigan Pier* (1937), George Orwell claimed that the British regional stereotypes stemmed from Nordic assumptions of superiority over southern peoples, based on climate and race. He did not allow, however, for complications based on gender. In these stereotypes, the ideal Briton was sturdily masculine but not as heavily so as the Germans or as stolidly as the Dutch; the Gallic and Latin peoples were effeminate. Since the 1950s such images have faded as Britain has become more involved with the Continent, simultaneously appreciating Latin expressiveness and the economic, technical, and design achievements of her neighbors.

39. See quotations by James T. Axtell, *The School upon a Hill* (1974), pp. 160–64. Kathryn Kish Sklar has argued that religious and moral prescriptions were less divided according to gender in seventeenth- and eighteenth-century New England than they became in the nineteenth century. Sklar, *Catherine Beecher* (1973), pp. 83–84 in the Norton paperback. For a different view, see Mary Beth Norton, *Liberty's Daughters* (1980). More tenuously Philip Greven has claimed that evangelicals in colonial America inveighed against effeminacy because of a "precariously established sense of masculinity." He attributed this in large measure to religious pressures to submit to the Lord in a feminine way as a "Bride of Christ" and to recognize the spiritual impotence of the self. All this, despite the "Soldier of Christ" conception and attempts to see piety as a manly endeavor. Greven provides very little evidence for what he asserts; some of his examples and quotations seen to contradict him; and he assumes too easily that religious submission and a belief in the Lord as a

source of strength contradicted men's basic sense of what constituted manliness. See Greven, *The Protestant Temperament* (1977), especially pp. 124ff, 140, 143–44.

40. Shakespeare gives us a comprehensive, anticourtier statement in *Henry IV*, Part I (Act I, Scene 3), where a battle-worn Sir Henry Percy castigates an interfering "popinjay" from the court. Percy was the son of an earl, but in the 1630s the muscular puritan William Prynne—himself a scourge of court effeminacy—criticized Shakespeare for overrespecting the mob. The common man element was there but did not dominate its gentry and burgher leadership. Despite the Levellers and Diggers' egalitarianism, anticourt sentiment was not primarily populist. Even Cromwell's famous remark, "I had rather have a plain russet-coated captain that knows what he fights for . . . than that which you call a gentleman and is nothing else," exemplified an officer—Cromwell himself was the son of a landowner and brewer.

The extent to which the settlement of colonial America involved a decline in class deference and a growth of individualist ambition is a matter of debate among colonial historians and depends partly on the region concerned. In general there were some such trends, but they accelerated after the Revolution. Cf. Richard D. Brown, *Modernization* (1976), especially chaps. 2–4; Marcus Cunliffe, "New World, Old World: The Historical Antithesis" (1974); and Eric Foner, *Tom Paine and Revolutionary America* (1976), pp. 28–45, 56–69, on artisans in Philadelphia.

41. The play's preamble insists that it is the creation of a citizen of America: "Where the proud titles of 'My Lord! Your Grace!' To humble *Mr* and plain *Sir* give place." Within this sentiment Tyler might be expected to favor Manly over Jessamy: a Federalist lawyer, he took part in the suppression of Shay's Rebellion and later became chief justice of Vermont.

42. James Henretta and others have argued that a "new type of modal personality" had emerged in the North before the Revolution—entrepreneurial, "dynamic . . . yet cautious and calculating." Puritan paternalism, Henretta says, was a "peculiar blend of timidity and assertiveness." It is consonant with this to argue that admired styles of strength did not become more openly aggressive till much later. See James A. Henretta, *The Evolution of American Society, 1700–1815* (1973), pp. 98–100; Henretta, "Families and Farms: Mentalité in Pre-Industrial America" (1978), pp. 3–32 (with further debate in the same journal, *William and Mary Quarterly* 37 (1980): pp. 688ff); and Edward Pessen, *Jacksonian America* (1969), chap. 2, cf. chap. 3.

43. An exception was Joseph B. Foraker, the Ohio boss. See Foraker, *Notes of a Busy Life* (1916), vol. 1, pp. 167–68. On the other hand, Richard Croker, the tough, brawling boss of Tammany in the 1880s and 1890s, showed that even an Irish-born politico could be susceptible to Anglophila and aristocracy: he acquired estates in England and unsuccessfully sought membership in Brit-

ish high society. Even when reformers were called "cold tea-sippers" (a favored epithet), the English connection was seldom made.

44. An early, popular example of this was Josiah Strong, *Our Country* (1885).

45. In presidential campaign biographies the insistence that the candidate had a "dirt farmer" (as well as athletic) background became more studied after the Civil War as the country became more urban. See William Burlie Brown, *The People's Choice* (1960), pp. 46–47, 84–85. Cf. R. Richard Wohl, "The 'Country Boy' Myth and Its Place in American Urban Culture" (1969); also Vivien Hart, *Distrust and Democracy* (1978), pp. 180–81, on the American term, "grass roots" (originated in the 1880s) and its connotations of vitality for the political system. Roger Butterfield, however, noted the retention of urban status in some politicians' countryboy acts. Butterfield, "The Folklore of Politics" (1950).

46. Sullivan, *A Pearl in Every Oyster* (1938). A very different fantasy, but really on the same subject (effete artifice), put the joke more squarely on the British: it used to be said that if you woke an upper-class Briton at 4:30 A.M. and shouted "Fire!" he would talk American.

47. The personal flavor of this was observed to me by my late father, Gerald Wilkinson, who travelled repeatedly between Britain, the United States, and the Pacific in that period, first on business and then on war intelligence. At the American embassy in London, Joseph P. Kennedy held this view.

48. Likewise his attack on the State Department's "lace handkerchief crowd" and his famous description of Truman's secretary of state, Dean Acheson, as a "pompous diplomat in striped pants, with a phoney British accent." *Congressional Record*, 81st Cong., 2d sess. (1950), 96, pt. 1957; ibid., 1st sess. (1951), 97, pt. 5579. The description of diplomats as "cookie-pushers" goes back at least to the early 1920s; in the 1930s and 1940s activist liberals such as Roosevelt and Hopkins used the term in exasperation against State Department bureaucracy. It originally meant any sissy who preferred easy work, feminine tea parties and social graces to masculine sports; it referred thence to bureaucratic apple-polishers. In 1905 Theodore Roosevelt criticized, perhaps with some reason, "pink tea types, who merely reside in the service. . . ." Like other foreign services the American one tended to recruit upper-class young men who wanted to travel and take in some foreign culture; it provided therefore a perfect target upon which fears of foreign subversion and bureaucratic parasitism could unite.

49. A striking use of court imagery, replacing scented courtiers with lotioned bureaucrats, is in *The Ugly American* by William Lederer and Eugene Burdick (1958). The same book uses the theme of artistic and sensual entrapment, mainly Asian but partly French. *The Ugly American* is discussed at more length in Chapter 2. Cf. David M. Kennedy, *Over Here* (1980), pp. 176–77, on General Pershing's attitude toward Europeans.

50. Comparative interpretations of Canadian culture and social character have variously stressed the physical harshness of the north, the forward position of governing institutions on the frontier, the peaceful use of Indians in the fur trade, the lack of a revolution, Scots puritan and French Catholic conservatism, and exaggerated Canadian views of American frontier violence. Cf. Samuel Delbert Clark, "The Canadian Community" (1954); Robert L. McDougall, "The Dodo and the Cruising Auk" (1963); John Porter, "Canadian Character in the Twentieth Century" (1967); Margaret Atwood, *Survival* (1972); George A. Rawlyck, *Nova Scotia's Massachusetts* (1973); and Sacvan Bercovitch, "The Rites of Assent" (1981), pp. 23–24. In the colonial period, however, because of the Canadian river system, the lone *coureur de bois* developed to a greater extent than did his American counterpart. Sergeant Preston of the Mounties was his juvenile fiction heir.

51. In his latter-day account of the Jamestown colony (*General History of Virginia, 1624*), Smith killed remarkably more Indians in single-handed combat than he did in his first report of it (*A True Relation . . . of Virginia, 1608*). See Bradford Smith, *Captain John Smith* (1953). On frontier figures who knew and publicized each other, see Kent Ladd Steckmesser, *The Western Hero in History and Legend* (1965); also Dixon Wecter, *The Hero in America* (1941), chap. 13, cf. chap. 8; and Henry Nash Smith, *Virgin Land* (1950), chap. 9.

52. The tendency to some of these views was particularly strong in colonial New England. See Clifford Shipton, "The New England Frontier" (1937), pp. 25ff. For a jaundiced view a century later, see the editorial in *Harper's Weekly*, 21 March 1875: "Are We as Great a Country as We Think We Are?" Walter Van Tilburg Clark, *The Ox-Bow Incident* (1940), is an important precursor of more recent attacks on frontier destructiveness.

53. Cf. Richard H. Thornton, *An American Glossary* (1912), entry on "Half-horse, half-alligator": also, Arthur K. Moore, *The Frontier Mind* (1957), chaps. 5 and 6.

54. For example, James Fenimore Cooper, *The Deerslayer* (1841); Francis Parkman, *The California and Oregon Trail* (1849), and other writings on the West; Zane Grey *The Lone Star Ranger* (1914); and Wallace Stegner, *The Big Rock Candy Mountain* (1943). Cf. Don D. Waller, "Wister, Roosevelt and James" (1960).

55. Steckmesser, *The Western Hero* (1965). Movie treatment of these figures has tended to become either unfavorable or psychologically complex, but some western legends have retained internal ambivalence. On the James brothers, for instance, see E. F. Bleiler, ed., *Eight Dime Novels* (1974), pp. xi, 34–40. In a forthcoming study of economic change and social conflict in nineteenth-century Missouri, David Thelen is tracing the popular support among Missourians for Jesse James in his raids on banks and railroads and the lack of it elsewhere.

56. These aspects and the related subject of self-control have been much written about. Cf. Cooper, *The Deerslayer* (1841); Roy Pearce, *Savagism and Civilization* (1967); John William Ward, *Andrew Jackson—Symbol for an Age* (1955), chap. 3; John Cawelti, *The Six-Gun Mystique* (1970); and Jenni Calder, *There Must be a Lone Ranger* (1974), especially chap. 6 ("Pas de Cheval, Pas de Cowboy").

57. Turner's paper, "The Significance of the Frontier in American History," given at the American Historical Association in 1893, is incorporated in his book, *The Frontier in American History* (1920). On eastern upper-class attractions to the West in the late nineteenth century (despite political fears of Populism), see G. Edward White, *The Eastern Establishment and the Western Experience* (1968); John E. Bauer, "The Health Seeker in the Westward Movement" (1959–60); and Bronwen J. Cohen, "Nativism and Western Myth" (1974). There were earlier parallels in the life of the historian Francis Parkman.

58. In the 1920s and 1930s, the highly urban stories of Damon Runyon made the tradition of the tenderfoot narrator into a tough guy's "reverse sell." The narrator uses a rough, terse language ("Runyonese") and hobnobs with dangerous characters, yet claims to be nervous and law-abiding: in a tight situation he just happens to be there to observe it. But it is often the narrator who saves the situation with a quick, quiet move, a phone call, a word in the right place.

59. Richard Slotkin, *Regeneration through Violence* (1973). Slotkin's last chapter makes other, complex extensions into the present. See also Max Brand's novel, *Singing Guns* (1938), where a hunted outlaw and pursuing sheriff ritually become blood brothers; and James Dickey's novel, *Deliverance* (1970), which telescopes numerous generations and uses of frontier myth, favorably and unfavorably, from inside and outside the myths, and with a thickly laid-on, sexual naturalism. On the whole question of relationships with the hunted, see "The Playboy Interview: James Dickey" (1971). On different aspects of this general subject, consider also the relationship between the young boy and the fish that got away in Ernest Hemingway, *Islands in the Stream* (1970, posthumous)—well presented in the movie with George C. Scott—and several of Howard Hawks's movies.

60. For example, Michael Paul Rogin, *Fathers and Children* (1975), especially "Introduction: Liberal Society and the Indian Question"; Slotkin, *Regeneration through Violence*; Leslie Fiedler, *The Return of the Vanishing American* (1968). Although the early popularity of stories about Indian capture contained a sexual element, the argument that Indians reached into mainstream white psyches by representing sensuality, affiliativeness, and harmony with nature underestimates the effect of their alienness and their reputation for asceticism. Even the better-documented argument about political guilt (see Rogin and oth-

ers) is qualified by the view that racialism complemented and supported an egalitarianism confined to whites. See John Ashworth, "The Jacksonian as Leveller" (1980).

61. Cf. Steckmesser, *The Western Hero in History and Legend*, chap. 14; George A. Custer, *My Life on the Plains* (1874), pp. 159, 176; Jay Monaghan, *Custer: The Life of General George Armstrong Custer* (1959), p. 333. Following Custer's Last Stand, an editorial in the reformist *Harper's Weekly* 20 (5 August 1876): 630–31, expressed a significant tension between a predominant wish to show humane honor toward the Indians and an underlying racialism and self-regarding realism.

62. I have explored the differences and overlaps between cognitive screening (aided by racial differences) and emotional suppression in a study of Heinrich Himmler's antisemitism: Rupert Wilkinson, *The Broken Rebel* (1972), pp. 170–76.

63. Stephen Fender, *Plotting the Golden West* (1982), notes the "blank page" possibilities of the far West yet observes that it suited certain literary traditions rather than others. See especially Fender, pp. 7–12. But see also John R. Milton, *The Novel of the American West* (1980), which envisages more open-ended possibilities for eastern romanticizers and myth weavers.

64. Cf. Daniel Bell, *The Cultural Contradictions of Capitalism* (1976), discussed in the Appendix.

65. For a striking impression of assault, in Ives's harsh-tender style, compare his work, "The Unanswered Question," with Beethoven's String Quartet no. 15 in A Minor, op. 132, third movement. Ives appears to set up and then attack and exploit the Beethoven work. Cf. Charles Ives, *Essays before a Sonata* (1961), especially the essays on transcendentalist writers; also the metaphors of mountain-climbing versus old ladies in his notes on composition, reprinted in the appendix of Wilfrid Mellers, *Music in a New Found Land* (1964). Two opposing views of Ives's declassé populism and revolt against feminine gentility are in Frank Rossiter, *Charles Ives and His America* (1975); and Richard Crawford, "Response to Frank Rossiter" (1974). Ives's contemporary, Carl Ruggles, was another American composer who attacked "sissy" music.

66. For example, the architect George Sullivan (1856–1924), the painter George Bellows (1882–1925), and the Ashcan School, alias the "black gang." Cf. after World War II, the action painting of abstract expressionism, and also the revolt against it by Jasper Jones and pop art.

67. For example, Emerson, "The American Scholar" (1837); Herman Melville, "Hawthorne and his Mosses" (1850); Walt Whitman, "The Eighteenth Presidency!" (1856); and Whitman, Letter to Emerson, August 1856 (no day given), often known as the 1856 Preface to *Leaves of Grass*. Similar calls, by writers as different as Wallace Stevens and Thomas Wolfe, were made in the twentieth century.

68. On Francis Bacon's view of knowledge and practice applied in early

American culture, see Merle Curti, *American Paradox* (1956). On a democratic "intellectualization of the mundane" in American culture, see Rupert Wilkinson, "Word-Choosing: The Sources of a Modern Obsession" (1982), pp. 82–83. On wider aspects of American intellectual pragmatism, see especially Morton White, *Social Thought in America (1957), and the articles by Jill Conway and Martin Malia in Daedalus 101* (Summer 1972), issue on intellectuals and change.

69. The aesthetic dimensions of the toughness-intellect fusion and the intellectual price paid for the fusion are both discussed in Rupert Wilkinson, "Connections with Toughness: The Novels of Eugene Burdick" (1977), pp. 223ff. Although World War I's use of intellectuals in Washington and the war effort gave academics a newly virile image in some quarters, the war period was short and the effect not so durable as that of the Cold War. In the long run, however, the trend in favor of intellectuals' potent image rested on some very basic sociobiological connections between cognition, exploration, and survival, a primitive factor that, ironically, became more important as society became more artificial, its crises more bewildering, its leaders more impotent, its people more in need of expert explanation.

70. Daniel Snowman, "The Jewish Stimulus to American Culture" (1967), gives a broader perspective on the convergence between Jewish and general American values and occupational structures.

71. Colin Brooks, a historian of eighteenth-century Britain and America, observes that British society at the time was more military and that its language may well have been more violent though possibly less concerned with mastery of nature.

72. In tracing the origins of tough and aggressive slang, I found a sharp increase around 1820 in the coining of such slang. This only applies, however, to slang which, whether or not obsolete, is fairly well known to us today.

73. Cf. Neil Harris, *Humbug: The Art of P. T. Barnum* (1973), especially chap. 3; David Brion Davis, "Some Themes of Countersubversion" (1960); Mark Twain, *The Adventures of Huckleberry Finn* (1883), chap. 23 ("Sold"). Ricky Elliott pointed out to me the parallel between Davis's "countersubversion" movements and Jacksonian fear of being a sucker. It is possible that each included projection of the other.

74. See George Horace Lorimer, *Letters from a Self-Made Merchant to His Son* (1902), especially Letter I-V. Lorimer was a meat-packing executive before becoming editor of the *Saturday Evening Post* and later president of the Curtis Publishing Co. Despite an anti-intellectual disdain for scholarship as an end in itself, Lorimer was a proponent of a broad, liberal education and pure scientific research.

75. Cf. Mary Roth Walsh, *"Doctors Wanted, No Women Need Apply"* (1977), pp. 138ff. Jill and John Conway pointed out to me this dimension including the effects on law schools.

76. In the late nineteenth century, romantic medievalism (Walter Scott, Arthurian legend, and so on) included the same twin appeals for Americans. Knight-errantry and the joust couched heroic individualism within a clear-cut institutional structure and placed it upon a cleanly pastoral setting.

77. Statements quoted and cited by Peter Gabriel Filene, *Him Her Self* (1975), chap. 4; Paul Van Dyke, "The College Man in Action" (1919).

78. This was part of a more general rise of heroes of light entertainment. Cf. Leo Lowenthal, "Biographies in Popular Magazines" (1944); Fred I. Greenstein, "New Light on Changing American Values" (1964), pp. 441–50. The rise of the athletic hero was only a relative change: consider the acclaim won in the late nineteenth century by the boxers John Sullivan ("the Boston Strong Boy", "The Great John L.") and "Gentleman Jim" Corbett, though Corbett also returned later on the movie screen.

79. An early precursor was the apostle of diet and discipline, Sylvester Graham (1794–1851), though his ideas were not popular at the time.

80. Such heroes helped to make the term "comics" a misnomer, and many of the strips have had a large adult as well as juvenile readership. The first major American comic-strip strong man was Popeye, who first appeared in 1919, but he was and is a lower-class character, not a classless and straight hero of the kind established in the 1930s. The first straight comic-strip hero of really superhuman strength was Tarzan, who began in strip form in 1929. (Edgar Rice Burroughs's first Tarzan book, *Tarzan of the Apes* was published in 1912.) British strips, too, produced a hero of superhuman strength in Garth, but not until 1943. Garth's origins had some similarity to Superman's. The Mighty Wilson, another British hero of amazing physical prowess though not really superhuman, started in 1941, but that was still after Superman (1938) and Batman (1939). Like Garth and some of the American strips, the Mighty Wilson reflected war-time desires for an individual savior and a special weapon.

81. About the same proportion of the population served in the armed forces in World War II as in the civil War, but the ratio of war-caused deaths to population was much higher in the Civil War. The Civil War lasted almost exactly four years—a little under four months longer than America's military participation in World War II.

82. See especially Dr. Keith's letter in Herman Wouk, *The Caine Mutiny* (1951), chap. 2—a book that is deliberately ambiguous toward military organization and authority.

83. For example, the last sentence of George Kennan's famous article (signed by 'X'), "The Sources of Soviet Conduct" (1947). Also the portraits of Father Finian and Gilbert MacWhite in William J. Lederer and Eugene Burdick, *The Ugly American* (1958), chaps. 3 and 9; and some of John F. Kennedy's Inaugural Address; also various writings of the 1950s and early 1960s on the need for excellence in government, sciences, and so on.

84. In the wake of Vietnam, the conservative English writer Henry Fairlie

(whose model might well be the Lord Melbourne that JFK himself admired) wrote a jaundiced view of the Kennedy administration's leading lights. Though not a fair and rounded view, it suggests that the Kennedys brought together a set of dualities that go far back in the main American traditions of toughness.

They wished to act . . . as rational men, unbemused and cool, skeptical and laconic, ironic and contained, the adjectives which persistently recur in the literature of the administration. . . . But the very energy, the very conviction, the very zeal, with which they pursued their purpose fatally contradicted it. Unbemused—yet bemused by the opportunities of power; cool—yet hot for action; sardonic—yet eager to move a nation; laconic—yet given to majestic periods in their utterance; ironic—yet surrendered to their own zeal; contained—yet exuberant performers in the public arena. [Fairlie, *The Kennedy Promise* (1973) p. 5]

85. Traditional support for this included Michael Maccoby's "Craftsman," the kind of exengineer executive who preferred to compete against nature or his own standards rather than against others and liked tinkering or hiking more than team sports. Maccoby, *The Gamesman* (1976), chap. 2. The varieties of convergence between counterculture and mainstream toughness in this period are indeed "mind-blowing." See, for instance, Adam Smith's marvellous account of a "Falstaffian"-sized yogi tough guy in the Oregon woods: Smith, *Powers of Mind* (1975), pp. 229–35, in the Ballantine paperback. Consider again the development of encounter groups and T-groups; aikido, "yoga tennis," and other athletic uses of new-type mind control; and some kinds of "heavy metal" music.

86. A succinct but rich analysis is Edmund White's essay "The Political Vocabulary of Homosexuality" (1980). White exaggerates the macho takeover but makes the interesting observation that homosexual men moved away from androgenous styles at the time that a number of young straight men began experimenting with them.

87. In the 1960s, a heterogeneous number of novels had mixed countercultural and anticonventional ideas with conventional aspects of toughness: For example, Ken Kesey, *Sometimes a Great Notion* (1964); James Drought, *The Enemy* (1964); and Charles Portis, *True Grit* (1968), whose youthful heroine (narrating the tale in old age) found an echo in Jodie Foster.

88. Cf. Robert L. Shook, *Winning Images* (1977).

89. On the history of American tough-guy exports, cf. Robert A. Fullerton, "Toward a Commercial Popular Culture in Germany" (1979); Richard Hoggart, *The Uses of Literacy* (1957), chap. 8.

90. *Tufff*, a gem of a play by Billie Brown, illustrates these aspects beautifully. Although set on an Australian beach, it is much less about Australian culture than about male adolescence per se in a modern consumer society. (Compare this with *Grease*, which is more about the specifics of American high school "making it" in the 1950s.) On adolescence, impulse control, and

authoritarianism, see R. Nevitt Sanford, "The Developmental Status of the Entering Freshman" (1962).

91. For more on male assertiveness and identity in industrial working-class life, see Peter N. Stearns, *Be a Man! Males in Modern Society* (1979), chap. 4; and parts of Andrew Tolson, *The Limits of Masculinity* (1977). In Britain, lower-class culture has also for decades enjoyed an ambivalent spoofing of "poofs" and "pansies," some of which shades into the more formal institution of "drag" and the "Widow Twankey" role (traditionally male-acted) in some local pantomimes. The practice carries with it an inverted daring, a fantasy wish to rebel "sideways" against sex roles, since the opportunities upward are so sparse. Some of the drag and homosexual spoofing is enjoyed by both sexes and fits trends to more shared husband-wife activities observed by John Goldthorpe et al., *The Affluent Worker* (1968).

92. This point is made by Michael Grant, ed., *Cicero: Murder Trials* (1975), p. 120.

93. The *plebeians* came to include rich political families whose ancestry in past consuls, tribunes, and dictators gave them high status, but they were still largely excluded from the closed, hereditary group of patricians.

94. In the second century B.C., Cicero postulated a broad "optimate" stratum, or "best citizens" leaders including public leaders, businessmen, landowners, ordinary citizens, and freedmen—people of "safe and sane" judgment and morals. This may sound like a common man formula, but Cicero was at pains to distinguish optimate public policies from those which aimed to "please the masses" or whip up popular excitement and agitation. Cicero himself was proud of being a "new man" in politics, chosen not by family tradition or a small minority but by "the will of the entire Roman people"; yet his fear of the masses was quite like that of elitist American Federalists. Writing much later, in the early second century A.D., the satirist Juvenal attacked economic inequality in Rome, but his ideal was the independent country gentleman, far from rich but with just enough means not to have to descend to manual work.

95. Oscar Lewis, *Five Families* (1959), p. 29 in the Mentor paperback; also the last chapter on the Castros.

96. This difference, of course, applied much less in the American South. Here again it is difficult to gauge Mexican influence.

97. Octavio Paz, *The Labyrinth of Solitude* (1962).

98. This is not to say that the Mexican heritage has no asceticism or moralism: the Spanish culture that produced Cortes had both. I must also qualify my stress on nonsexual alternatives in American tough-guy styles by observing the linguistic traffic in America between sexual and nonsexual spheres. In addition to the well-known use of competitive and acquisitive language in sexuality ("making it," "scoring," "deliver"), there is much displacement of male sexuality into nonsexual spheres. Thus American usage is particularly prone to images of penetration (to be "into" a subject, to "put a call in" or a loan

"into" a client, even to be "deeply involved in" something). Consider also the "thrust" of an argument or report, so popular in the Kennedy sixties, and the liquid as well as logistical "pour it on" (that replaced the nineteenth-century "pile it on" after gasoline engines appeared). Such displacement, however, can be a way of limiting and replacing open sexuality, just as the stress on anality can be a diversion away from primary sexual areas. There is likewise a neopuritan aspect to the traditional American use of "hot" terms ("hot stuff," he's "hot at it," "hot shit") for dynamic success; covertly they suggest sexuality but also have an origin in the large number of "hell" terms produced from the nineteenth century on ("hell-to-spit," "hell-fired," "hell-bent," "hell of a time," "give 'em hell").

99. Not all public schools were boarding schools, and like British prep schools (nonstate primary schools), they have increasingly become day schools. But the most famous and influential public schools have predominantly been boarding schools.

100. David Newsome, *Godliness and Good Learning* (1961), chap. 4.

101. Student subcultures in American secondary schools have stressed adult-like maturity in competitive techniques—in drinking, dating, driving, and so on—while turning away from broader adult imitation, which has sometimes been seen as "milk and cookies." Cf. Gary Schwartz and Don Merten, "The Language of Adolescence" (1967).

102. The term "wet" was renewed politically by the right-wing Monday Club, which used it against MPs deemed soft on the Rhodesian issue in the 1960s and 1970s. It was then used by Thatcher's monetarists against conservative colleagues who were inclined to more public spending and who sometimes applied the label to themselves in the same spirit that an American might have called himself "doveish" or "soft-nosed." In his *Dictionary of Historical Slang* Eric Partridge classifies "wet" (meaning "soft, silly, dull or stupid") as a public school term of the late nineteenth and early twentieth century, and he suggests it may have come from "wet goose," a rural term for a poor, simple fellow, dating from the mid-nineteenth century. Like most British observers, however, Partridge underestimates the reach of prep school (as distinct from public school) language into upper-class, adult styles. In the twentieth century at least, "wet" was mainly a prep school term, subsequently borrowed by upper and upper-middle class mothers to denounce fecklessness in their offspring. "James, pick up that pullover and stop being wet."

103. James McLachlan, *American Boarding Schools* (1970), gives examples and discussion of this in America from the early nineteenth century: pp. 116–17, 125–26, 256–57, 276–77.

104. I know of no comparative study of British and American boarding school cultures; the above statement is based on my own impressions of both systems gathered before writing my book on British public schools: *The Prefects* (1964). One of the most searching depictions of an American-style "win ethic" in a

Briton is the characterization of Peter Savage in John Masters's novel, *Far, Far The Mountain Peak* (1957): the case is presented as a pathology and Savage's redemption at the end requires failure.

105. Cf. Maurice L. Farber. "English and Americans" (1953); Geoffrey Gorer, "English Character in the Twentieth Century" (1967); Daniel Snowman, *Britain and America* (1977), pp. 90–96, 132–39. At the level of child-rearing, the idea of self-control *is* highly articulated in Britain: "control yourself!" has been for decades a common command in British middle-class homes. In adult society, however, institutions have meshed smoothly to make controls on aggressiveness a matter of implicit procedure (even in the routinized area of labor disputes). In America, by contrast, institutions are more apt to be burdened with the dual function of promoting and controlling personal assertiveness. Thus, the recent development of television debates in presidential elections dramatizes personal contest yet mutes it by having the contestants answer press interrogators rather than each other. Contrast the American debates of 1976 with the German election debates of the same year, when the contestants for the chancellorship directly argued.

APPENDIX

1. Some of my own arguments about toughness in America were previewed in an *Encounter* article in February 1976. Cady's essay is imaginative and useful but it attributes strenuosity to an indiscriminate list of historical and literary figures, and it does not set out to trace changes and phases in strenuous values. Paul Gardner's book on sports in American life, *Nice Guys Finish Last* (1974), makes some telling, if necessarily incomplete, historical points about American competitiveness, concern with winning, and "he-man" toughness: see chapter 3 in that book. Other works that deal with aspects of the subject in passing include Orrin E. Klapp, *Heroes, Villains and Fools* (1962); Ronald Segal, *The Americans* (1969); and John Fraser, *America and the Patterns of Chivalry* (1982). My review of Fraser's book in the *Times Higher Education Supplement*, London, 28 May 1982, p. 18, contrasts it with other perspectives on American toughness.

2. Lucy Komisar's article, "Violence and the Masculine Mystique" (1970), links American male concerns with toughness to violence levels, the win ethic, and technological power in America; but even she—understandably in a short piece—does not set out to explain the American historical factors. Her main explanations are not specific to America.

3. Some of these studies note wide-ranging sources and ramifications of their subjects without dwelling on values of toughness and mastery as a problem in long-term historical causation. Cf. Richard Hofstadter, *Anti-Intellectualism in American Life* (1963); Peter Shaw, "The Tough Guy Intellectual" (1966); John

A. Barsness, "Theodore Roosevelt as Cowboy: The Virginian as Jacksonian Man" (1969); T. J. Jackson Lears, *No Place of Grace* (1981).

4. Cf. Rupert Wilkinson, "American Character Revisited" (1983). John Higham made a similar point against historians and writers on social character in the 1950s: he accused them of subjectivizing class conflict into "psychological tensions running through the society as a whole." Higham, "The Cult of the American Consensus" (1959). On the differences between the 1950s and 1970s in this regard, see my article cited above.

5. A study in 1967 found that the favorite TV programs of clerks were significantly more apt to be sports, adventure, or Westerns than those of either managers or skilled craftsmen. The only big difference was in the popularity of sports programs (chosen by 46 percent of clerks versus 26 percent of managers and 23 percent of craftsmen), but it seemed that people with the most demanding or physical jobs tended to prefer programs with less strenuous content. See Gavin Mackenzie, *The Aristocracy of Labor* (1973), pp. 92–94 (sample based on Providence, Rhode Island).

6. Clancy Sigal, "Little Italy Gets It Together" (1979). Various writers have suggested that gangsters and policemen have imitated their fictional and screen counterparts and that moviemakers have then used the imitations.

7. A *Washington Post*-ABC News poll in October 1981 found that respondents tended to see President Reagan as taking more aggressive foreign policy positions than they themselves would, but nonetheless admiring Reagan for this.

8. Media Institute, *Crooks, Conmen and Clowns* (1981), found that big business bosses were portrayed as crooked, their executives as malevolent, and small businessmen as fools. This ties in with the tendency in both American and British television drama to portray lower-class people in a humorous light, but class bias is not synonymous with business or corporate bias. The Media Institute study found that business practices as well as business people were depicted unfavorably.

BIBLIOGRAPHY

Aaron, Daniel. *Writers on the Left: Episodes in American Literary Communism.* New York: Harcourt, Brace and World, 1961.

Aberle, David D., and K. D. Naegele. "Middle-Class Fathers' Occupational Role and Attitudes towards Children." *American Journal of Orthopsychiatry* 22 (1952): 76ff.

Adams, Abigail, and John Adams. *The Book of Abigail and John: Selected Letters of the Adams Family, 1762–1784.* Edited by L. H. Butterfield, Marc Friedlander, and Mary-Jo Kline. Cambridge: Harvard University Press, 1975.

Adams, Brooks. *The Law of Civilization and Decay: An Essay on History.* New York: Macmillan Co., 1895.

Adams, John. *The Adams-Jefferson Letters.* Edited by Lester J. Cappon, II. Chapel Hill: University of North Carolina Press, 1959.

Adams, Michael C. *Our Masters the Rebels: A Speculation on Union Military Failure in the East, 1861–1865.* Cambridge: Harvard University Press, 1978.

Aiken, Albert W. *Kit Carson: King of Guides.* New York: Beadle's, 1882.

Alexander, Franz. *Our Age of Unreason: A Study of the Irrational Forces in Social Life.* Philadelphia: Lippincott, 1942.

Allen, H. C. *Bush and Backwoods: A Comparison of the Frontier in Australia and the United States.* East Lansing: Michigan State University Press, 1959.

Ambrose, Stephen E. *Rise to Globalism: American Foreign Policy, 1938–1970.* Baltimore: Penguin, 1971.

Andersen, U. S. *Success Cybernetics.* West Nyack: Parker, 1966.

Anderson, Sherwood. "An Apology for Crudity," *Dial,* 8 November 1917.

Arbuthnot, John. *The History of John Bull.* Edited by Alan W. Bower and Robert E. Erickson. Oxford: Oxford University Press, 1976. Five pamphlets first published 1712.

Aristophanes. "The Frogs." In *Aristophanes: "The Wasps"; "The Poet and* the Woman"; "The Frogs," edited by David Barrett. Harmondsworth: Penguin, 1964.

Armitage, Shelley. "Rawhide Heroines: The Evolution of the Cowgirl and the Myth of America." In *The American Self: Myth, Ideology and Popular Culture*, edited by Sam B. Girgus. Albuquerque: University of New Mexico Press, 1981.

Ashton, Robert, ed. *James I by His Contemporaries: An Account of His Career and Character as Seen by Some of His Contemporaries*. London: Hutchinson, 1969.

Ashworth, John. "The Jacksonian as Leveller." *Journal of American Studies* 14 (1980): 407–41.

Atwood, Margaret. *Survival: A Thematic Guide to Canadian Literature*. Toronto: Anansi, 1972.

Auchincloss, Louis. *Venus in Sparta*. Boston: Houghton Mifflin, 1958.

Axtell, James T. *The School upon a Hill: Education and Society in Colonial New England*. New Haven, Conn.: Yale University Press, 1974.

Babbitt, Irving. *Literature and the American College: Essays in Defense of the Humanities*. Boston: Houghton Mifflin, 1908.

Bach, Richard. *Jonathan Livingston Seagull*. New York: Macmillan Co., 1970.

Bakal, Carl. *The Right to Bear Arms*. New York: McGraw-Hill, 1966.

Barnet, Richard. "The Game of Nations." *Harper's Magazine* 243 (November 1971): 55–59.

Barnett, Correlli. "The Education of Military Elites." In *Governing Elites*, edited by Rupert Wilkinson. New York: Oxford University Press, 1969.

Barsness, John A. "Theodore Roosevelt as Cowboy: The Virginian as Jacksonian Man." *American Quarterly* 21 (1969): 606–19.

Bartlett, John Russell. *Dictionary of Americanisms: A Glossary of Words and Phrases, Usually Regarded as Peculiar to the United States*. New York: Bartlett and Welford, 1848.

Barton, Bruce. *The Man Nobody Knows*. Indianapolis: Bobbs-Merrill, 1925.

Bateson, Gregory. "Morale and National Character." In *Civilian Morale*, edited by Goodwin Watson. Boston: Houghton Mifflin, 1942.

Bauer, John E. "The Health Seeker in the Westward Movement." *Mississippi Valley Historical Review* 46 (1959–60): 91–110.

Beard, George M. *American Nervousness*. New York: Putnam, 1881.

Beardslee, David C., and Donald O'Dowd. "Students and the Occupational World." In *The American College: A Psychological and Social Interpretation of the Higher Learning*, edited by R. Nevitt Sanford. New York: Wiley, 1962.

Bell, Daniel. *The Cultural Contradictions of Capitalism*. New York: Basic Books, 1976, new foreword, 1978.

Benchley, Peter. *Jaws*. Garden City, N.Y.: Doubleday, 1974.

Bercovitch, Sacvan. "The Rites of Assent." In *The American Self: Myth, Ide-*

ology and Popular Culture, edited by Sam B. Girgus. Albuquerque: University of New Mexico Press, 1981.

Berle, A. A., Jr. "The Social Economics of the New Deal." *New York Times Magazine*, 29 October 1933.

Bertolome, Fernando. "Executives as Human Beings." *Harvard Business Review* 50 (November-December 1972): 62–69.

Best, Geoffrey. "Militarism and the Victorian Public School." In *The Victorian Public School: Studies in the Development of an Educational Institution*, edited by Brian Simon and Ian Bradley. Dublin: Gill and Macmillan, 1975.

Bethell, Tom. "Hard-Money Men." *Harper's Magazine*, February 1981, 33–40.

Biderman, Albert D. *March to Calumny: The Story of American POWs in the Korean War*. New York: Macmillan, 1963.

Billington, Ray. *The American Frontiersman*. Oxford: Oxford University Press, 1954.

Bishop, T.J.H., and Rupert Wilkinson. *Winchester and the Public School Elite: a Statistical Analysis*. London: Faber and Faber, 1967.

Black, Jonathan. *Oil*. New York: Morrow, 1974.

Blackie, William. "Is American Stamina Declining?" *Harper's New Monthly Magazine* 79 (1899): 241–49.

Blair, Clay, Jr. *The Atomic Submarine and Admiral Rickover*. New York: Holt, 1954.

Bleiler, E. F., ed. *Eight Dime Novels*. New York: Dover, 1974.

Blumberg, Paul. *Inequality in an Age of Decline*. New York: Oxford University Press, 1980.

Boorstin, Daniel J. *The Americans: The National Experience*. New York: Random House, 1965.

Bowman, Claude C. "The College Professor in America: An Analysis of Articles Published in General Magazines, 1890–1938." Ph.D. diss., University of Pennsylvania, 1938.

Brand, Max [Frederick Faust]. *Destry Rides Again*. New York: Dodd, Mead, 1930.

———. *Singing Guns*. New York: Dodd, Mead, 1938.

———. *The Dude*. New York: Dodd, Mead, 1940.

———. *Larramee's Ranch*. New York: Dodd, Mead, 1966. First published as serial in *Western Story* (starting 13 September 1924).

Brandt, Anthony. "What It Means to Say No." *Psychology Today*, August 1981, 70–77.

Braverman, Harry. *Labor and Monopoly Capital: The Degradation of Work in the Twentieth Century*. New York: Monthly Review Press, 1974.

Bridwell, E. Nelson, ed. *Batman: From the 30s to the 70s*. New York: Crown, 1971.

————. *Superman: From the 30s to the 70s*. New York: Crown, 1971.

Brenton, Myron. *The American Male*. New York: Coward-McKann, 1966.

Brogan, D. W. *The American Character*. New York: Time, 1962.

Brooks, John. "The New Snobbery: How to Show Off in America." *Atlantic Monthly* 247 (January 1981): 37–48.

————. *Showing Off in America: From Conspicuous Consumption to Parody Display*. Boston: Little, Brown, 1981.

Brown, Richard D. *Modernization: The Transformation of American Life, 1600–1865*. New York: Hill and Wong, 1976.

Brown, William Burlie. *The People's Choice: The Presidential Image in the Campaign Biography*. Baton Rouge: Louisiana State University Press, 1960.

Brunt, P.A. *Ancient Culture and Society: Social Conflicts in the Roman Republic*. London: Chalto and Windus, 1971.

Burdick, Eugene. *The Ninth Wave*. Boston, Houghton Mifflin, 1956.

————. *The Blue of Capricorn*. Boston: Houghton Mifflin, 1961.

————. *The 480*. New York: McGraw-Hill, 1964.

Burdick, Eugene, and William J. Lederer. *Sarkhan*. New York: McGraw-Hill, 1965.

Burdick, Eugene, and Harvey Wheeler. *Fail-Safe*. New York: McGraw-Hill, 1962.

Burnett, Frances Hodgson. *Little Lord Fauntleroy*. New York, Scribner's, 1886.

Burroughs, Edgar. *Tarzan of the Apes*. Chicago: McClurg, 1914. First published in *All Story Magazine*, October 1912.

————. *The Return of Tarzan*. Chicago: McClurg, 1915.

————. *Tarzan and the Leopard Men*. Tarzana, Calif.: Burroughs, 1935.

Butterfield, Roger. *The American Past: A History of the United States . . . Told with the Aid of Eleven Hundred Pictures Reproduced from Original Photographs, Paintings, Cartoons, Lithographs, Engravings and Drawings*. New York: Simon and Schuster, 1947, revised 1957, 1966.

————. "The Folklore of Politics." *Pennsylvania Magazine of History and Biography* 74 (1950): 164–77.

Cady, Edwin. "The Strenuous Life." In *New Voices in American Studies*, edited by Ray B. Browne. West Lafayette, Ind.: Purdue University Press, 1966.

Caidin, Martin. *Cyborg*. New York: Arbor House, 1972.

Calder, Jenni. *There Must be a Lone Ranger: The Myth and Reality of the Wild West*. London: Hamish Hamilton, 1974.

Camp, Walter. *Walter Camp's Book of College Sports*. New York: Century, 1893.

Campbell, Bruce. "The Ideology of the Ante-bellum Northern Democrats." *Journal of American Studies* 11 (1977): 103–21.

Cannon, Ida M. *On the Social Frontier of Medicine*. Cambridge: Harvard University Press, 1952.

Cannon, Walter Bradford. *The Way of an Investigator: A Scientist's Experience in Medical Research*. New York: Norton, 1945.

Cash, W. J. *The Mind of the South*. New York: Knopf, 1941.

Cather, Willa. *O Pioneers!* Boston: Houghton, Mifflin, 1913.

Catullus, Gaius Valeius. *The Poems of Catallus*. Edited by Peter Wrigham. Harmondsworth: Penguin, 1966.

Cawelti, John. *The Six-Gun Mystique*. Bowling Green, Ohio: Bowling Green University, Popular Press, 1970.

Chandler, Raymond. *Farewell, My Lovely*. New York: Knopf, 1940.

———. *The High Window*. New York: Knopf, 1942.

———. "The Simple Art of Murder." *Atlantic Monthly* 174 (December 1944): 53–59.

———. *Playback* Boston: Houghton Mifflin, 1958.

Chapman, Stephen. "Hard Nose." *New Republic*, 31 March 1979, 10–12.

Chinoy, Ely. *Auto Workers and the American Dream*. Garden City, N. Y.: Doubleday, 1955.

Churchill, Winston S. *My Early Life: A Roving Commission*. London: Butterworth, 1930.

Cicero, Marcus Tullius. *Cicero: Murder Trials*. Edited by Michael Grant. Harmondsworth: Penquin, 1975.

Clark, Samuel Delbert. "The Canadian Community." In *Canada*, edited by George W. Brown. Berkeley: University of California Press, 1954.

Clark, Walter Van Tilburg. *The Ox-Bow Incident*. New York: Random House, 1940.

Clough, S. DeWitt, ed. *Backbone Hints for the Prevention of Jelly-Spine Curvature and Mental Squint: A Straight-up Antidote for the Blues and a Straight-Ahead Sure Cure for Grouch*. Chicago: Clough, 1908.

Cohen, Bronwen J. "Nativism and Western Myth: The Influence of Nativist Ideas on the American Self-Image." *Journal of American Studies* 8 (1974): 23–39.

Coles, Robert. *The Middle Americans*. Boston: Little, Brown, 1971.

Collins, Bruce. "The Ideology of the Ante-bellum Northern Democrats." *Journal of American Studies* 11 (1977): 103–21.

Conkling, Alfred R. *The Life and Letters of Roscoe Conkling*. New York: Webster, 1889.

Conway, Jill. "Intellectuals in America: Varieties of Accommodation and Conflict." *Daedalus* 101 (Summer 1972): 199–205.

Cooke, Alistair. "Epitaph for a Tough-Guy." *Atlantic Monthly* 199 (1957): 31ff. On Humphrey Bogart.

Cooper, James Fenimore. *The Deerslayer: Or, The First War-Path, a Tale*. Philadelphia: Lea and Blanchard, 1841.

Cottle, Thomas. "Zero Man: Anatomy of an Academic Failure." *Change* (November 1972): 49ff.

Cox, LaWanda, and John M. Cox. "Negro, Suffrage and Republican Politics." *Journal of Southern History* 33 (1967): 303–30.

Craig, Patricia, and Mary Cadogan. *The Lady Investigates: Women Detectives and Spies in Fiction.* London: Gollanz, 1981.

Crawford, Richard. "Response to Frank Rossiter." Paper given at the American Musicological Society, New York, November 1974.

Crevecoeur, Hector St. John de. *Letters from an American Farmer.* Dublin: Exshaw, 1782.

Cunliffe, Marcus. *George Washington: Man and Monument.* Boston: Little, Brown, 1958.

———. "American Watersheds." *American Quarterly* 13 (1961): pp. 480–94.

———. *Soldiers and Civilians: The Martial Spirit in America, 1775–1865.* Boston: Little, Brown, 1968.

———. "New World, Old World: The Historical Antithesis." In *Lessons from America: an Exploration*, edited by Richard Rose. London: Macmillan, 1974.

———. "The Two or More Worlds of Willa Cather." In *The Arts of Willa Cather*, edited by Bernice Slote and Virginia Faulkner. Lincoln: University of Nebraska Press, 1974.

Cunliffe, Marcus, and Robin Winks, eds. *Pastmasters: Some Essays on American Historians.* New York: Harper and Row, 1969.

Curti, Merle. *American Paradox: The Conflict of Thought and Action.* New Brunswick, N.J.: Rutgers University Press, 1956.

Cusick, Philip A. *Inside High School: The Student's World.* New York: Holt, Rinehart & Winston, 1973.

Custer, George A. *My Life on the Plains, or, Personal Experiences with Indians.* New York: Sheldon, 1874.

Dahl, Robert A. *Who Governs? Democracy and Power in an American City.* New Haven, Conn.: Yale University Press, 1961.

Darrow, Clarence. "Salesmanship." *American Mercury*, August 1925.

Davidson, Thomas. "The Ideal Training of an American Boy." *Forum* 17 (July 1894).

Davis, David Brion. "Some Themes of Countersubversion: An Analysis of Anti-Masonic, Anti-Catholic and Anti-Mormon Literature." *Mississippi Valley Historical Review* 47 (1960): pp. 205–24.

Davis, Richard Harding. "The Thanksgiving Day Game." *Harper's Weekly* (9 December 1893).

Dean, John. *Blind Ambition: The White House Years.* New York: Simon and Schuster, 1976.

DeCharms, Richard, and Gerald H. Moeller. "Values Expressed in American

Children's Readers: 1800–1950." *Journal of Abnormal and Social Psychology* 64 (1962): 136–42.

Degler, Carl N. "The Sociologist as Historian: Riesman's *The Lonely Crowd*." *American Quarterly* 15 (1963): 483–97.

————.*At Odds: Women and the Family in America from the Revolution to the Present*. New York: Oxford University Press, 1980.

Devlin, Patrick. *Too Proud to Fight: Woodrow Wilson's Neutrality*. New York: Oxford University Press, 1974.

DeVos, George. "National Character." In *The International Encyclopedia of the Social Sciences*. New York: Collier Macmillan, 1968, 2:14–19.

Dickey, James. *Deliverance*. Boston:Houghton Mifflin, 1970.

————."The Playboy Interview: James Dickey." *Playboy*, November 1973. *See also* Norman, Geoffrey.

Dingwall, Eric John. *The American Woman: An Historical Study*. London: Duckworth, 1956.

Dizikes, John. *Sportsmen and Gamesmen*. Boston: Houghton Mifflin, 1981.

Dornbusch, Sanford M., and Lauren C. Hickman. "Other-Directedness in Consumer-Goods Advertising: A Test of Riesman's Historical Theory." *Social Forces* 38 (1959): 99–102.

Doughty, Howard. *Francis Parkman*. New York: Macmillan, 1962.

Douglas, Ann. *The Feminization of American Culture*. New York: Knopf, 1977.

Dreiser, Theodore. *The Titan*. New York: Lane, 1914.

————. *Twelve Men*. New York: Boni and Liveright, 1919.

Drought, James. *The Enemy*. Norwalk, Conn.: Skylight, 1964.

Dyer, Wayne. *Your Erroneous Zones*. New York: Crowell, 1976.

Ellis, Edward S. *Nathan Todd: Or, the Fate of the Sioux Captive*. New York: Beadle's, 1860.

————. *Seth Jones: Or, the Captives of the Frontier*. New York: Beadle's, 1877.

————. *The Lost Trail*. New York: Beadle's, 1885.

Emerson, Ralph Waldo. *Selected Prose and Poetry*. Edited by Reginald L. Cook. San Francisco: Rinehart, 1950. Includes "The American Scholar (1837), "Self-Reliance" (1841), and "Circles" (1841).

————. "Success." In *Society and Solitude*. Boston: Fields, Osgood, 1880.

————. "Wealth." In *The Conduct of Life*. Boston: Houghton Mifflin, 1860.

Epstein, Joseph. *Ambition: The Secret Passion*. New York: Dutton, 1980.

Eriksman, Fred. "The Strenuous Life in Practise: The School and Sports Stories of Ralph Henry Barbour." *Rocky Mountain Social Science Journal* 7 (1970): 29ff.

Erikson, Erik H. *Childhood and Society*. New York: Norton, 1950.

Eysenck, H. J. *The Psychology of Politics*. London: Routledge and Kegan Paul, 1954.

Fairlie, Henry. *The Kennedy Promise*. Garden City, N.Y.: Doubleday, 1973.

Farber, Maurice L. "English and Americans: A Study in National Character." *Journal of Psychology* 32 (1951): 241–49.

———. "English and Americans: Values in the Socialization Process." *Journal of Psychology* 36 (1953): 243–50.

Farrell, James T. *Studs Lonigan*. 3 vols. New York: Vanguard, 1932, 1934, 1936.

Fasteau, Marc Feigen. *The Male Machine*. New York: McGraw-Hill, 1975.

Feiffer, Jules, ed. *The Great Comic Book Heroes*. New York: Dial, 1965.

Fellman, Michael. *The Unbounded Frame: Freedom and Community in Nineteenth Century Utopianism*. Westport, Conn.: Greenwood, 1973.

Fender, Stephen. *Plotting the Golden West: American Literature and the Rhetoric of the California Trail*. Cambridge: Cambridge University Press, 1982.

Fiedler, Leslie A. *Love and Death in the American Novel*. New York: Criterion, 1960.

———. *The Return of the Vanishing American*. New York: Stein and Day. 1968.

Filene, Peter Gabriel. *Him Her Self: Sex Roles in Modern America*. New York: Harcourt, Brace, Johanovich, 1975.

Finlay, John L. "The American Nature of Football." *Intellectual Digest*, June 1972. First published in *Queen's Quarterly*, Ontario.

Fischer, David Hackett. *The Revolution of American Conservatism: The Federalist Party in the Era of Jeffersonian Democracy*. New York: Harper and Row, 1965.

———. *Growing Old in America*. New York: Oxford University Press, 1977, expanded 1978.

Fischer, David Hackett, and Lawrence Stone. "Growing Old: An Exchange." *New York Review of Books*, 15 September 1977, 47–49.

Foner, Eric. *Tom Paine and Revolutionary America*. New York: Oxford University Press, 1976.

Foraker, Joseph. *Notes of a Busy Life*. Cincinnati: Stewart and Kidd, 1916.

Fox, Daniel M. *The Discovery of Abundance: Simon N. Patten and the Transformation of Social Theory*. Ithaca, N.Y.: Cornell University Press, 1967.

Fraser, John. *America and the Patterns of Chivalry*. Cambridge: Cambridge University Press, 1982.

Fredrickson, George M. *The Inner Civil War: Northern Intellectuals and the Crisis of the Nation*. New York: Harper and Row, 1965.

French, Philip. *Westerns: Aspects of a Movie Genre*. New York: Oxford University Press, 1973.

Friedman, Bruce Jay. *The Dick*. New York: Knopf, 1970.

Friedsan, H. J. "Bureaucrats as Heroes." *Social Forces* 32 (1954): 269ff.

Fromm, Erich, and Michael Maccoby. *Social Character in a Mexican Village.* Englewood Cliffs, N.J.: Prentice-Hall, 1970.

Fullerton, Ronald A. "Toward a Commercial Popular Culture in Germany: The Development of Pamphlet Fiction, 1871–1914." *Journal of Social History* 12 (1979): 490ff.

Gaddis, William "The Rush for Seond Place." *Harper's Magazine*, April 1981, 31–39.

Gans, Herbert J. *The Urban Villagers: Group and Class in the Life of Italian-Americans.* New York: Free Press, 1962.

———. "Symbolic Ethnicity: The Future of Ethnic Groups and Cultures in America." In *On the Making of Americans: Essays in Honor of David Riesman,* edited by Gans, Nathan Glazer, Joseph R. Gusfield, and Christopher Jencks. Philadelphia: University of Pennsylvania Press, 1979.

Gardner, Paul. *Nice Guys Finish Last: Sport and American Life.* London: Lane, 1974.

Gerry, Christopher. "Becoming Adult: Social Roles and Values in Selected American Adolescent Fiction, 1865–1915." Ph.D. diss., University of Sussex, 1982.

Gilder, George. *Wealth and Poverty.* New York: Basic Books, 1981.

Gilmore, Michael T. "Eulogy as Symbolic Biography: The Inconography of Revolutionary Leadership, 1776–1826." In *Studies in Biography,* edited by Daniel Aaron. Cambridge: Harvard University Press, 1978.

Golde, Roger A. "Are Your Meetings Like This One?" *Harvard Business Review* 50 (1972): 68ff.

Goldthorpe, John, David Lockwood, Frank Beckhofer, and Jennifer Platt. *The Affluent Worker: Political Attitudes and Behavior.* Cambridge: Cambridge University Press, 1968.

Goldwater, Barry. *The Conscience of a Conservative.* New York: Victor, 1960.

Gorer, Geoffrey. *The American People: A Study in National Character.* New York: Norton, 1948.

———. "English Character in the Twentieth Century." *Annals of the American Academy of Political and Social Science* 44 (1967): 77ff.

Gossett, Thomas F. *Race: The History of an Idea in America.* Dallas: Southern Methodist University Press, 1965.

Grand, Sara. "The Man of the Moment." *North American Review* 158 (1894): 626–27.

Graney, Marshall. "Role Models in Children's Readers." *School Review* 85 (1977): 247ff.

Grant, Michael. *See* Cicero, Marcus Tullius.

Greene, Theodore. *America's Heroes: The Changing Models of Success in American Magazines.* New York: Oxford University Press, 1970.

Greenstein, Fred. "New Light on Changing American Values: A Forgotten Body of Survey Data." *Social Forces* 42 (1964): 441–50.

Greven, Philip. *The Protestant Temperament: Patterns of Childrearing, Religious Experience, and the Self in Early America.* New York: Knopf, 1977.

Grey, Zane. *The Last Trail: A Story of Early Days in the Ohio Valley.* New York: Burt, 1909.

———. *The Heritage of the Desert.* New York: Harper, 1910.

———. *Riders of the Purple Sage: A Novel.* New York: Grosset and Dunlap, 1912.

———. *The Lone Star Ranger: A Romance of the Border.* New York: Grosset and Dunlap, 1914.

———. *The Man of the Forest: A Novel.* New York: Grosset and Dunlap, 1920.

———. "The Man Who Influenced Me Most." *American Magazine* 102 (August 1926): 52–55, 130–36.

———. *The Dude Ranger.* New York: Black, 1931.

Grieg, Peter. "So Soft, So Pampered." *Daily Express*, (London) 11 November 1972.

Grund, Francis J. *Aristocracy in America: From the Sketch-Book of a German Nobleman.* London: Bentley, 1839.

Gunderson, Robert Gray. *The Log-Cabin Campaign.* Lexington, Ky.: University of Kentucky Press, 1957.

Gurko, Leo. *Heroes, Highbrows, and the Popular Mind.* Indianapolis: Bobbs-Merrill, 1953.

Guttman, Allen. *From Ritual to Record: The Nature of Modern Sports.* New York: Columbia University Press, 1976.

Guzzardi, Walter. "The Young Executive." *Fortune* series, June, July, September, and October, 1964.

Hailey, Arthur. *Hotel.* Garden City, N.Y.: Doubleday, 1965.

———. *Airport.* Garden City, N.Y.: Doubleday, 1968.

Halberstam, David. *The Best and the Brightest.* New York: Random House, 1972.

Hale, Nathan C. *Freud and the Americans: The Beginnings of Psychoanalysis in the United States, 1876–1917.* New York: Oxford University Press, 1971.

Haley, Bruce. *The Healthy Body and Victorian Culture.* Cambridge: Harvard University Press, 1979.

Hall, G. Stanley. *Adolescence: Its Psychology and Its Relationships to Physiology, Anthropology, Sociology, Sex, Crime, Religion and Education.* 2 vols. New York: Appleton, 1904.

Hamilton, W. J. *Old Avoirdupois: Or, Steel Coat, the Apache Terror.* New York: Beadle's, 1872.

Hammett, Dashiell. *The Dain Curse*. New York: Knopf, 1928.

———. *Red Harvest*. New York: Knopf, 1929.

———. *The Maltese Falcon*. New York: Knopf, 1930.

Hannerz, Ulf. *Soulside: Enquiries into Ghetto Culture and Community*. New York: Columbia University Press, 1969.

Harris, Neil. *The Artist in American Society: the Formative Years, 1790–1860*. New York: Braziller, 1966.

———. *Humbug: The Art of P. T. Barnum*. Boston: Little, Brown, 1973.

Harrison, William H. *A Discourse on the Aboriginees of the Valley of the Ohio*. Cincinnati: Historical Society of Ohio, 1839.

Hart, James D. *The Popular Book: A History of America's Literary Taste*. New York: Oxford University Press, 1950.

Hart, Vivien. *Distrust and Democracy: Political Distrust in Britain and America*. Cambridge: Cambridge University Press, 1978.

Hartshorne, Thomas L. *The Distorted Image: Changing Conceptions of the American Character Since Turner*. Cleveland: Press of Case Western Reserve University, 1968.

Hartz, Louis. *The Liberal Tradition in America: An Interpretation of American Political Thought since the Revolution*. New York: Harcourt, Brace and World, 1955.

Hawkins, M. J. "The Government: Its Role and Its Aim." In *The Origins of the English Civil War*, edited by Conrad Russell. London: Macmillan, 1973.

Hawley, Cameron. *Executive Suite*. Boston: Houghton Mifflin, 1954.

Hawthorne, Nathaniel. *Mosses from an Old Manse*. New York: Wiley and Putnam, 1846.

Heilbroner, Robert L. *Marxism: For and Against*. New York: Norton, 1980.

Hemingway, Ernest. *Death in the Afternoon*. New York: Scribner's, 1932.

———. *To Have and Have Not*. New York: Scribner's, 1937.

———. *Islands in the Stream*. New York: Scribner's, 1970. Posthumously published.

Henretta, James A. *The Evolution of American Society, 1700–1815: An Interdisciplinary Analysis*. Lexington, Mass.: Heath, 1973.

———. "Families and Farms: Mentalité in Pre-industrial America." *William and Mary Quarterly* 35 (1978): pp. 3–32.

Henty, G. A. *Beric the Briton: A Story of the Roman Invasion*. London: Blackie, 1893.

Herrick, Robert. *The Master of the Inn*. New York: Scribners, 1913.

Higginson, Thomas Wentworth. *Army Life in a Black Regiment*. Boston: Field, Osgood, 1870.

Higham, John. "The Cult of the American Consensus." *Commentary* 27 (February 1959): 93–100.

————. "The Reorientation of American Culture in the 1890s." In *Writing American History: Essays on Modern Scholarship*. Bloomington: Indiana University Press, 1970.

Himes, Chester. *Pinktoes*. New York: Putnam, 1965.

Himmelfarb, Gertrude. *Victorian Minds*. New York: Knopf, 1968.

Hoffman, Stanley. *Gulliver's Troubles, or the Setting of American Foreign Policy*. New York: McGraw-Hill, 1968.

Hofstadter, Richard. *Social Darwinism in American Thought*. Philadelphia: University of Pennsylvania Press, 1944.

————. *The American Political Tradition and the Men Who Made It*. New York: Knopf, 1948.

————. "Commentary: Have There Been Discernable Shifts in American Values during the Past Generation?" In *The American Style: Essays in Values and Performance*, edited by Elting Morison. New York: Harper and Row, 1958.

————. *Anti-Intellectualism in American Life*. New York: Knopf, 1963.

Hoggart, Richard. *The Uses of Literacy: Aspects of Working-Class Life, with Special Reference to Publications and Entertainments*. London: Chatto and Windus, 1957).

Holmes, Oliver Wendell, Sr. *Elsie Venner: A Romance of Destiny*. Boston: Ticknor and Fields, 1861.

Holmes, Oliver Wendell, Jr. *The Mind and Faith of Justice Holmes: His Speeches, Essays, Letters and Judicial Opinions*. Edited by Max Lerner. New York: Random House, 1943.

Honey, J. R. *Tom Brown's Universe: the Development of the Public School in the 19th Century*. London: Millington, 1977.

Hoover, Herbert. *American Individualism*. New York: Doubleday, Page, 1922.

————. "Rugged Individualism." Speech presented on 22 October 1928, in New York. Reprinted in *Great Issues in American History: from Reconstruction to the Present Day, 1864–1969*, edited by Richard Hofstadter. New York: Knopf, 1958, revised 1969, Part VI, Document 8.

Hough, Emerson. *The Story of the Cowboy*. New York: Appleton, 1897.

Houghton, Walter E. *The Victorian Frame of Mind, 1830–1870*. New Haven, Conn.: Yale University Press, 1957.

Household, Geoffrey. *Rogue Male*. London: Chatto and Windus, 1939.

Howells, W. D. *A Boy's Town: Described for Harper's Young People*. New York: Harper, 1890.

Hsu, Francis L. K. "American Core Value and National Character." In *Psychological Anthropology*, edited by Francis L. K. Hsu. Homewood, Ill.: Dorsey, 1961.

Hubbard, Elbert. *No Enemy But Himself*. New York: Putnam, 1894.

————. "A Message to Garcia." *Philistine* March 1889. Reprinted in *Back-*

bone Hints for the Prevention of Jelly-Spine Curvature and Mental Squint, edited by S. DeWitt Clough. Chicago: Clough, 1908.

————. *The Olympians: A Tribute to 'Tall, Sun-Crowned Men*. East Aurora, N.Y.: Roycrofters, 1921.

Hudson, Liam. *The Cult of the Fact*. London: Cape, 1972.

Hughes, Thomas. *Tom Brown's School Days. By an Old Boy*. Cambridge, England: Macmillan, 1857.

————. *The Manliness of Christ*. London: Macmillan, 1879.

Hulbert, Ann. "Friends for Now." *Harper's Magazine*, April 1982, 101–3.

Hutt, Corinne. *Males and Females*. Harmondsworth: Penguin, 1972.

Ilchman, Warren F. *Professional Diplomacy in the United States, 1779–1939*. Chicago: Chicago University Press, 1961.

Ives, Charles. *Essays Before a Sonata*. Edited by Howard Boatright. New York: Norton, 1961.

Jackson, Andrew. *Correspondence of Andrew Jackson*. Edited by John Spencer Bassett, II. Washington, D. C.: Carnegie Institution, 1926–35.

Jahoda, Marie. "The Migration of Psychoanalysis: Its Impact on American Psychology." *Perspectives in American History* 2 (1968): 420–45.

James, William. *Pragmatism: A New Name for Some Old Ways of Thinking*. New York: Longman, Green, 1907.

————. "The Moral Equivalent of War" (1910). In *Essays on Faith and Morals*, edited by Ralph Barton Percy. New York: Longmans, Green, 1943.

Jefferson, Thomas. *The Adams-Jefferson Letters*. Edited by Lester J. Cappon, II. Chapel Hill: University of North Carolina Press, 1959.

Jenkins, Dan. *Semi-Tough*. New York: Athenaeum, 1972.

Jennings, Eugene Emerson. *Routes to the Executive Suite*. New York: McGraw-Hill, 1971.

Jerome, John. *Truck: On Rebuilding a Worn-Out Pickup and Other Post-Technological Adventures*. Boston: Houghton Mifflin, 1977.

Johnson, Hugh. *The Blue Eagle from Egg to Earth*. Garden City, N.Y.: Doubleday, 1935.

Johnson, Owen. *The Varmint: A Lawrenceville Story*. Boston: Little, Brown, 1910.

————. *Stover at Yale*. New York: Grosset and Dunlap, 1912.

Jones, Howard Mumford. *The Pursuit of Happiness*. Cambridge: Harvard University Press, 1953.

Kammen, Michael. *People of Paradox: An Enquiry Concerning the Origins of American Civilization*. New York: Knopf, 1972.

————. *A Season of Youth: The American Revolution in the Historical Imagination*. New York: Knopf, 1978.

Kammen, Michael, ed. *The Contrapuntal Civilization: Essays towards a New Understanding of the American Experience*. New York: Crowell, 1971.

Kasson, John. *Civilizing the Machine: Technology and Republican Values in America, 1776–1900*. New York: Grossman, 1976.

Kearns, Doris. *Lyndon Johnson and the American Dream*. New York: Harper and Row, 1976.

Kennan, George. "The Sources of Soviet Conduct." *Foreign Affairs* 25 (July 1947): 566–82. Under pseudonym, "X."

Kennedy, David M. *Over Here: The First World War and American Society*. New York: Oxford University Press, 1980.

Kennedy, John F. "We Must Climb to the Hilltop." *Life*, 26 September 1960, 68ff.

———. "The Soft American" (1960). In *Sport and Society: An Anthology*, edited by John T. Talamini and Charles H. Page. Boston: Little, Brown, 1973.

Kerber, Linda. "The Republican Mother: Women and the Enlightenment—an American Perspective." *American Quarterly* 28 (1976): 187ff.

Kesey, Ken. *Sometimes a Great Notion*. New York: Viking, 1964.

Kidder, Tracy. "Flying Upside Down." *Atlantic Monthly* 248 (July 1981): 54–64.

———. *The Soul of a New Machine*. Boston: Little, Brown, 1981.

King, Florence. "The Niceness Factor: Good Guyism in America." *Harper's Magazine*, October 1981, 60–64.

Kingsley, Charles. *Hereward the Wake*. Cambridge, England: Macmillan, 1866).

———. *His Letters and Memoirs of His Life*. Edited by Mrs. Charles Kingsley. London: King, 1877.

Kipling, Rudyard. *Captains Courageous: A Story of the Grand Banks*. London: Macmillan, 1898.

Kirkendall, Richard. "Franklin D. Roosevelt and the Service Intellectual." *Mississippi Valley Historical Review* 49 (1962–63):456–71.

Kissinger, Henry. *The White House Years*. Boston:Little, Brown, 1979.

Klapp, Orrin E. "The Folk Hero." *Journal of American Folklore* 62 (1949): 17–25.

———. "The Clever Hero." *Journal of American Folklore* 67 (1954): 21–34.

———. *Heroes, Villains and Fools: The Changing American Character*. Englewood Cliffs, N.J.: Prentice-Hall, 1962.

Kleiman, Robert. "The Air War in Indochina." *New York Times*, 28 August 1972.

Kluckhohn, Clyde. "Have There Been Discernable Shifts in American Values during the Past Generation?" In *The American Style: Essays in Values and Performance*, edited by Elting Morison. New York: Harper and Row, 1958.

Komisar, Lucy. "Violence and the Masculine Mystique." *Washington Monthly*, July 1970, 39–48.

Kraft, Joseph. "The Two Worlds of McGeorge Bundy." *Harper's Magazine* 231 (November 1965): 106–16.

Kramer, Jane. *The Last Cowboy*. New York: Harper and Row, 1977.

Kyne, Peter B. *The Go-Getter: A Story That Tells You How to Be One*. New York: Cosmopolitan, 1921.

Lacey, Robert. "Monkey Business." *Sunday Times Magazine* (London), 19 April 1972, 54–69. On Tarzan and Edgar Rice Burroughs.

L'Amour, Louis. *Hondo*. New York: Fawcett, 1953.

Lane; R. E. "The Fear of Equality." *American Political Science Review* 53 (1959): 35ff.

Lapham, Lewis. "Intimations of Mortality: Notes on the Restoration of Harper's Magazine." *Harper's Magazine*, September 1980.

———. "Gilding the News." *Harper's Magazine*, July 1981.

LaPorte, Todd, and Daniel Metlay. *They Watch and Wonder: Public Attitudes towards Advanced Technology*. Berkeley: University of California Press, 1975.

Lasch, Christopher. *The Culture of Narcissism: American Life in an Age of Diminishing Expectations*. New York: Norton, 1979.

———. "Politics and Social Theory: A Reply to the Critics." *Salmagundi* 46 (Fall 1979):194–202. Symposium on The Culture of Narcissism.

Leach, William. *True Love and Perfect Union: The Feminist Reform of Sex and Society*. New York: Basic Books, 1980.

Lears, T. J. Jackson. *No Place of Grace: Antimodernism and the Transformation of American Culture, 1880–1920*. New York: Pantheon, 1981.

Lederer, William J. *Ensign O'Toole and Me*. New York: Norton, 1957.

———. *A Nation of Sheep*. New York: Norton, 1961.

———. *Our Own Worst Enemy*. New York: Norton, 1968.

Lederer, William J., and Eugene Burdick. *The Ugly American*. New York: Norton, 1958.

Lederer, Wolfgang. *The Fear of Women*. New York: Grune and Stratton, 1968.

Lee, Harper. *To Kill a Mockingbird*. Philadelphia: Lippincott, 1960.

LeMasters, E. E. *Parents in Modern America*. Homewood, Ill.: Dorsey, 1970, revised 1977.

———. *Blue-Collar Aristocrats: Life Styles at a Working-Class Tavern*. Madison: University of Wisconsin Press, 1975.

Letwin, William. "The Past and Future of the American Businessman." *Daedalus* 98 (Winter 1969): 1–22.

Leuchtenburg, William E. *Franklin D. Roosevelt and the New Deal: 1932–1940*. New York: Harper and Row, 1963.

———. "The New Deal and the Analogue of War." In *Change and Continuity in Twentieth-Century America*, edited by John Braeman, Robert H. Bremner, and Everett Walters. Columbia: University of Ohio Press, 1964.

Levine, Lawrence W. *Black Culture and Black Consciousness: Afro-American Thought from Slavery to Freedom*. New York: Oxford University Press, 1977.

Lewis, Oscar. *Five Families: Mexican Case Studies in the Culture of Poverty*. New York: Basic Books, 1959.

Lewis, Sinclair. *Babbitt*. New York: Harcourt, Brace and World, 1922.

———. *Arrowsmith*. New York: Harcourt, Brace and World, 1924.

Lilienthal, David. *The Journals of David Lilienthal*. Vol. 1, *The TVA Years, 1939–1945*. New York: Harper and Row, 1964.

Lipset, Seymour Martin. "Three Decades of the Radical Right: Coughlinites, McCarthyites, and Birchers." In *The Radical Right*, edited by Daniel Bell. Garden City: Doubleday, 1963.

———. *The First New Nation*. New York: Basic Books, 1963.

Lipset, Seymour Martin, and Richard B. Dobson. "The Intellectual as Critic and Rebel," *Daedalus* 101 (1972): 137–98.

Lipset, Seymour Martin, and Leo Lowenthan, eds. *Culture and Social Character: The Works of David Riesman Reviewed*. New York: Free Press, 1961.

Livius, Titus. *Livy: The Early History of Rome*. Introduction by R. M. Ogilvie. Harmondsworth: Penguin, 1960.

Lohoff, B. A. "Herbert Hoover, Spokesman of Humane Efficiency: The Mississippi Flood of 1927." *American Quarterly* 22 (1970): 690–700.

London, Jack. *A Daughter of the Snows*. Philadelphia: Lippincott, 1902.

———. *The Call of the Wild*. New York: Macmillan, 1903.

———. *The Sea-Wolf*. New York: Macmillan, 1904.

———. *The Game*. New York: Macmillan, 1905.

———. *Before Adam*. New York: Macmillan, 1906.

———. *The Iron Heel*. New York: Macmillan, 1907.

———. *The Road*. New York: Macmillan, 1907.

———. *The Valley of the Moon*. New York: Macmillan, 1913.

———. *Letters from Jack London*. Edited by King Hendricks and Irving Shepard. New York: Odyssey, 1965.

Longmate, Norman. *The G.I.s: The Americans in Britain, 1942–1945*. New York: Scribner's, 1975.

Lorimer, George Horace. *Letters from a Self-Made Merchant to His Son*. Boston: Small, Maynard. 1902.

Lowenthal, Leo. "Biographies in Popular Magazines." In *Radio Research, 1942–43*, edited by Paul F. Lazarsfeld and Frank N. Stanton. New York: Essential Books, 1944.

Lydall, Harold, and John B. Lansing. "A Comparison of Personal Income and Wealth in the United States and Great Britain." *American Economic Review* 49 (1959): 43ff.

Lynd, Robert S. *Knowledge for What: The Place of Social Science in American Culture*. Princeton: Princeton University Press, 1939.

Lynn, Kenneth S. *The Dream of Success*. Boston: Little, Brown, 1955.

Lyttelton, E. "Endure Hardness." In *Essays on Duty and Discipline*. London: Cassell, 1910.

McClelland, David. *The Achieving Society*. New York: Free Press, 1961.

Maccoby, Eleanor Emmons, and Carol Nagy Jacklin, *The Psychology of Sex Differences*. Stanford, Calif.: Stanford University Press, 1974.

Maccoby, Michael. *The Gamesman: The New Corporate Leaders*. New York: Simon and Schuster, 1976.

Macdonald, Dwight. *Against the American Grain*. New York: Random House, 1962.

MacDonald, Ross. *The Moving Target*. New York: Knopf, 1949.

McDougall, Robert L. "The Dodo and the Cruising Auk: Class in Canadian Literature." *Canadian Literature* (Autumn 1963): 6–20.

MacFarlane, Rob. "Mid-Victorian Ideals of Manliness: A Study of Two Exponents—Thomas Hughes and Samuel Smiles." Master's thesis, University of Sussex, 1981.

McGiffert, Michael, ed. *The Character of Americans: A Book of Readings*. Homewood, Ill.: Dorsey, 1964, revised 1970.

McGovern, James R. "David Graham Phillips and the Virility Impulse of Progressives," *New England Quarterly* 39 (1966): 334–55.

Mackenzie, Gavin. *The Aristocracy of Labor: The Position of Skilled Craftsmen in the American Class Structure*. New York: Cambridge University Press, 1973.

Mackenzie, Norman. *Women in Australia*. London: Angus and Robertson, 1963.

McKern, Sharon. *Redneck Mothers, Good Ol' Girls, and Other Southern Belles: A Celebration of the Women in Dixie*. New York: Viking, 1979.

McLachlan, James. *American Boarding Schools: A Historical Study*. New York: Scribner's 1970.

McPartland, John. "Footnote on Sex." *Harper's Magazine*, March 1942, 212ff.

Macrae, Norman. "Intrapreneurial Now." *Economist* 17 April 1982, 47–82.

Madden, David, ed. *Tough Guy Writers of the Thirties*. Carbondale: University of Southern Illinois Press, 1968.

Mailer, Norman. *Advertisements for Myself*. New York: Putnam, 1959.

Malia, Martin. "The Intellectuals: Adversaries or Clerisy?" *Daedalus* 101 (Summer 1972): 206–16.

Maliver, Bruce L. "Encounter Groupers Up Against the Wall." *New York Times Magazine*, 3 January 1971.

Mallan, John P. "Roosevelt, Brooks Adams, and Lea: The Warrior Critique of Business Civilization." *American Quarterly* 8 (1956): 216–30.

Marckwardt, Albert H. *American English*. New York: Oxford University Press, 1958.

Marden, Orison. *Architects of Fate, or Steps to Success and Power*. Boston: Houghton Mifflin, 1895.

Marinetti, Filippo Tommaso. *Selected Writings*. Edited by R. W. Flint. London: Secker and Warburg, 1972.

Martineau, Harriet. *Society in America*. New York: Saunders and Otlay, 1837.

Marx, Leo. "Two Kingdoms of Force." *Massachusetts Review* 1 (1959): 62–95.

———. *The Machine in the Garden: Technology and the Pastoral Ideal in America*. New York: Oxford University Press, 1964.

———. "Noble Shit": The Uncivil Response of American Writers to Civil Religion in America." *Massachusetts Review* 14 (1973): 709ff.

Masters, John. *Far, Far the Mountain Peak*. London: Joseph, 1957.

Mathews, Mitford M. *A Dictionary of Americanisms, on Historical Principles*. Chicago: University of Chicago Press, 1951.

Matusow, Allen J., ed. *Joseph R. McCarthy*. Englewood Cliffs, N.J.: Prentice-Hall, 1970.

Matza, David, and Gresham Sykes. "Juvenile Delinquency and Subterranean Values." *American Sociological Review* 26 (1961): 712–19.

Mead, Margaret. *And Keep Your Powder Dry: An Anthropologist Looks at America*. New York: Morrow, 1941, expanded 1965.

———. "Why We Americans 'Talk Big.' " *Listener*, 28 October 1943.

———. *Male and Female: A Study of the Sexes in a Changing World*. New York: Morrow, 1949, new introductions 1962, 1967.

Media Institute. *Crooks, Conmen and Clowns: Businessmen in TV Entertainment*. Washington, D.C.: Media Institute, 1981.

Mellen, Joan. *Big Bad Wolves: Masculinity in the American Film*. New York: Pantheon, 1978.

Mellers, Wilfred. *Music in a New Found Land: Themes and Developments in the History of American Music*. London: Barrie and Rockliffe, 1964.

Melville, Herman. "Hawthorne and His Mosses, by a Virginian Spending July in Vermont" (1850). Reprinted in *The Portable Melville*, edited by Jay Leyda. New York: Viking, 1952.

Menzies, Hugh O. "The Ten Toughest Bosses." *Fortune*, 21 April 1980, pp. 62–72.

Middlekauf, Robert. "The Ritualization of the American Revolution." In *The Development of an American Culture*, edited by Stanley Coben and Lorman Ratner. Englewood Cliffs, N.J.: Prentice-Hall, 1970.

Miller, Lillian B. "Paintings, Sculpture and the National Character, 1815–1860." *Journal of American History* 53 (1967): 696ff.

Miller, Perry. "From Government to Revival." In *The Shaping of American*

Religion, edited by James Ward Smith and A. Leland Jameson. Princeton: Princeton University Press, 1961.

Millett, Kate. *Sexual Politics*. New York: Doubleday, 1970.

Mills, C. Wright. *The Power Elite*. New York: Oxford University Press, 1956.

Milton, John R. *The Novel of the American West*. Lincoln: University of Nebraska Press, 1980.

Minturn, Leigh, and William W. Lambert. *Mothers of Six Cultures: Antecedents of Child Rearing*. New York: Wiley, 1964.

Moley, Raymond. *After Seven Years*. New York: Harper, 1939.

Monaghan, Jay [James Monaghan]. *Custer: The Life of General George Armstrong Custer*. Boston: Little, Brown, 1959.

Moore, Arthur K. *The Frontier Mind: A Cultural Analysis of the Kentucky Frontiersman*. Lexington, Ky.: University of Kentucky Press, 1957.

Morgan, Edmund S. "The Puritan Ethic and the American Revolution." *William and Mary Quarterly* 24 (1967): 3ff.

Morris, Willie. *North toward Home*. Boston: Houghton Mifflin, 1967.

Muensterberg, Hugo. *American Traits from the Point of View of a German*. Boston: Houghton Mifflin, 1901.

Nash, Roderick. *Wilderness and the American Mind*. New Haven, Conn.: Yale University Press, 1967.

Nevins, Allan, and Frank Weitenkampf, eds. *A Century of Political Cartoons*. New York: Scribner's, 1944.

Newsome, David. *Godliness and Good Learning: Four Studies on a Victorian Ideal*. London: Murray, 1961.

Niles, Hezekiah, ed. *Centennial Offering Republication of the Principles and Acts of the Revolution in America*. Chicago: Barnes, 1876.

Norman, Geoffrey. "The Stuff of Poetry: James Dickey." *Playboy*, May 1971.

Norris, Frank. *Moran of the Lady Letty: A Story of Adventure off the California Coast*. New York: Doubleday, 1898.

————. *McTeague: A Story of San Francisco*. New York: Doubleday, 1899.

————. *The Octopus: A Story of California*. New York: Doubleday, 1901.

————. *The Pitt: A Story of Chicago*. New York: Doubleday, 1903.

————. *The Responsibility of the Novelist, and Other Literary Essays*. New York: Doubleday, 1903.

————. *Vandover and the Brute*. New York: Doubleday, 1914. Written probably before 1897.

Norton, Mary Beth. *Liberty's Daughters: The Revolutionary Experience of American Women, 1750–1800*. Boston: Little, Brown, 1980.

Nye, Russell B. "The Juvenile Approach to American Culture, 1870–1930." In *New Voices in American Studies*, edited by Ray B. Browne. West Lafayette: Purdue University Press, 1966.

Ong, Walter J. *Fighting for Life: Contest, Sexuality and Consciousness*. Ithaca: Cornell University Press, 1981.

Opinion Research Corporation. *Attitudes of the U.S. Public toward Science and Technology*, Study III. Princeton: Opinion Research Corp., 1976.

Orwell, George [Eric Blair]. *The Road to Wigan Pier*. London: Gollancz, 1937.

Oxford English Dictionary. *On Historical Principles*. 13 vols. Edited by James A. H. Murray, Henry Bradley, W. A. Craigie, and C. T. Onions. Oxford: Oxford University Press, 1933.

Parkman, Francis. *The California and Oregon Trail: Being Sketches of Prairie and Rocky Mountain Life*. New York: Putnam, 1849.

――――. *The Journals of Francis Parkman*. Edited by Mason Wade. Vol 1. New York: Harper, 1947.

――――. *The Letters of Francis Parkman*. Ed. by Wilbur R. Jacobs. Vol. 1, 1841–1865. Norman: University of Oklahoma Press, 1960.

――――. *La Salle and the Discovery of the Great West*. Boston: Little Brown, 1879.

Parsons, Talcott. "Certain Primary Sources and Patterns of Aggression in the Social Structure of the Western World." *Psychiatry* 10 (1947): 167–81.

Parsons, Talcott, and R. F. Bales. *Family, Socialization and Interaction*. Glencoe, Ill.: Free Press, 1953.

Partridge, Eric. *Dictionary of Historical Slang*. Harmondsworth: Penguin, 1972.

Pascale, Richard Tanner, and Anthony G. Athos. *The Art of Japanese Management: Applications for American Executives*. New York: Simon and Schuster, 1981.

Patten, Simon N. *The New Basis of Civilization*. New York: Macmillan, 1907.

Paz, Octavio. *The Labyrinth of Solitude: Life and Thought in Mexico*. New York: Grove, 1962.

Peale, Norman Vincent. *The Power of Positive Thinking*. Englewood Cliffs, N.J.: Prentice-Hall, 1952.

Pearce, Roy. *Savagism and Civilization: A Study of the Indian and the American Mind*. Baltimore: John Hopkins Press, 1967.

Peck, John M. "The Life of Daniel Boone." In *The Lives of Daniel Boone and Benjamin Lincoln*, edited by Jared Sparks. Boston: Little, Brown, 1847.

Perry, George, and Alan Aldridge, eds. *The Penguin Book of Comics: A Slight History*. Harmondsworth: Penguin, 1967, revised 1971.

Pessen, Edward. *Jacksonian America: Society, Personality and Politics*. Homewood, Ill.: Dorsey, 1969.

Phelps, Stanlee, and Nancy Austin. *The Assertive Woman*. San Luis Obispo, Calif.: Impact, 1975.

Phillips, David Graham. *The Second Generation*. New York: Appleton, 1907.

Pirsig, Robert M. *Zen and the Art of Motorcycle Maintenance: An Enquiry into Values*. New York: Morrow, 1974.

Pleck, Joseph, and Jack Sawyer, eds. *Men and Masculinity*. Englewood Cliffs, N.J.: Prentice-Hall, 1974.

Pocock, P.G.A. *The Machiavellian Moment: Florentine Republican Thought and the Atlantic Republic Tradition*. Princeton: Princeton University Press, 1975.

Porter, John. "Canadian Character in the Twentieth Century." *Annals of the American Academy of Political and Social Science* 370 (March 1967): 77ff.

Portis, Charles. *True Grit*. New York: Simon and Schuster, 1968.

Potter, David M. *People of Plenty: Economic Abundance and the American Character*. Chicago: University of Chicago Press, 1954.

———. "The Quest for the National Character." In *The Reconstruction of American History*, edited by John Higham. New York: Harper and Row, 1962.

———. "American Individualism in the Twentieth Century." *Texas Quarterly* (Summer 1963). Revised and reprinted in *Innocence and Power: Individualism in Twentieth-Century America*, edited by Gordon Mills. Austin: University of Texas Press, 1965.

Priestley, J. B. *Victoria's Heyday*. London: Heinemann, 1972.

Pringle, Henry F. *Theodore Roosevelt: A Biography*. New York: Harcourt, Brace, 1931.

Pringle, John Douglas. *Australian Accent*. London: Chatto and Windus, 1958.

Puzo, Mario. *The Godfather*. New York: Putnam, 1969.

Pyke, Rafford. "What Men Like in Men." *Cosmopolitan* 33 August 1902.

Pyles, Thomas. *Words and Ways of American English*. New York: Random House, 1952.

Rahv, Philip. *Literature and the Sixth Sense*. Boston: Houghton Mifflin, 1969.

Rand, Ayn. *The Fountainhead*. Indianapolis: Bobbs-Merrill, 1943.

———. *For the New Intellectual: The Philosophy of Ayn Rand*. New York: Random House, 1961.

Rapson, Richard L. "The American Child as Seen by British Travellers, 1845–1935." *American Quarterly* 17 (1965): 520–34.

Rauson, Hugh. *A Dictionary of Euphemisms and Other Double Talk: Being a Compilation of Linguistic Fig Leaves and Verbal Flourishes for Artful Users of the English Language*. New York: Croun, 1981.

Rawlyck, George A. *Nova Scotia's Massachusetts: A Study of Massachusetts-Nova Scotia Relations, 1630–1784*. Montreal: McGill-Queen's University Press, 1973.

Riesman, David. "Some Observations on Changes in Leisure Attitudes." *Antioch Review* 12, no. 4 (1952). Reprinted in Riesman, *Individualism Reconsidered, and other Essays*. Glencoe, Ill.: Free Press, 1954.

———. "Egocentrism: Is the American Character Changing?" *Encounter*, August-September 1980, 19–28.

Riesman, David, and Reuel Denney. "Football in America: A Study in Culture Diffusion." *American Quarterly* 3, no. 4 (1951). Reprinted in Riesman, *Individualism Reconsidered, and Other Essays*. Glencoe, Ill.: Free Press, 1954.

Riesman, David, with Nathan Glazer. *Faces in the Crowd: Individual Studies in Character and Politics*. New Haven, Conn.: Yale University Press, 1952.

Riesman, David, with Nathan Glazer and Reuel Denney. *The Lonely Crowd: A Study of the Changing American Character*. New Haven, Conn.: Yale University Press, 1950.

Ringer, Robert J. *Winning through Intimidation*. Los Angeles: Los Angeles Book Publishers, 1973.

———. *Looking Out for Number One*. New York: Funk and Wagnalls, 1977.

Roberts, Gerald F. "The Strenuous Life: The Cult of Manliness in the Era of Theodore Roosevelt." Ph.D. diss., Michigan State University, (1970).

Rodgers, Daniel T. *The Work Ethic in Industrial America, 1850–1920*. Chicago: University of Chicago Press, 1978.

Rogin, Michael Paul. *The Intellectuals and McCarthy: The Radical Specter*. Cambridge: MIT Press, 1967.

———. *Fathers and Children: Andrew Jackson and the Subjugation of the Indians*. New York: Random House, 1975.

Roosevelt, Theodore. *The Winning of the West: An Account of the Exploration and Settlement of Our Country from the Alleghanies to the Pacific*. 6 vols. New York: Putnam, 1889–97.

———. *The Strenuous Life: Essays and Addresses*. New York: Century, 1900.

———. *An Autobiography*. New York: Macmillan, 1913.

———. *The Writings of Theodore Roosevelt*. Edited by William H. Harbaugh. Indianapolis: Bobbs-Merrill, 1967.

Rosecrance, Richard N. "The Radical Culture of Australia." In *The Founding of New Societies*, edited by Louis Hartz. New York: Harcourt, Brace and World, 1964.

Rosenberg, Charles. "Sexuality, Class and Role in Nineteenth-Century America. *American Quarterly* 25 (1973): 131ff.

Rossiter, Frank. *Charles Ives and His America*. New York: Liveright, 1975.

Rourke, Constance. *American Humor: A Study of the National Character*. New York: Harcourt, Brace, 1931.

Runyon, Damon. *Runyon on Broadway*. Edited by E. C. Bentley. London: Constable, 1970. Contains all stories from *More Than Somewhat* (1937), *Take It East* (1938), and *Furthermore* (1941).

Safire, William. *Safire's Political Dictionary*. New York: Random House, 1978.

Sallust [Gaius Sallustius Crispus]. "The Conspiracy of Cataline." In *Sallust: The Jugurthine War, The Conspiracy of Cataline*, edited by S. A. Handford. Harmondsworth: Penguin, 1963.

Sanford, Charles L. *The Quest for Paradise: Europe and the American Moral Imagination*. Urbana: University of Illinois Press, 1961.

Sanford, R. Nevitt. "The Developmental Status of the Entering Freshman." In *The American College: A Psychological and Social Interpretation of the Higher Learning*, edited by R. Nevitt Sanford. New York: Wiley, 1962.

Sapper [Cyril McNeile]. *Jim Maitland*. London: Hodder and Stoughton, 1923.

Scaduto, Tony. *Frank Sinatra*. London: Joseph, 1976.

Schaefer, Jack. *Shane*. Boston: Houghton Mifflin, 1949.

Schlesinger, Arthur M., Jr. *The Age of Jackson*. Boston: Little, Brown, 1945.

———. *The Age of Roosevelt*. Vol 2, *The Coming of the New Deal*. Boston: Houghton Mifflin, 1958.

———. *The Age of Roosevelt*. Vol. 3, *The Politics of Upheaval*. Boston: Houghton Mifflin, 1960.

———. *Robert Kennedy and His Times*. Boston: Houghton Mifflin, 1978.

Schlissel, Lillian. "Frontier Families: Crisis in Ideology." In *The American Self: Myth, Ideology, and Popular Culture*, edited by Sam B. Girgus. Albuquerque: University of New Mexico Press, 1981.

Schneider, Louis, and Sanford Dornbusch, *Popular Religion: Inspirational Books in America*. Chicago: University of Chicago Press, 1958.

Schrag, Peter. *The Decline of the WASP*. New York: Simon and Schuster, 1971.

Schwartz, Gary, and Don Merten. "The Language of Adolescence: An Anthropological Approach to the Youth Culture." *American Journal of Sociology* 72 (1967): 453–68.

Sebald, Hans D. *Momism: The Silent Disease of America*. Chicago: Nelson-Hall, 1976.

Segal, Ronald. *The Americans: A Conflict of Creed and Reality*. New York: Viking, 1969.

Sexton, Patricia Cayo. *The Feminized Male: Classrooms, White Collars and the Decline of Manliness*. New York: Random House, 1969.

Shannon, William V. *The American Irish: A Political and Social Portrait*. New York: Macmillan, 1963.

Shaw, Peter. "The Tough Guy Intellectual." *Critical Quarterly* 8 (1966): 13–28.

Sherwood, Roert E. *Roosevelt and Hopkins: An Intimate History*. New York: Harper and Row, 1948.

Shipton, Clifford. "The New England Frontier." *New England Quarterly* 10 (1937): 25ff.

Shook, Robert L. *Winning Images*. New York: Macmillan, 1977.

Sigal, Clancy. "Little Italy Gets It Together." *Observer* Magazine. Special issue on "American Style." 13 May 1979.

Sklar, Kathryn Kish. *Catherine Beecher: A Study in American Domesticity*. New Haven, Conn.: Yale University Press, 1973.

Sklar, Robert, ed. *The Plastic Age, 1917–1930*. New York: Braziller, 1970.

Slay, General Alton D. "The Air Force Systems Command Statement on Defense Industry Base Issues." Speech before Preparedness Panel of the House Armed Services Committee, House, 96th Congress, 2d Sess. 13 November 1980.

Slotkin, Richard. *Regeneration through Violence: The Mythology of the American Frontier, 1600–1800*. Middletown, Conn.: Wesleyan University Press, 1973.

Smith, Adam. *Powers of Mind*. New York: Random House, 1975.

Smith, Bradford. *Captain John Smith: His Life and Legend*. Philadelphia: Lippincott, 1953.

Smith, Henry Nash. *Virgin Land: The American West as Symbol and Myth*. Cambridge: Harvard University Press, 1950.

Smith, Manuel J. *When I Say No, I Feel Guilty*. New York: Dial, 1975.

Snowman, Daniel. "The Jewish Stimulus to American Culture." *Jewish Chronicle* Supplement, 5 May 1967, vi–vii.

———. *Britain and America: An Interpretation of British and American Culture, 1945 to 1975*. New York: Harper and Row, 1977.

Sofer, Elaine Graham. "Inner-Direction, Other-Direction, and Autonomy: A Study of College Students." In *Culture and Social Character: The Work of David Riesman Reviewed*, edited by Seymour Martin Lipset and Leo Lowenthal. New York: Free Press, 1961.

Soule, George. "Hard-Boiled Radicalism." *New Republic* 65 (1931): 261–65.

Spate, O.H.K. *Australia*. London: Benn, 1968).

Spillane, Micky [Frank Morrison Spillane]. *My Gun Is Quick*. New York: Dutton, 1950).

———. *The Girl-Hunters*. New York: Dutton, 1962.

Spoto, Donald. *Camerado: Hollywood and the American Man*. New York: New American Library, 1978.

Springall, John O. "Youth and Empire: A Study of the Propagation of Imperialism to the Young in Edwardian Britain." Ph.D. diss., University of Sussex, 1968.

Standish, Burt L. [Gilbert Patten]. "Frank Merriwell's Nobility: Or the Tragedy of the Ocean Tramp."*Tip Top Weekly*, 22 April 1899. Reprinted in *Eight Dime Novels*, edited by E. F. Bleiler. New York: Dover, 1974.

———. *Frank Merriwell's School Days*. New York: Street and Smith, 1901.

———. "On College Battlefields." In *The College Life Series*, vol. I. (New York: Barse and Hopkins, 1917.)

Stearns, Peter N. *Be a Man! Males in Modern Society*. New York: Holmes and Meier, 1979.

Steckmesser, Kent L. "The Frontier Hero in History and Legend." *Wisconsin Magazine of History* 46 (Spring 1963).

———. *The Western Hero in History and Legend*. Norman: University of Oklahoma Press, 1965.

Stegner, Wallace. *The Big Rock Candy Mountain*. New York: Duell, Sloane and Pearce, 1943.

———. "The Personality." In Catherine Drinker Bowen, E. R. Mirrielies, Arthur Schlesinger, Jr., and Wallace Stegner, *Four Portraits and One Subject: Bernard De Voto*. Boston: Houghton Mifflin, 1963.

Steinbeck, John. *The Grapes of Wrath*. New York: Viking, 1939.

Steinem, Gloria. "The Myth of Masculine Mystique." *International Education* 1 (1972): 30–35. Reprinted in *Men and Masculinity*, edited by Joseph H. Pleck and Jack Sawyer. Englewood Cliffs, N.J.: Prentice-Hall, 1974.

Stephens, C. A. "A Terrible Temper." *Youth's Companion*, 25 June 1891.

Stevens, Evelyn P. "Mexican Machismo: Politics and Value Orientations." *Western Political Quarterly* 18 (1965): 484–87.

Stevens, William K. "The Urban Cowboy, 1978 Style." *New York Times*, 10 June 1978, Cl.

Stone, Gregory P. "Halloween and the Mass Child." *American Quarterly* 11 (1959): 372–79.

Stone, Lawrence. "Walking over Grandma." *New York Review of Books*, 12 May 1877, 10–16.

Storr, Anthony. *Human Aggression*. Harmondsworth: Penguin, 1968.

Stout, Rex. *The Hand in the Glove: A Dol Bonner Mystery*. New York: Farrar and Rhinehardt, 1937. Published in the U.K. as *Crime on Her Hands*.

———. *Death of a Dude: A Nero Wolfe Novel*. New York: Viking, 1969.

Strong, Josiah. *Our Country: Its Possible Future and Its Present Crisis*. New York: Home Missionary Society, 1885.

Strout, Cushing. "A Note on Degler, Riesman, and Tocqueville." *American Quarterly* 16 (1964): 100–102.

Sullivan, Frank. *A Pearl in Every Oyster*. Boston: Little, Brown, 1938.

Sumner, William Graham. *"Discipline" and Other Essays from the Collected Works of William Graham Sumner*. New Haven, Conn.: Yale University Press, 1923.

Sykes, Gresham. *The Society of Captives: A Study of a Maximum Security Prison*. Princeton: Princeton University Press, 1958.

Tarkington, Booth. *Penrod*. New York: Doubleday, 1914.

Taviss, Irene. "A Survey of Popular Attitudes toward Technology." *Technology and Culture* 13 (1972): 606ff.

Taylor, Frederick Winslow. *The Principles of Scientific Management*. New York: Harper and Row, 1911.

Taylor, William R. *Cavalier and Yankee: The Old South and American Character*. New York: Braziller, 1961.

Terkel, Studs. *Working: People Talk about What They Do All Day and What They Feel about What They Do*. New York: Pantheon, 1974.

Thomas, John L. "Romantic Reform in America, 1815–1865." *American Quarterly* 17 (1965): 656ff.

Thomas, P. W. "Two Cultures: Court and Country under Charles I." In *The Origins of the English Civil War*, edited by Conrad Russell. London: Macmillan, 1973.

Thompson, Daniel P. *The Green Mountain Boys: A Historical Tale of the Early Settlement of Vermont*. Montpelier, Vt.: Walton, 1839.

Thompson, Robert. *No Exit From Vietnam*. New York: McKay, 1969.

Thompson, Roger. *Women in Stuart England and America: A Comparative Study*. London: Routledge and Kegan Paul, 1974.

Thomson, James C., Jr. "How Could Vietnam Happen: An Autopsy." *Atlantic Monthly* 221 (April 1968): 47–53.

Thornton, Richard H. *An American Glossary: Being an Attempt to Illustrate Certain Americanisms Upon Historical Principles*. Philadelphia: Lippincott, 1912.

Thurber, James. "The Secret Life of Walter Mitty." In *My World—and Welcome to It*. New York: Harcourt, Brace, 1942.

Thurow, Lester C. *The Zero-Sum Society: Distribution and the Possibilities for Economic Change*. New York: Basic Books, 1980.

Tiger, Lionel. *Men in Groups*. New York: Random House, 1969.

Toby, Jackson. "Violence and the Masculine Ideal: Some Qualitative Data." *Annals of the American Academy of Political and Social Science* 364 (1966): 19ff.

Tocqueville, Alexis de. *Democracy in America*. London: Saunders and Ofley, 1835.

Tolson, Andrew. *The Limits of Masculinity*. London:Tavistock, 1977.

TRB. "The Macho of Time." *New Republic* 172 (20–27 August 1977): 2, 42.

Trow, Martin. "Small Businessmen, Political Intolerance and Support for McCarthy." *American Journal of Sociology* 64 (1958): 270–81.

Tuchman, Barbara. *Stilwell and the American Experience in China, 1911–1945*. New York: Macmillan, 1971.

Turner, Frederick Jackson. *The Frontier in American History*. New York: Holt, 1920.

Twain, Mark [Samuel L. Clemens]. *Roughing It*. Hartford, Conn.: American Publishing, 1871.

———. *The Adventures of Tom Sawyer*. Hartford, Conn.: American Publishing, 1876.

———. *Life on the Mississippi*. Boston: Osgood, 1883.

———. *The Adventures of Huckleberry Finn, Tom Sawyer's Comrade*. New York: Webster, 1885.

———. *A Connecticut Yankee in King Arthur's Court*. New York: Webster, 1889.

Tyler, Royall. "The Contrast: The American Son of Liberty" (1787). Reprinted in *Dramas from the American Theater, 1762–1909*, edited by Richard Moody. Cleveland: World, 1966.

Vance, Norman. "The Ideal of Manliness." In *The Victorian Public School: Studies in the Development of an Educational Institution*, edited by Brian Simon and Ian Bradley. Dublin: Gilland Macmillan, 1975.

Van Dyke, Paul. "The College Man in Action." *Scribner's* 65 (May 1919).

Veblen, Thorstein. *The Theory of the Leisure Class: An Economic Study of Institutions*. New York: Macmillan, 1899.

Veroff, Joseph, Elizabeth Douvain and Richard Kulka. *The Inner America: A Self-Portrait, 1956 to 1976*. New York: Basic Books, 1981.

Villa, Pancho. *Memoirs of Pancho Villa*. Edited by Martin Luis Guzman. Austin: University of Texas Press, 1965.

Waldo, Samuel Putnam. *Memoirs of Andrew Jackson*. Hartford, Conn.: Russell, 1818.

Waller, Don D. "Wister, Roosevelt and James: A Note on the Western." *American Quarterly* 12 (1960): 385ff.

Walsh, Mary Roth. *"Doctors Wanted, No Women Need Apply": Sexual Barriers in the Medical Profession, 1835–1975*. New Haven, Conn.: Yale University Press, 1977.

Ward, John William. *Andrew Jackson—Symbol for an Age*. New York: Oxford University Press, 1955.

———. *Red, White and Blue: Men, Books and Ideas in American Culture*. New York: Oxford University Press, 1969.

Ward, Russell. *The Australian Legend*. Melbourne: Oxford University Press, 1958.

———. *The Penguin Book of Australian Ballads*. Harmondsworth: Penguin, 1964.

Warren, Robert Penn. *All the King's Men*. New York: Harcourt, Brace, 1946.

Watts, William and Lloyd Free, eds. *State of the Nation*. New York: Universe, 1973.

Waugh, Coulton. *The Comics*. New York: Macmillan, 1947.

Webb, Walter Prescott. *The Great Plains*. Boston: Ginn, 1931.

Wechsler, James A. *Revolt on the Campus*. New York: Covici, Friede, 1935.

Wecter, Dixon. *The Hero in America: A Chronicle of Hero-Worship*. New York: Scribner, 1941.

Weigley, Russell F. *The American Way of War: A History of U.S. Military Strategy and Policy*. Bloomington: Indiana University Press, 1973.

Wentworth, Harold, and Stuart Berg Flexner. *Dictionary of American Slang*. New York: Crowell, 1960. supplemented 1967.

Wheeler, Edward J. *Deadwood Dick, the Prince of the Road*. New York: Beadle's, 1877.

———. *Deadwood Dick on Deck; or, Calamity Jane, the Heroine of Whoop-Up: A Story of Dakota*. New York: Beadle's, 1885.

———. *Deadwood Dick's Leadville Lay*. New York: Beadle's, 1889.

White, Edmund. "The Political Vocabulary of Homosexuality." In *The State of the Language*, edited by Leonard Michaels and Christopher Ricks. Berkeley: University of California Press, 1980.

White, G. Edward. *The Eastern Establishment and the Western Experience: The West of Frederick Remington, Theodore Roosevelt, and Owen Wister*. New Haven, Conn.: Yale University Press, 1968.

White, Morton. *Social Thought in America: The Revolt against Formalism*. Cambridge, Mass.: Beacon, 1957.

White, Theodore H. *The Making of the President, 1960*. New York: Athenaeum, 1961.

Whiting, Charles. *Patton*. New York: Ballantine, 1970.

Whitley, John S. "Stirring Things Up: Dashiell Hammett's Continental Op." *Journal of American Studies* 14 (1980): 443–55.

Whitman, Walt. "The Eighteenth Presidency!" (1856). In *Walt Whitman's Workshop: a Collection of Unpublished Manuscripts*, edited by Clifton Joseph Furness. Cambridge: Harvard University Press, 1928.

———. *Leaves of Grass*. Edited by [Edward] Scully Bradley and Harold Blodgett. New York: Norton, 1968. Includes Preface to 1856 edition (open letter to Emerson).

Whyte, William H., Jr. *The Organization Man*. New York: Simon and Schuster, 1956.

Wilkinson, Rupert. *The Prefects: British Leadership and the Public School Tradition. A Comparative Study in the Making of Rulers*. London: Oxford University Press, 1964. Published in the U.S. as *Gentlemanly Power*.

———. *The Prevention of Drinking Problems: Alcohol Control and Cultural Influences*. New York: Oxford University Press, 1970.

———. *The Broken Rebel: A Study in Culture, Politics and Authoritarian Character*. New York: Harper and Row, 1972.

———. "On the Toughness of the Tough Guy." *Encounter*, February 1976, 34–42.

———. "Connections with Toughness: The Novels of Eugene Burdick." *Journal of American Studies* 2 (1977): 223–39.

———. "Word-Choosing: The Sources of a Modern Obsession." *Encounter*, May 1982, 80–87.

———. "American Character Revisited." *Journal of American Studies* 17 (August 1983).

Williams, William Carlos. "Descent." In *In the American Grain*. New York: Boni, 1925.

Willingham, Calder. *End as a Man*. New York: Vanguard, 1947.

Wills, Garry. "The Kennedy Imprisonment: 1. The Prisoner of Charisma." *Atlantic Monthly*, January 1982, 27–40.

———. "The Kennedy Imprisonment: 2. The Prisoner of Toughness" *Atlantic Monthly* February 1982. 52–66.

Wilmot, Chester. *The Struggle for Europe*. London: Collins, 1952.

Wilson, Edmund. *Patriotic Gore: Studies in the Literature of the Civil War*. New York: Oxford University Press, 1962.

Wilson, John Dover, ed. *Life in Shakespeare's England: A Book of Elizabethan Prose*. Harmondsworth: Penguin, 1944.

Wilson, Meredith. "Wrong Number." *Scribner's* 65 (1919): 549ff.

Wister, Owen. *The Virginian*. New York: Grosset and Dunlap, 1902.

Wohl, R. Richard. "The 'Country Boy' Myth and Its Place in American Urban Culture," *Perspectives in American History* 3 (1969): 77–156.

Wolfe, Bernad. *Limbo '90*. New York: Random House, 1953.

Wolfe, Tom. *Mauve Gloves and Madmen, Clutter and Vine, and Other Stories, Sketches and Essays*. New York: Farrar, Straus, and Giroux, 1976. Includes "The Truest Sport," "The Perfect Crime," "The Me Decade and the Third Great Awakening," and "Honks and Wonks."

———. *The Right Stuff*. New York: Farrar, Straus, and Giroux, 1979.

Wolfenstein, Martha. "Fun-Morality: An Analysis of Recent Child-Training Literature." In *Childhood in Contemporary Culture*, edited by Margaret Mead and Martha Wolfenstein. Chicago: University of Chicago Press, 1953. Revised article of 1951.

Wolfenstein, Martha, and Nathan Leites. *Movies: A Psychological Study*. Glencoe, Ill.: Free Press, 1950, new preface 1970.

Woodward, C. Vann. *Tom Watson: Agrarian Rebel*. New York: Macmillan, 1938.

———. "The Aging of America." *American Historical Review* 82 (1977): 583ff.

Wouk, Herman. *The Caine Mutiny: A Novel of World War II*. Garden City, N.Y.: Doubleday, 1951.

Wubben, H. H. "American Prisoners of War in Korea," *American Quarterly* 22 (1970) : 3–19.

Wylie, Philip. *Gladiator*. New York: Knopf, 1930.

———. *Generation of Vipers*. New York: Rinehart, 1942.

Yankelovich, Daniel. "New Rules in American Life: Searching for Self-Fulfillment in a World Turned Upside Down." *Psychology Today*, April 1981, 35ff.

———. *New Rules: Searching for Self-Fulfillment in a World Turned Upside Down*. New York: Random House, 1981.

Zagorin, Perez. *The Court and the Country: The Beginnings of the English Revolution*. London: Routledge and Kegan Paul, 1969.

Ziff, Larzer. *The American 1890s: The Life and Times of a Lost Generation*. New York: Viking, 1966.

Zuckerman, Michael. "The Fabrication of Identity in Early America." *William and Mary Quarterly* 34 (1977): 184–214.

INDEX

Fictional characters are listed alphabetically by their first names or nicknames unless only their surnames are well known.

About the Author

RUPERT WILKINSON, former chairman of American Studies at the University of Sussex, England, is currently Visiting Professor at Smith College. His previous books include *Gentlemanly Power: British Leadership and the Public School Tradition; The Prevention of Drinking Problems;* and *The Broken Rebel: A Study in Culture, Politics and Authoritarian Character.*